CENTERED RIDING 2

Sally Swift at a horse show in Medfield, Massachusetts in the late 1930's. She is riding Douchka.

CENTERED RIDING 2
FURTHER EXPLORATION

Sally Swift

ILLUSTRATIONS BY SUSAN E. HARRIS

TRAFALGAR SQUARE PUBLISHING
North Pomfret, Vermont

First published in 2002 by
Trafalgar Square Publishing
North Pomfret, Vermont 05053

Printed in China

Library of Congress Cataloging-in-Publication Data

Swift, Sally, 1913-
  Centered Riding 2 : further exploration / Sally Swift.
      p. cm.
  ISBN-13: 978-1-57076-226-0
  ISBN-10: 1-57076-226-0
  1. Horsemanship. I. Title.
SF309 .S995 2002
798.2'3--dc21
                                2002004979

Cover and book design by Carrie Fradkin
Typeface: Poppl-Pontifex, Tiepolo

Color separations by Tenon & Polert Colour Scanning Ltd.

10 9 8 7 6 5

CONTENTS

DEDICATION

To my Centered Riding Level IV Senior Instructors who all apprenticed with me personally, and to all the present and future generations of Level IV Instructors who will, in turn, develop ever-increasing numbers of Centered Riding instructors to spread the word.

ACKNOWLEDGMENTS

There are many people who I want to thank for their share in helping me produce this book. First, my thanks goes to all those students and friends who talked me into it and persevered in prodding me to finish, in spite of many intermissions. Susan Harris and I put together the original outline as we drove between clinics when she was apprenticing with me. Susan also is responsible for all the artwork as well as many suggestions in the text, and for the entire chapter on jumping, which I did not feel qualified to write. Lucile Bump, my student from before the start of Centered Riding, spent many hours critiquing what I had written, and helping me formulate different ways to explain the thinking, feeling, and performing of the activities in Centered Riding. Furthermore, most of the photographs in the book were taken at her Southmowing Stables, many of the horses work in her school, and the riders are Southmowing riders.

Thanks goes to my photographers. Darrell Dodds took two-thirds of the photographs. Most of the others were taken by Bob Langrish, Mike Maloney, and Margaret Halpert. Judy Britton, Gail Allen, and Amy Boemig helped sort through many hundreds of slides picking the ones we used. Amy Dillon and Denise Manning recorded the captions.

Thanks to another important group—the riders who were the subjects in all these photographs: Jineen Walker, Cynthia Crawley, Beth McElwee, Beth Kinney, Amanda Pettingill, Claudia Heiss, Val Deane, and Lucile Bump all worked long, hard, and patiently through the inevitable retakes needed. Bless them.

Many thanks go to my good friend, Francois Lemaire de Ruffieu, for so generously sharing with me his vast knowledge of horsemanship. His input profoundly enhanced and rounded out my teaching of Centered Riding.

As for the text, thanks goes to Huntley Hashagen for typing up most of the hard-to-decipher copy. A large thanks to Karen McCollom for putting some order to that mass of material and preparing it for my editor and publisher Caroline Robbins' eagle eye, and Martha Cook, her "right hand man."

The biggest thanks of all goes to Caroline Robbins, who, after reading through the book, came down 80 miles to my house (I do not drive anymore) twice a week for three months to clarify every small detail—taking a little out here, or asking me for a little more there. It all reads so beautifully when you are finished, Caroline, and it sounds just like me. How can I thank you enough?

Why a Second Book?

Since the publication of my first book, *Centered Riding* in 1985, the concept of Centered Riding has helped many people improve their riding, and consequently the communication with their horses. This approach to riding enables people to use their bodies more efficiently and fluidly, and to understand more clearly the relationship between their own, and their horse's bodies. The emphasis is essentially on the rider. It makes it clear how profoundly you influence your horse by the way you use your own body.

Centered Riding 2: Further Exploration does not replace the first book, it complements it. The books belong side by side, and readers will do well to have read *Centered Riding*. This second book includes more about the horse. It explains in broad terms how you can improve your horse's musculature and way of going through your expanded understanding and application of Centered Riding. You cannot fail to improve your horse's body as you progress in your riding skills. They are interchangeable and can produce a lovely interplay between horse and rider.

As I continue to teach Centered Riding, I have discovered that this approach to riding keeps evolving in new and interesting ways. The basics and the philosophy remain constant, but new ways of using or expressing them have emerged continually through the teaching process. Over the years, I have frequently found myself developing a whole new direction of teaching a familiar concept. This book not only reviews the all-important basics, but also presents these expanded applications of the Centered Riding method.

Very importantly, I want to emphasize that Centered Riding is not a special form of riding. It is a most effective way to learn to ride a horse classically well in all disciplines. Excellence in riding is achieved when a rider is able to ride in harmony with a horse and thus allow him to achieve his maximum potential of dynamic movement, athleticism, and obedience. Centered Riding lies at the core of all good riding, from beginner to Olympic level, from dressage and jumping to reining or endurance riding.

Occasionally I ask myself, "How did this happen? Why am I excitedly working at this project in my retirement years?" Chance and circumstances do surprising things. The fact that I have had a back problem since childhood (a scoliosis) led me to work with some remarkable people who helped me use my awkward body well. Through this exposure to methods of movement and body control, I developed a deep interest in the way the human body works. So, when I retired at age sixty-two from office work, I began playing with my concepts. I had meant to travel a bit and "teach a few of my friends riding, for fun." When people recognized that I was teaching something that was largely missing in riding instruction, the demand for my ideas simply swept me along.

People have said it is a pity I did not introduce this teaching twenty years earlier. I wonder, however, if I would have had such a receptive audience back then. By chance I began teaching and developing these concepts when the demand for this sort of knowledge was growing.

When I was young in the 1920's and 30's, there was a lot of discussion about Federico Caprilli[1] and his revolutionary "forward seat." Caprilli had changed riding in a major way in the early part of the twentieth century, but sixty years later one seldom hears the words "forward seat." The concept is taken for granted; it is simply the way to ride. I hope this will happen over time to Centered Riding—that the philosophy and concepts of this approach will merge into all forms of riding and teaching, and it too will be taken for granted.

---

1 Federico Caprilli (1868-1907). An Italian cavalry officer who introduced the forward seat jumping style in 1907.

1

The Validity of Centered Riding

I am sure you have a dream horse. What do you see in this dream creature? You probably see beauty and balance, rhythm, lightness and power, and you probably see all of these qualities demonstrated with confidence, attentiveness, and delight.

To achieve these wonderful attributes in a living, breathing horse, you must first fully understand the animal: a gorgeous creature, born to live and run free and wild, but kind enough to share his abilities with us. Since he is willing to work with us, we have a responsibility to make his work as easy, free of pain, and as pleasant as possible, even in times of great effort such as cutting cattle, galloping over jumps across country, in the jumper ring, or competing in dressage at the Grand Prix level. Here is where Centered Riding fits in. The finesse and techniques of Centered Riding allow for maximum harmony between horse and rider in all circumstances.

Centered Riding is not a "style" of riding as Western, hunter seat, saddle seat, and dressage are examples of styles. Rather, Centered Riding is a way of reeducating the mind and body toward greater balance and integration, which in turn opens up a new dimension in the world of equestrian arts. It gives you a new way of expressing the old classical principles in whatever your style of riding. It is essential that horsemanship maintain the purity of the classical principles within each style and discipline. Centered Riding very simply makes this easier to do.

Peggy Brown *riding centered. Because she was wearing this "bone suit" to appear in the video,* Anatomy in Motion: The Visible Rider, *which she produced with Susan Harris, you can well see her correct anatomy and her beautifully balanced seat.*

A centered, balanced rider with good awareness of her body and that of her horse can help her horse develop correct musculature, and move with balance and freedom of motion. The horse has a chance to work in harmony with his rider and take pleasure in his work rather than develop stress, and all too often, pain. This freedom of motion leads to efficiency of movement, which in itself produces beauty.

It is important for you to remember that a horse knows how to be a horse. You don't need to teach him how to trot, canter, or even pirouette. He learned all these things in his first few days of life, partly through the joy of being alive and, if he was born in the wild, in order to escape predators. The natural horse is able to run, cavort, and balance at all times.

When you get on your horse's back, you change the situation. The horse now must balance himself

Robin Brueckmann
A beautiful, centered rider and student of mine since her late teens, she is now a Centered Riding instructor, combined-training, and dressage judge. Robin is known for her dressage exhibitions riding "David" (shown here), without bridle, or stirrups, which she cannot use because of an injury to her foot. By special permission, she is allowed to compete in high-level dressage without stirrups, and has won a US Dressage Federation Gold Medal.

efficiently with your weight on his back, and respond to your aids. His ability to manage this depends on your carrying yourself in balance with him.

The practice of Centered Riding can help you develop the ability you will need to transform your horse into your dream horse. Through Centered Riding, you will improve your balance—forward, back, and sideways; learn to stay calm and mentally balanced even in stressful moments; develop the ability to use precise, comfortable, and appropriate aids, and to ride with positive intent.

Centered Riding will also help you develop an awareness, which will greatly improve your ability to "read" your horse, to understand his moods and his responses. A horse expresses himself a great deal through his body movements. He can express pain and discomfort, tension and fatigue, and he can express confusion, fear, and distrust. On the other hand, he can also express joy, trust, and enthusiasm ranging from willing cooperation to keenness.

The horse's expression through movement is a result of a combination of his body balance and his state of mind. A horse suffering from discomfort, tension, or confusion, for instance, will not have a free, supple, balanced body. On the other hand, a comfortable horse can express joy, trust, and enthusiasm for his work with a body that is essentially balanced, fluid, and free. He can be receptive to your aids.

Only when a horse is physically and mentally comfortable in his work can he give you his maximum potential of the moment. To quote Xenophon,[1]

---

1 Xenophon (427–354 BC) A Greek cavalry officer, writer, and horseman famed for his essays on horsemanship, most notably, *The Art of Horsemanship*.

Marcia Kulak A gorgeous rider, she is also a longtime student who came to me when she was 16. She is now an international three-day-event rider and has represented the US. Opposite, Marcia is riding Talk Back very fast cross-country at the North Georgia International Horse Trials, and above, over a show-jumping fence on Night Watch, winning the Groton House Horse Trials. She has soft contact with both the horses, who look happy, relaxed, and with no evident tension.

"For what the horse does under compulsion is done without understanding; and there is no beauty in it either, any more than if one should whip and spur a dancer."

Since the horse's movement is a result of a combination of his body balance and his state of mind, both of which are deeply influenced by the rider—in many cases dependent on the rider—you carry an immense responsibility. You must use your body in such a way that you do not interfere with his balance and movement, while at the same time indicating your intentions with clarity. This is

what encourages the horse to work happily. This is where Centered Riding can be of enormous help.

In order to attain and keep your dream horse, you will also need to maintain obedience and control as well as allowing your horse full freedom of movement and expression. To do this, you will need his total cooperation. That will involve motivating him to want to do what you want him to do.

Many of us are apt to fall into the trap of anthropomorphism, certain that our horses will enjoy doing the things we enjoy. Sometimes this is true. Surely, many horses enjoy fox hunting. A friend tells me this is one reason she loves hunting, because she and her beloved horse can enjoy it together. Cutting horses also seem to like their work. And, of course, most horses love to go out for a trail ride—ears pricked, and walking fast. But all too often we see horses doing their work because they must; it will be worse for them if they don't. This is essentially the premise of training through reward and punishment. The result is a horse that is doing what you want but without joy. It is not true cooperation, though it is obedience, and you do have control. This is projecting your motives on your horse.

In order to understand the nature of the horse and to avoid anthropomorphizing, it is important to keep in mind the horse's instinctive characteristics. One of these, for instance, is its powerful herd instinct. Horses naturally live in groups and herds. They are not loners. Yet, so often a horse's job causes him to live, and work alone. You can both use and fulfill your horse's desire for company by developing a trusting relationship between horse and rider. Your horse's herd instinct becomes a source of motivation for him, and you can, in some ways, replace the members of the herd for him using the Centered Riding approach.

Now compare for a moment a horse approaching a jump with ears back and body stiff, to another horse coming to the same fence with ears pricked, his body balanced, and the strides flowing. Think, too, about the Grand Prix dressage horse going through all the figures accurately but with minimal movement, a dead tail, eyes looking inward, and a lackluster performance. Then remember another horse performing the same figures with what seems joyful abandon,

accurate but buoyant, as if hardly touching the ground. The difference between these performances finds its basis in joyful cooperation, versus dull obedience. The ability to more accurately "read" your horse, and understand his motivation, will help you achieve this sort of joyful cooperation. As the FEI's [2] rules state so elegantly in the dressage section, "The horse thus gives the impression of doing of his own accord what is required of him." This phrase can certainly apply to any horse in any discipline, or to the horse ridden purely for the joy of riding. This is an exciting concept.

It is also important to become aware of how your horse is using himself. Does he move with some flow and balanced energy, impulsion, with harmony and buoyancy? What is the quality of his gaits and movement? Good quality of movement results in forward energy flow and allows the horse to come into balance.

What constitutes good quality of movement? The horse must have the appropriate balance for his job; his center of balance must be more forward for a hunter, more back and elevated for a jumper, more forward for Western Pleasure, more elevated through the withers for the cutting horse. But wherever his balance, the hind legs must be free, through all joints, to elastically step forward and help lighten the load on the front end. An unbalanced horse will audibly pound the ground. A balanced horse, whatever he is doing, is light on his feet. Good quality gaits have ease and rhythm, and it is necessary for the rhythm to be light and regular.

I remember watching Bent Jensen,[3] a deeply centered rider, and a big man on a big horse, sail

---

2 Fédération Equestre Internationale (FEI), the international governing body for officially recognized international horse competitions, including the equestrian events in the Olympic Games.

3 Bent Jensen. Two-time Danish national dressage champion, and Olympic competitor. He now teaches and competes in the US.

Bent Jensen What a joy to look at this picture of Bent Jensen on his horse, Grand Garcon! Here is Centered Riding at its best. The rider is balanced, grounded, deep yet light, with man and horse moving in fluid harmony.

across the diagonal at the Devon Dressage Show at a powerful extended trot and with almost invisible aids, come in one stride quietly to a walk in perfect balance. It looked as if eggs would not have broken under that horse's feet.

When the horse has balance, rhythm, flow, and regularity in his movement, forward energy and impulsion will start in the push of the cupped hind foot from the ground and go up through his center (which lies below his lumbar spine between diaphragm and the pelvis), through his back, between his shoulders, through his withers, and out through the soft, pulsing poll. Alois Podhajsky[4] says "Success will be revealed to the rider in the pleasant way he will feel the back of his horse swinging rhythmically beneath his seat—what Xenophon described as a 'divine sensation.'"

Good self-use in a horse means higher performance, and a longer life at a high level of performance in any field. However, good self-use and correct movement can be spoiled. Furthermore,

4 Alois Podhajsky (1899-1973). Director of the Spanish Riding School in Vienna for 26 years, he won an Olympic medal in Berlin in 1936.

John Lyons This shows John Lyons, an instinctively centered rider and person, siting tall with a deep, soft, and balanced seat, no tension anywhere, on a happy, free-moving horse. John tells me that he has admired Centered Riding concepts for a long time.

habits that have been "taught" are the hardest to lose, whether they are bad habits you would like to lose, or good habits you would like to keep. That, of course, means that it can be difficult to remake a spoiled horse.

With this in mind, before you go any further in the development of your dream horse, you need to take an honest look at yourself in relation to your own specific horse. Is he really suited to you, or you to him? Do you love him from a sentimental point of view because he is your first horse or because he is so beautiful, even if he is a bit of a rogue? Is it pride that motivates you to continue, even though your rides are often alarming or frustrating? It is true that many problems can be overcome with time and improved riding, but the hours you spend on your horse are precious, and perhaps you could enjoy these hours more with a different horse. Be honest with yourself. Do you love your horse because you have so much fun working with him, or because you cannot resist a challenge? Besides, if your horse is not suitable for you he could well be much happier with someone else, or with a different job.

Assuming that you are satisfied with your equine partner, Centered Riding will help you achieve a greater harmony with him, improve his movement, and help you to ride correctly in a classical manner through body control and improved awareness. Without constant awareness of yourself and your horse, you all too easily interfere with his movement in a way that will detract from good

Sue Ashley working with Colonel Albrecht Von Ziegner, a well-known German instructor. They are teaching Jae to piaffe. Jae is working happily—note his attentive ears that are not pinned back in discomfort.

quality performance. If you work to put him in positions and situations to constantly learn and improve his self-use, you will be approaching the goal of your dream horse.

Discussing the qualities of the dream horse reminds me of a student named Sue Ashley and her dandy little horse, Jae. Sue wanted to progress in dressage and Jae was the horse she had to work with. Jae had a wonderful temperament and Sue had a lot of sense and persistence. She was also enamored with Centered Riding and kept coming back to refine her Centered Riding capabilities to help in her training. Methodically and correctly, she trained him. She never pushed him beyond what he could deal with at any given moment, so he always enjoyed his work.

She brought Jae along through Training, First, and Second Level dressage. Then she was urged to get another horse, as Jae "couldn't really go much higher." But she kept coming back every year, working at Third Level and then Fourth Level and so on up, and each year she was told that Jae was going very well at that level but she should get another horse if she wanted to go further. The year she turned up doing all the Grand Prix movements very correctly she also had a chance to take a clinic with Robert Dover.[5] When asked what she especially wanted help on she said she would like to improve Jae's piaffe-passage transitions. After she demonstrated them for Robert he said thoughtfully, "If my horse could do those transitions that well I'd be very happy. In fact, they are better than most I

5 Robert Dover. Dressage rider who has represented the US in five Olympic Games, winning three team Bronze medals.

see from horses in Europe." Then he turned to the audience and said, "If more of you people would take the time, patience, and persistence to train your horses as Sue has done with Jae, when you get the horse of your dreams you won't ruin him." She had savored and enjoyed every step of the way; no steps were sidetracked, and the goal came to her.

This book is not about "what to do" with your horse to achieve your goal. There are many excellent books available that do this. It is about "how to do" what is needed—not only with your body, but also with your horse's body—to produce the greatest efficiency of movement for you both. You will find that not until you are centered, balanced, and in harmony within your own body, will you be able to avoid interfering with the balance of your horse. The horse can only move with his maximum efficiency and grace if you, the rider, are centered and in balance and harmony on and with him. He can only move as well as you move.

2

Mechanics of Learning

Understanding the physical process of learning, how the brain and body incorporate new information and movement, is vital not only to your progress as a rider but also to your success as your horse's trainer. Before Centered Riding can help you use yourself effectively, you need to have a good understanding of the actual mechanics of learning.

The human brain is divided into two halves, which are connected by the corpus callosum, a two-way bridge of nerve fibers. On the whole, the two sides of the brain have different functions. The left side uses information in an organized, linear fashion, processing details rationally, analytically, and verbally. In contrast, the right side of the brain is more intuitive and full of imagery. It deals with wholes and concepts rather than parts and words, and tends to integrate and synthesize rather than list.

The two sides of the brain work together in the processing and use of information. New information is entered in the left brain in separate details. If you use your left brain to recall this new information, you will find yourself listing particulars. This approach, though appropriate for some disciplines, is an imperfect way to approach a physical activity like riding. If, for instance, you were riding a circle, by the time you listed all the six or seven details required for a correct circle, you would be halfway around the circle before you finished your checklist! If, instead, you allow your right brain to control the movement by giving it the desired image, you will find your body responding automatically with simultaneous and synchronized actions. This is not to say that a beginner rider can simply conjure up an image of the perfect half-pass, and suddenly begin to float effortlessly across the ring. Before your right brain can help your performance, you must learn the details; your left brain must be given the information for your right brain to use. In other words, you must learn the aids first and then learn to coordinate them. Once you have learned a movement and stored its execution in your right brain during the learning process, the simple use of an image will trigger your body to co-ordinate and perform the movement. This is a sim-plified explanation of a complicated process.

Bearing this in mind, how do you learn in the most efficient way? All too often, we see riding stu-dents (or students in any field) suffering from con-fusion, frustration, and fear of failure. Any of these reactions can result in a dead end in the student's ability to learn. What usually causes these difficul-ties is trying to learn too much at one time. The same is true of your horse. To learn effectively, both you and your horse need to be given infor-mation in incremental doses.

I try to teach any new movement or exercise in small segments. First, I explain the overall move-ment you are going to work on. Let us say that you will be riding circles. Instead of explaining all the aids at once, I pick just one or two. Each new seg-ment of learning the method and pattern of that circle is done first while standing still. When that is clear in your mind you then practice it at the walk, and later at the trot and canter. You learn the most basic part of the movement and give your body a chance to practice just that much. Then you learn another part and practice the two to-gether. Then comes a third part, first learning and understanding, then putting it into practice com-bined with the other two, and so on.

By learning in small segments, you have time for clear understanding of the project. You have given your body time to learn the coordination necessary and to develop the muscles needed for the new movement. You are learning in a non-threatening way without being overwhelmed with information that you cannot incorporate or re-member all at once. As a result, these details are available for synthesis by the right brain when you are ready to call them up to help you ride the whole movement. With this gradual build-up, you will find you need to do little else but think of making a circle and your horse will follow your intent.

I had a clear example of the success of this method when asked to help a young man who was working to become an advanced level three-day-event rider. Although he had achieved his goal by riding at this level, he came to me because his body was stiff and locked. I worked with him bit by bit, with time between each segment to feel the results. By the end of the lesson, he was totally changed, and riding with balance, flexibility, and softness throughout his body. We were both delighted, but he said, "I could never have done this if you had just told me to relax. It worked only because you did it focusing on each small part at a time."

You can apply this teaching approach equally well when schooling your horse. Teach him only what he is physically and mentally ready to learn. Teach him in small segments and give him practice in each segment so he is comfortable with it both physically and mentally. For instance, when he can work easily in a large, 20-meter circle, make one or two smaller circles, which will be harder for him. Go back to the bigger one again to relieve the effort and regain his self-confidence. Then ride a few smaller circles again, and back to the larger. This gives him non-threatening time to develop new techniques, coordination, and muscle. If you ask for too much, or for too long a time, he will become frustrated, and you will undermine his self-confidence and his con-fidence in you, and he will not enjoy his work. Without keeping joy in his work, you will not suc-ceed in developing his full potential.

Move forward step by step, and keep it simple. Simplicity can have great power. As you and your horse progress, what seemed hopelessly difficult earlier will become not only possible, but simple.

WHAT ARE THE ESSENTIALS OF **Mechanics of Learning?**

- ▶ There are two sides of the brain.
- ▶ The left brain takes in knowledge of details.
- ▶ The right brain amalgamates details into a whole, which can be used as a complete image.
- ▶ Learn and teach in small segments—too much at one time can be frustrating to both you and your horse.

WHAT ARE THE RESULTS?

- ▶ By keeping information simple, learning becomes easy and fun.

3

Four Basics and Grounding

All of Centered Riding work stems from the concepts of its *Four Basics*, and *grounding*. The *Four Basics* are: *centering; breathing; soft eyes;* and *building blocks*. Living in our hurrying, hectic, pressured society exacerbates the tendency to interfere. The lack of any one of these *Four Basics* and *grounding* can cause interference. If you lose one of these *Basics* you may find yourself tense, with hard eyes, rigid joints, or you may be breathless and out of balance. Though trying to decide which basic comes first can produce a bad case of the "chicken and the egg," it is usually best to find your center and understand the concept of *centering* before establishing the other *Basics*.

Centering Yourself

The *Four Basics* provide an armament of awareness through which you can more easily find your center. They work together in a way that allows the center to perform freely and, in turn, your center can bring the other *Basics* into line and allow your body to operate in a natural and fluid way.

You can find your center easily by placing your thumb over your navel and spreading your hand below it so your little finger rests on your pubic arch. Your center will lie behind the palm of your hand. Put your other hand over the top of your sacrum (the part of the vertebral column that is directly connected with the pelvis) where the fifth lumbar vertebra rests on it. Your center lies between your hands as shown in the photograph (fig. 3.1). This area contains a large nerve center, which controls the entire body. When you perform an activity, your brain controls your intent and gives the larger directions, but the details of how you do it—the coordination that is needed to perform the movement of your intent—comes from your center. If the desired movement is to be performed efficiently you must allow your center to direct the coordination with what I call *clear intent,* a precise, positive understanding, and picture of what you want.

All too often, the way in which we use our bodies and brains interferes with this coordination.

As you find your center between your hands, let yourself simply be aware of the area of your center. I usually sense the center as a *ball floating in a liquid*—any consistency you like. Sometimes it is small but heavy like a t'ai chi ball. Other times I imagine the *ball* as large as a softball. Any size, texture, or density that fits your fancy will do.

Some people are not comfortable with the concept of the center as a ball. They conceive of it as a mass of energy in the upper pelvis, or even a sun with rays. Any of these images will serve the purpose of helping to find your center. I call this *"finding the ball in your center,"* and in Centered Riding vocabulary, refer to it quickly as the *ball!* This is how you *center yourself.*

Not long ago, Saundra, a friend, student, and now a Centered Riding instructor, told me about an incident that highlighted how *centering* can coordinate our efforts. After a long day of teaching Centered Riding, Saundra was pressed by friends to go bowling with them. She really wanted to go home, did not know how to bowl, and had absolutely no interest in learning to bowl. Yet, here she was in the bowling alley, sucked in by her jovial friends. Terri insisted that Saundra try her hand at the sport and showed her how to hold the ball and swing her arm. Each time when her turn came, the ball shot out of Saundra's hand and sputtered down the gutter, a total loss. Finally, Terri suggested, "Use your center, Saundra."

In her displeasure, she hadn't thought of using her center for bowling. Now the idea intrigued her. She took time to go deep within her low, quiet center, and discovered that her body was no longer upright and awkward, but easily dropped low to the floor, one knee well ahead, the other back, balanced with hip, knee, and ankle joints deeply closed and back, neck, and head long and free, her arm and hand quietly swinging the ball. Then came the follow-through with open pointing fingers sending

<u>3.1</u> *Finding your center: place one hand on your lower abdomen, and the other hand behind you over the top of your sacrum.*

her energy sliding slowly down the alley with the ball. The motion was one of beauty and control, and instead of crashing down the gutter, this ball went with an unhurried roll down the center of the alley exactly to where it was directed by that totally extended hand, body, and center (fig. 3.2). Saundra had executed a perfect strike!

3.2 Saundra is using her center, and is well grounded with energy flowing through her torso out through her fingertips.

The incredulous applause was instant. Saundra continued to bowl, *centering* herself with each turn. Time and again, she made a perfect strike. Everyone, her friends, the other bowlers in the alley, and Saundra herself, were dumbfounded at such success by a total novice.

How had she done it? Her friends, and even the other seasoned bowlers were asking. She explained to them as well as she could and although they improved their performances, none of them had quite as dramatic results as Saundra. Although she is still amazed at the magnitude of the difference in the way her body managed itself between her first awkward tries and the successes, Saundra suspects that her long practice of meditation, which involves much use of the center, combined with her Centered Riding training, made her efforts so particularly effective. She knew what she wanted to do, but she was able to relinquish to her center the control of how to do it. It can be a difficult task, but if we can let our minds give the directives and allow our centers to take over the job of coordinating without interference, the results can be extraordinary.

I have always been aware of the importance of my center. When in my upper teens, I knew that if I wanted to do something special with my horse, get him balanced, or approach a jump, I needed to take the *ball* from my upper body and drop it down into my pelvis where it landed with a "plop" as if into mud (fig. 3.3). With it there, I could do anything. I did not think of it as *centering* at that time. It was just my special feeling of the *ball*. Years later, when I was developing Centered Riding as a technique, I realized how fundamental the *ball* was to effective riding.

So, how to do you *find your center*? And, how do you *center yourself*? You just *think* about it. Your mind alerts your center.

Breathing

The next of the *Four Basics* is *breathing*, and it involves the use of the whole torso. The diaphragm stretches across the torso at the bottom of the rib cage, moving well up within the rib cavity with the exhalation, and down again with the inhale (fig. 3.4). It has a powerful root extending down into the area of the center. If you find yourself breathing shallowly only in the top of your rib cage, you will note a feeling of restricted body use. Any time you hold your breath, you create stiffness and rigidity. If, on the other hand, you allow your breath to feel as if it is filling up the whole area down through the back of your lower body, as if you could breathe into the back of your pelvis or even your feet, you help release multiple tensions. This is not a case of taking big, deep breaths, but rather of allowing each normal breath to travel softly throughout your body and to integrate the rhythms of your body, and of your horse.

This quality of breathing has many positive results. Sit quietly on your horse (or on a straight,

3.3 "Ball" dropping into your center: when you allow the "ball" to drop from your upper torso right through your body, it will land with a "thunk" as if into mud in your pelvis.

FRONT VIEW

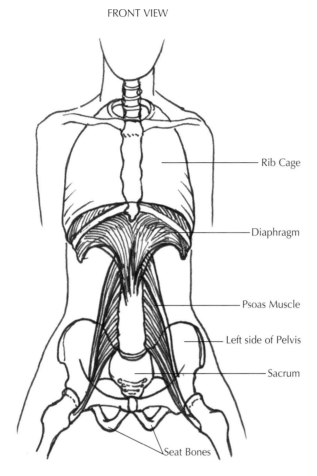

Rib Cage

Diaphragm

Psoas Muscle

Left side of Pelvis

Sacrum

Seat Bones

3.4 This diagram shows how the diaphragm attaches to the spine and "cups" up into the rib cage.

Soft Eyes

The third *Basic, soft eyes,* allows you to expand your awareness. While looking toward an object, let your eyes relax. Let the object be the general center of your gaze, but look at it with your peripheral vision taking in the largest possible expanse around it (fig. 3.5). You will become simultaneously aware of your surroundings and your inner body, the relationship of its parts to each other, and to your horse. The use of *soft eyes* opens the way for proprioception and awareness. Proprioception is the ability to sense where all your body parts are in relation to one another. Identity, a sense of self, is organically anchored with proprioception.

You will find that it is much easier to feel how the horse moves your body when you are using *soft eyes.* Using *soft eyes* becomes almost a philosophy rather than just a new way of seeing. It is a method of becoming distinctly aware of what is going on around you, beneath you, and inside of you. With hard, intently focused eyes, you will tend to hold your breath, lose your center, and be less aware of the relationship of your body to your surroundings, including your horse.

A number of people working in a small area can ride complicated movements independently without bumping into each other if they use *soft*

hard-backed chair) and breathe into your lower back. Notice that your pelvis rocks gently on your seat bones (ischia) front-to-back. With each breath, your sacrum drops slightly down, then goes back to balance again. Each time this happens, it softens your lower back across the top of the buttocks, expands the lower back, lengthens the spine, and releases tension in the hip joints. Under many circumstances in Centered Riding, you will hear me asking you to *drop your sacrum; breathe into your lower back*; and *let your spine lengthen.*

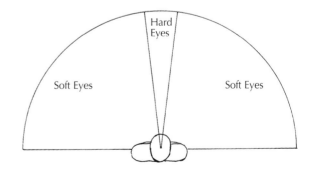

Hard Eyes

Soft Eyes   Soft Eyes

3.5 "Soft eyes" versus "hard eyes": note the wide peripheral vision for soft eyes as compared to the narrow, concentrated vision of hard eyes.

eyes. If they use hard eyes—probably focusing intently on their horses' ears—they will collide and crash.

Building Blocks

Finally, you can add the fourth *Basic—building blocks.* When you are "built" correctly, you will be in balance. If you don't have balance, your entire ride will become involved either in trying to find it, or in using extra muscular effort to avoid falling off your horse.

As I wrote in *Centered Riding,* "Your bottom *building blocks* are your legs and feet. The next block is your pelvis, then rib cage, shoulders, and last, your head and neck. For flatwork, the correct lineup of the blocks (viewing the body sideways) will allow you to drop a plumb line from the ear through the tip of the shoulder, hip joint, and ankle. Just before it passes through your hip joint, you will find it going straight through your center (fig. 3.6)." As is the case with each of the *Basics,* without balance you lose efficiency. Without the other *Basics,* you lose balance. You need them all.

Grounding

The results from using the *Four Basics* will be maximized by allowing yourself to become "grounded." *Grounding* is a sensation of connection with the ground, and offers you increased stability. There is a story in my family of my looking up at my father and saying, "I may not go up as far as you do, but I go down just as far." That connection with the ground will allow you to find your center, to breathe more easily, to use *soft eyes,* to be balanced, and to feel tall. I am constantly being impressed by the importance of being grounded in everything we do.

In recent years, I started to think that *grounding* should become the fifth *Basic,* but some of my students said I couldn't do that because "the *Four Basics* are 'classic'." I thought about this and realized that *grounding* was actually the founda-

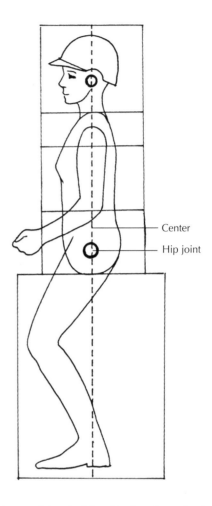

3.6 The balance of the "building blocks": from the feet up through the hip joints, the center, the tip of the shoulder, and the ear, they must stack one above the other.

tion on which the *Four Basics* depend. *Grounding* gives everything else security. It is a feeling that your well-established center is dropping energy down through your legs and feet into the ground, while the energy in the ground comes up to your feet. An image (or feeling) of *grounding* has your legs and feet sucked gently down and down, from your open hip joints into the ground where the soles of your feet are secured as if by magnets. The magical part is that the ground—as it holds you—

can move with your feet anywhere you wish, giving you total stability at all times. You know that nothing, and no one, can knock you over. (This happens just as easily when you are on your horse and your feet are not actually touching the ground.)

Grounding does not involve being heavy. I'll explain. Have you ever had to deal with a small child who does not want to go to bed, and somehow makes herself inseparable from the floor? And what about the daughter of George Leonard who wrote *The Ultimate Athlete*? Weighing just 110 lbs, she made herself so heavy that a weightlifter could not pick her up! One way to experience being grounded is to try the exercise, *Feet in the Sand* (see p. 37). You can also ground different parts of your body—your feet, your knees, and your seat. As I said above, the sensation of *grounding* is also just as easy to feel when you are on your horse. It is a powerful tool.

Results of the Four Basics

Recently, I have become even more acutely aware of the power of the center through working with disabled riders. I worked with Pam who had lost a significant degree of control of her body and limbs in a car accident. I made no effort to teach her how to ride—I simply worked with her as she sat on the horse. I put my hands on her lower body, front and back, to locate her center as you did when you found your own center. I also paid a lot of attention to myself—my *centering, grounding* and balance, *breathing,* and *soft eyes.* I talked quietly about her allowing herself to be aware of the area between my hands, especially toward the hand on the sacrum, and discover peace and quiet there. I persisted, being careful to keep 75 percent of my attention on my center, grounding, and myself, and only 25 percent on the rider. More attention on her than that appeared to cause her to overload and block her body, but the 25 percent seemed to quiet her frantically active center.

As I concentrated on our centers in that way, her body began to find more normal patterns. Her buttocks relaxed, her hamstrings and the muscles down the front of her legs released. This in turn released her hip joints so her legs dropped down under her, and her torso stopped tipping forward, back, or sideways, and came into balance. Her seat settled all over the saddle, and when she was led off at the walk her back rippled and she moved with the horse with a following seat.

This happened with each rider. It seemed like a miracle. My hypothesis is that the senses of the disabled, and of all of us in varying lesser degrees, are peripheral more than centered. There tends to be a lot of extraneous activity and disorientation in the periphery. When we can bring awareness and quiet into the center, the center seems to be able to draw this extraneous activity into itself, reorganize it, and send it out again in better order.

The way in which *centering* is helpful to disabled riders indicates not only that the center can be a powerful area of reorganization, but that the body would like to be normal. If we can remove or reduce interferences, the body will return to as close to normal as possible.

With this finding, I was curious to discover what would happen if I used the same technique that I had done on Pam, with the able-bodied. In some of my clinics, I tried doing the hands-on work first, unmounted, so less would have to be done on the horse. The riders worked in pairs, with one putting her hands on the front and back of the other's lower torso. The first partner paid careful attention to her own *grounding, centering, breathing, soft eyes,* and *building blocks.* As a result, the second partner felt a nice warmth and stability. This stable feeling dissolved into overload and discomfort if the first partner focused all her attention on the second partner.

Back on their horses, the able-bodied riders melted into lovely deep seats with tall, balanced bodies. I then had them move into slow work on the horses, with a lot of walking at first, but later with the full quota of activity. The one criterion, especially at first, was if the rider lost any of the *Four Basics*, or if there was any resistance in the horse, that the horse be brought back to a walk, or sometimes a halt, for *centering* and reorganization of the rider—and therefore of the horse—before moving off again. By the end of a two- or three-day clinic, the riders were wonderfully balanced and fluid, and the horses were balanced, forward, and straight at all gaits.

This experience was strong proof of how valuable work on the ground is in learning Centered Riding. First, you can concentrate on yourself only. There are no distractions from a horse being underneath you. Second, a horse does not have to put up with, in some cases endure the seemingly endless mistakes you make, which are inevitable when you are learning.

A local vet, Pamela, has a very determined Morgan horse, Buster, whom she brought to one of my first clinics after my discovery with the disabled. Pamela tends to be crooked from an old injury. She complained that Buster had been leaning heavily on her outside rein on one side all summer and she was fed up with it. We did some intensive *centering* work both on the ground and mounted, with no mention of inside or outside reins, or of corrective work on horses or riders. (By the way, in this book when I refer to the *inside* rein or leg, I mean the hand or leg on the *inside* of the circle or turn you are riding.) At the end of the class, I asked each rider, as I always do, what had been special during the lesson. Pamela burst into a big smile and said, "I'm straight (which she was) and Buster didn't once lean on the outside rein—he's straight, too!"

Another one of my students was Alexandra who was a 14-year-old hunter-seat rider working into the Medal/Maclay classes. She was ambitious, talented, and with a good foundation in the techniques needed in major eqitation classes. But she was full of tension, which was interfering with her further progress. In her first lesson with me, we spent a long time on the ground working through the *Four Basics*, learning to move from her center, and exploring the correct use of her joints. Once on the horse, we spent a long time at the walk sorting out how to stay centered, how she could avoid holding her breath under stress, and how to maintain the use of the *Four Basics,* and *grounding.* We took the same objectives into the trot and canter. She became nicely fluid and balanced. She came back two weeks later having competed in a Medal/Maclay class on the flat. She had won the blue ribbon despite stiff competition against experienced, competent equitation riders. When her mother asked what she had done differently, Alexandra replied, "I didn't think at all about my equitation. All I did was think about *centering* the whole time, and my horse went like silk."

This begins to sound as if all we have to do to learn how to ride is to learn how to be centered. This, of course, is not true. Pam, Alexandra, and the people in the clinics were already riders. During the clinic sessions, I inserted many directives for specific situations, but the emphasis was on doing it *all* from the center. The result of this approach indicates that riders can learn and apply the myriad of details involved in riding more easily and efficiently through *centering,* and achieve beautiful results.

I often have people tell me, "You have not only helped my riding; you have changed my whole life." Usually, this is simply because they have been able to increase their awareness or because of the relief of being able to allow things, their bodies and their lives, to function on their own after years of struggling to be in control of everything. You will discover in your own way what *centering* can accomplish when you open up to awareness and quiet. ❧

WHAT ARE THE ESSENTIALS OF Four Basics and Grounding?

► Use all *Four Basics.* They depend on each other.

► They are important in all types of riding.

CENTERING

► Find your center between your hands.

► Be aware of your center.

► Thinking about your center brings it into activity.

BREATHING

► Involve the whole torso, not just the chest.

► Understand the importance of the diaphragm.

► Keep breathing. Do not hold your breath.

► Breathe normally into your lower back and pelvis.

SOFT EYES

► Use peripheral vision.

► Become aware of your surroundings and your inner body.

► Find your identity, a sense of self.

► Use *soft eyes* in all you do, and particularly in crowded areas.

BUILDING BLOCKS

► Must balance one above the other.

► A plumb line should go from your ear through the tip of the shoulder, hip joint, and ankle.

► Are essential for balance and efficiency.

GROUNDING

► A sensation of connection with the ground.

► The foundation on which the *Four Basics* rest.

► Essential at all times.

WHAT ARE THE RESULTS?

► If you open yourself up to become aware of them, you will free your body, and allow it to move and function without restriction.

4

Use of Self

There are three primary ways of learning—auditory, visual, and kinesthetic (the sense of muscular effort). With this in mind, I use words, pictures, and sensations in teaching. I explain, I use my model skeleton and drawings, and I demonstrate and help people to feel, sometimes with my hands, and sometimes by positioning people and then letting them learn through the motion of the horse.

These three ways of learning combine to create an improved *use of self*. How you use your body is obviously of vital importance in any athletic venture as well as in everyday life. The concept of *use of self*, however, extends beyond the function of physical skills and includes the idea of an interactive mind-body relationship. Improvement in the performance of a physical activity such as riding, or simply getting up out of a chair, can best be achieved by first fully understanding the facets of an activity, and then by consciously avoiding focusing on the difficulties so that the right skills can develop. You can think of good *use of self* as "educated body language with intent." Good *use of self* results in efficiency of movement, which in turn allows fluid grace in all that you do.

In each teaching session in this book, you will have a chance to learn a little better *use of self*, first in the awareness session on the ground, and then on your horse. For the best *use of self*, you need to have learned to use the *Four Basics: centering, breathing, soft eyes,* and *building blocks.* You also need to be well *grounded* and to allow the feeling of a free, growing, and open body. These are the directives that will give you good *use of self*, which in turn will allow you to improve your riding skills.

You may feel stuck in your body and that learning a new way of using it will be hopelessly difficult. In fact, as I have discovered over the years this sort of learning is an ongoing process. The development of Centered Riding reflects my lifetime of gathering input from varied sources related to body movement and control. When I was a child with scoliosis, I worked with an innovative woman named Mabel Todd, who developed her own method of physical and occupational therapy after injuring herself falling down the stairs while sleepwalking during a flying dream! She taught me about anatomy and breathing as well as muscle development through exercises. Later, in my fifties, when I had lost some of what Miss Todd had taught me, I worked with Jean Gibson who helped me learn to release blocked sections of my body and to redevelop muscles that I had been using improperly for years.

Even later, I began to work with a man named Peter Payne who taught me the *Alexander Technique.* The *Alexander Technique* is a method of reeducating the mind and body toward greater balance and integration, with special reference to posture and movement. With the help of these methods of body control, combined with my own discovery of the power of *centering,* and after many years of finding my way through some pitfalls, I am much more able to use my body in an efficient way.

F.M. Alexander, who developed the *Alexander Technique,* was originally an actor striving for improved efficiency and body control in his craft (fig. 4.1). His premise stated that the body innately likes to be correct, but that we tend to develop habits, which ultimately distort our carriage and movement. We frequently are unaware of our bad habits because the familiar feels correct. In acquiring better *use of self,* Mr. Alexander developed a sequence that can be well applied to everything you learn in Centered Riding. First, you need to develop an awareness of your body and its movement. You can actually do much of this on your own, but an instructor can help you recognize bad habits, which inhibit your free body movement. An example might be something as simple as holding your breath when you ride.

If you can then experience, maybe only briefly at first, the sensation of a new way of movement, such as following the motion of your horse's back while continuing to breathe, you will be able to compare the old way with the new way. I hesitate to call these "good" or "bad" ways of performing an activity, because there is really no totally good or bad way, though there is always a choice between better or worse. When you accept this concept, you can avoid becoming judgmental and interfering with your progress by questioning, "Am I right?" or, "Am I wrong?" Instead, you can allow yourself to move on by noting changes such as, "That feels better," or, "That didn't feel as good."

As soon as you begin to use this comparison method, you will realize you have a choice. Do you want to stay on the old route or take the new one? Taking a moment to consciously make this decision will substantially help you to progress and to make the results of your efforts clear-cut. Since habits can be very strong and persistent, you may have to make a concerted effort to leave an old habit behind. Then you must give your body time to sort out the change. Leave the old way behind, and wait and allow the body to function in the new way. The steps toward improving your *use of self* can be listed in the following way:

1. Allow yourself to become aware.
2. Wait.
3. Make a choice.
4. Leave the old way behind.
5. Wait.
6. Allow the new movement to emerge.

The more you can work with sensations, especially of the whole rather than the left-brained lists of things, the more accurate and effective your riding will become. If you ride most of the time with consciousness of self, you will find that you use your aids more efficiently and simply, and therefore more clearly. Your horse will become your partner more completely than you have ever found before. When you ride with this good *use of self* and your horse comes into balance, you will find that you begin to dance in harmony together.

4.2 Peggy Brown is driving Ulie in competition. All the Centered Riding Basics apply to driving as well. In this picture, you can see the lovely centered connection between horse and driver. This is a perfect example of "use of self."

WHAT ARE THE ESSENTIALS OF Use of Self?

▶ There are three primary ways of learning: auditory, visual, and kinesthetic.
▶ Good use of self is "educated body language."
▶ It develops awareness of your body, and you learn an improved way of movement.
▶ Choose which way to move—the old way, or the new way.
▶ Let the old way go, and the new way emerge.

WHAT ARE THE RESULTS?

▶ An enhanced partnership with your horse.

On the Ground and On the Horse

In this section of the book, I will lead you through a progression of work and activity that will allow you to futher understand the concepts and practice of Centered Riding. The first part of each session will be on the ground, followed by a mounted section. The groundwork session will give you the opportunity to totally concentrate on yourself without the distraction of the horse. The mounted section will give you the chance to put into practice what you have learned on the ground.

Doing the work on the ground, you will develop greater awareness about yourself that will allow you to recognize tensions and resistances in your body, and ultimately realize your potential for fluid movement. You will learn how your body operates—both generally and specifically—before applying this new knowledge through simple exercises on your horse.

The mounted work gives you the opportunity to improve your horse's use of his body with the newly learned use of your own body. Although it is not my intent to make this a book about training horses, it is hard to separate the training of the rider from training the horse—one leads to the other—so you'll learn about the major elements of training that are common to all disciplines, such as up-and-down transitions, and circles and turns. These help a horse's body balance, as well as strengthen his back so he can raise it for improved movement. I do not go into the details of specific movements as these often vary with each discipline of riding.

Take your time learning this material because the work will become the foundation for your riding. You can use this solid *grounding* at any level or type of riding, from beginning dressage to higher level jumping, from Western pleasure to endurance riding.

Two words, which keep appearing in Centered Riding, are "aware" and "allow." In our society, we are often too busy trying to accomplish our objectives to take the time to become aware of the sensations along the way. We often become too goal-oriented and mechanical in our approach to an end result. Fortunately, because we are not machines, we can change and learn to be aware.

As you learn to be *aware*, you can begin to *allow* things to happen in your riding rather than *making* them happen. Through relinquishing total control of every situation, you may find new directions that will work well for you and your horse. You can begin to allow your horse to share the work with you. For instance, if you are in balance yourself and rebalance your horse before a corner, you can allow him to carry you both through the turn without "riding" him each step of the way. Or, for instance, if you soften your jaw, hands, and feet, you might find that your breathing pattern has changed radically. This change will surely affect your horse, and the work becomes more fun for both of you. This idea of allowing developments to occur, both unexpected and expected, may be a revolutionary concept for you and it may take some courage to implement. Give it a try and discover what happens. You are allowed to experiment and make mistakes, because, like a child learning to walk, it is through making mistakes that you learn.

It is best to do "awareness work" in comfortable, loose-fitting clothes, without shoes, in a warm, well-carpeted room. I have, however, found myself teaching in cold, covered arenas with students in riding clothes and down jackets, so any convenient setting will work. Though you can do much of this groundwork alone, sometimes you will need a partner. In fact, it can be advantageous to work in a group so that you can share your experiences.

5

Learning Balance
and Relaxation

We are now ready to start actual work in learning how to improve your use of your body so that you can help your horse improve the use of his. In order to attain *pure balance,* you will need to work on various exercises presented in this chapter.

ON THE GROUND

As you prepare for your first session of awareness work on the ground, stand comfortably with your feet apart. If there are several of you, make a circle, giving yourselves plenty of room. Close your eyes. Mentally search your body from the bottom-up for places that are tightened in an effort to keep you upright. Check your feet, toes, ankles, calves, knees, thighs, and buttocks for any spots of tension. Go on up through your hip joints, loin, stomach, ribs, shoulders, neck, jaw and head. Are you surprised to find a number of places tight for no real reason? Much of this tightness is an unconscious and unnecessary effort to contend with gravity. Gravity is always trying to pull us downward. You can learn to manage the problem of gravity without tension through an understanding of the body and correct balance.

Finding Your Sun

Muscles are long, stringy affairs that stretch from one bone across a joint or space to another bone. Each muscle has a counterpart. As the joint opens or closes, a muscle contracts (thereby shortening and thickening) and its counterpart lengthens. Unless muscles are in use, they should be long, relaxed, and just taut enough so that pairs of opposing muscles can balance the joint appropriately. Let us see if you can release your tight spots where you muscles are short and tense and allow them to become longer.

To begin to release some of your overall tension, try putting your fingertip on your sternum (breastbone) in the center of your chest. Now trace your finger about halfway down the length of your sternum until you find an indentation. With your finger in that indentation, become completely aware of that spot. This awareness will produce a release of tension in all directions. To help establish this awareness you can imagine a sun in that spot. Let your sun send warm rays upward and outward in a broad radius. You should feel a release in your chest and the front of your shoulders as well as your rib cage, abdomen and hip joints. I call this *Finding Your Sun*. Doing it frequently as you work, both on the ground and on your horse, is a good way to lighten your upper body and encourage forward and upward balance.

The Elastic Suit

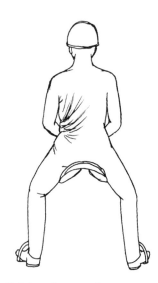

5.1 *Imagine wearing an "elastic suit" that doesn't fit. It pinches on one side so the whole suit is pulled out of shape. This makes it uncomfortable and restricting.*

Now imagine that you are wearing an *elastic suit* that covers your entire body (5.1). Does it fit you? If it fits, it will be smooth and stretchy all over. However, suppose there is a place that has been pinched together like a tuck, or a snag in a sweater where the pulled yarn puckers the stitching and puts the whole sweater out of line. Such a pinch in your elastic suit will make it uncomfortable and restricting. Each one of those tight spots you are finding in your body is like one of those little pinched places in your elastic suit causing you to be less comfortable and efficient. We are going to see how to eliminate these tense places in a simple way.

The Shake Out
ARMS
Test the freedom of one arm by moving it around through space—up, down, and around in circles, back and forth. Feel the weight of it. Does it feel light or heavy? Now lets do a *Shake Out*. Remember that any time you have freed muscles

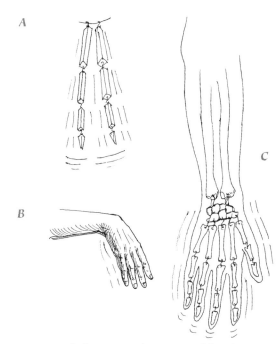

5.2 A–C *"Shaking Out" the wrist and hand.*

(A) *Allow the bones from the wrist to dangle as if they are prisms on a chandelier.*
(B & C) *Let your hand and wrist hang loose.*

that extend over a joint, you have lengthened them, and therefore given the joint more room for movement. Tight muscles across a joint jam the bones together and make them more difficult to use with coordination and balance. Keeping this in mind, shake out one wrist, moving your forearm to do so. Moving the bone and joint above a certain joint enables you to free that joint. Thus, when you shake the elbow and your forearm to free the wrist, your hand will bobble in all directions (figs. 5.2 A–C). Shake the wrist slowly at first until you are familiar with the feeling, and then gradually speed it up. Ultimately you can shake it quite hard in all different directions.

Pause for a moment and put some tension in your fingers. Try to shake the wrist again. You will find that it is no longer free to shake. Free your fin-

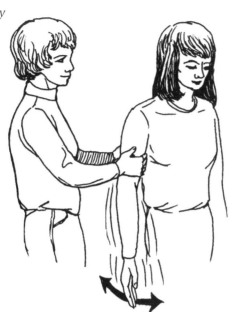

5.3 Free your elbow by moving your upper arm and shoulder in a forward-and-back, or slightly circular motion. It helps, at first, if you have someone else move your upper arm for you. This way, you will get the correct feeling before trying it on your own.

5.4 "Shake Out" the lower arm. Move the upper arm and allow the lower arm to remain limp from the elbow down.

gers and tighten your toes on one foot. Free the toes, and tighten and set your jaw. You will quickly find that when you tighten any part of your body it affects all other parts in some way.

To free up the elbow, you are going to have to move the upper arm and shoulder, and probably your torso too, in a forward and back, or slightly circular motion. Let the arm from the elbow down hang as if it were a *stone on a string* (fig. 5.3). Only then can you really free the elbow. If you are voluntarily moving the forearm around, you are not freeing it; you are using muscles and working it. Instead, let the forearm dangle and wobble freely as you shake the upper arm (fig. 5.4). When that feels free, you can move on up to the shoulder. Since the shoulder does not have a bone above it that you can move, you will have to move the whole torso. You should do this with a rotary motion. Take your right shoulder back, your left shoulder forward, then the left shoulder back and the right shoulder forward, and repeat this movement several times (fig. 5.5). If you try to loosen your shoulder by wiggling it around over the ribs, it won't work because you are

making it move instead of allowing it to flop. It helps to lean a little out over the arm as you rotate your body. Your whole arm at this point will dangle loosely.

When you have that whole arm shaken out, stand quietly for a moment and move the arm around in space the way you did at the beginning.

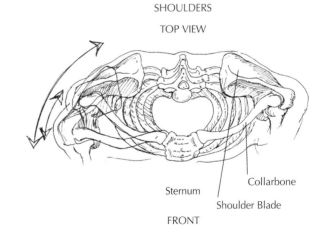

SHOULDERS

TOP VIEW

Sternum

Collarbone

Shoulder Blade

FRONT

5.5 "Shake Out" the whole arm by wobbling the shoulder back and forth.

ABOVE

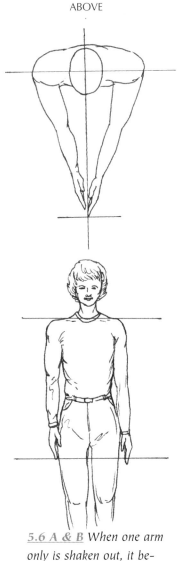

5.6 A & B When one arm only is shaken out, it becomes longer than the other.

Test how it feels. Does it feel different? It probably feels lighter, more airborne, and free, and has a greater range of motion. Now, let it drop to your side, and notice how it feels. Does it feel heavier and longer than the other arm, or tingly and lighter? Some people feel it one way, and some another. Either way is all right. If there are other people around you who have also shaken out one arm, look at them. Notice how funny they look now that they have one arm longer than the other, some of them quite a lot longer (figs. 5.6 A & B). None of them will be as even as they were before they started. If you are alone, look at yourself in the mirror. This may be a bit disconcerting because you will realize how tight you have been until now. To even up the arms, go through the same routine with the other arm.

LEGS

Next, try freeing the legs. Find your balance and stand on one foot. If you need help in balancing, put your hand on a chair or on somebody's shoulder. With your knee bent slightly in front, start loosening one ankle by shaking your lower leg. Let the foot hang with the toes and ankles all "flippy floppy" as if you were shaking water off your toes (fig. 5.7). Then try tightening up your toes. It is a hopeless situation. You can no longer shake your foot and ankle. They are now stiff. Just for a moment, contemplate yourself on a horse with your feet in the stirrups. How often do you tighten your feet, especially your toes, inside your

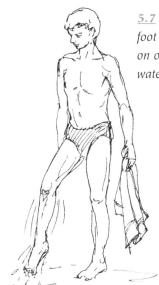

5.7 "Shake Out" one foot and ankle standing on one leg as if shaking water off your toes.

5.8 Release the knee. Rather than simply swinging your lower leg back and forth, use this alternative method of holding your thigh.

boots? You will probably find that you do this quite often. It takes training to keep the feet and ankles relaxed when you are riding, especially in moments of stress. While shaking your foot, try curling the toes of the foot you are standing on. You will find this devastating to your coordination and balance, and you will notice again the effect of one body part upon another. Now, free the toes again and finish shaking the ankle.

To release your knee, move the thigh and hip a little, letting the knee, lower leg, and foot just dangle softly. Unlike the ankle, wrist, and elbow, the knee has no rotary mobility so don't try any circular motion with it. Simply swing it gently back and forth without snapping it forward. Knees are delicate joints that need to be treated with respect (fig. 5.8).

5.9 *Finding the edge of the hip socket with fingers at the correct location.*

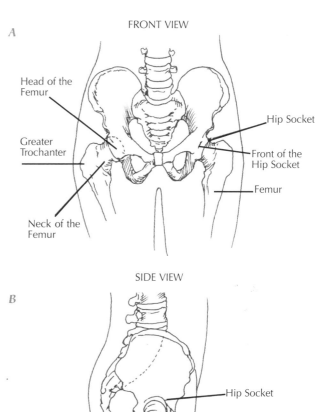

FRONT VIEW

Head of the Femur

Hip Socket

Greater Trochanter

Front of the Hip Socket

Femur

Neck of the Femur

SIDE VIEW

Hip Socket

Greater Trochanter

5.10 A & B *Hip joint anatomy.*

(A) Front view. (B) Side view.

HIPS

When your knee feels loose, you can begin to work on your hip. We should pause a moment here to make sure you know where your hip joint is. With your fingers pressed into the front bend of your hip socket, lift your knee up and down. This motion will flex your leg a little at the hip joint. You will feel a tendon that lines up with your knee tighten under your fingers. Move your fingers to the inner edge of this tendon, and you will be touching the front of your hip socket. You will find it is quite low (fig. 5.9). The joint itself consists of the ball at the end of the femur (thighbone), which slides in a deep, smooth socket in the pelvis. This socket extends back and up into your pelvis, and

you can only touch the front of it. From the hip joint, the femur goes out to the side almost horizontally for a couple of inches before it angles sharply down toward the knee (figs. 5.10 A & B). Put the palm of your hand on the outside of your hip, about on the seam of your pants, as shown, and rotate your knee out and in. When you find the right spot under your hand, you will feel the greater trochanter, the corner of the femur, move back and forth as it pivots in the hip joint. Put your

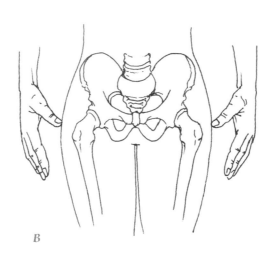

B

<u>5.11 A–C</u> *Locating the hip joint.*

First, find the greater trochanters with the flat of your hands (A); then put your thumbs on top pointing them into the depths of the hip sockets (B & C)

thumbs on the tops of the greater trochanters, and point them at each other. Your actual hip joints are a couple of inches directly to the inside from your thumbs (figs. 5.11 A–C).

Now that you have located your hip joint, you can release it. Balance on one leg, holding onto something. Let the other leg hang loosely. Remember that if you move the leg around purposefully, you are not loosening it. It must hang in a floppy manner from deep in the hip joint. You will have to tip away a little from this leg to keep it off the ground, or leave just the toe of this foot on the ground. Now wobble your hips a little but not excessively. When you put your foot down on the ground again, close your eyes, and think about that leg. How does it feel? I am sure it feels longer than the other, fully active, and tingly. It is longer, just as your arm was longer. To even yourself up, you need to do the same routine with the other leg (fig. 5.12).

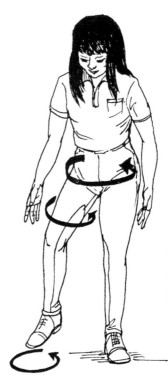

<u>5.12</u> *"Shaking Out" the hip joint. Wobble the thigh in the hip joint as shown.*

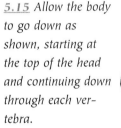

5.13–5.16 "Shaking Out" the Spine.

5.13 "Shaking Out" the spine causes a ripple effect the same as beads being shaken on a string.

SPINE

Lastly, you must free the 24 joints of the spine. You can think of them as *beads on a string* that will rattle if you shake them (fig. 5.13). You need to choose one of two ways to do this exercise–depending on your physical condition. Unless you have a strong back (see below), and many people do not, you should stay upright. Place your feet slightly turned out about a shoulder width apart. Flex both knees forward and slightly out, letting the hip joints and pelvis go softly back as needed. Begin to flex your knees alternately forward and back allowing this motion to wobble your pelvis

softly and comfortably on your hip joints (fig. 5.14). This will in turn begin to send ripples up your spine and through your neck to your head balanced between your ears. Let your torso slosh and ripple up through your body. You may find that you are allowing yourself an amazing amount of motion and activity, fun and laughter.

If you have a strong back, after you get your knees and pelvis wobbling, allow your spine to bend down starting with your head and neck and gradually going down one vertebra at a time until your sacrum is above your head and your spine hangs from your sacrum like those rattling *beads on a string* (fig. 5.15). Let your arms hang down, your hair fall off, your teeth fall out,

5.14 Start by flexing one knee, then the other. Wobble the sacrum and create a ripple effect up the spine.

5.15 Allow the body to go down as shown, starting at the top of the head and continuing down through each vertebra.

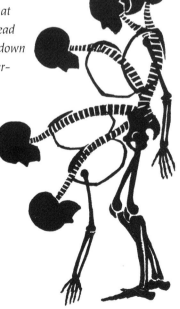

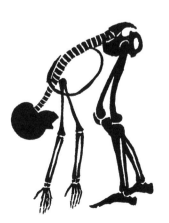

5.16 With your body hanging from your sacrum, "Shake Out" your beads-on-the-string-feeling spine by flexing first one knee, and then the other.

and your cheeks slide off (fig. 5.16). Shake a moment from your pelvis, not too long, and then keeping your knees active, gradually come to the upright one vertebra at a time, starting at the bottom, your head coming up the very last.

How do you feel? Do you feel light, free, and open? You probably do. Gravity is no longer pulling you down so hard. And, your *elastic suit* fits much better.

The Teeter-Totter

For further awareness experiences, try this *Teeter-Totter* exercise. Stand quietly and comfortably erect, feet slightly apart. With your whole body straight, tip forward as far as you can without having to take a step to catch yourself. Hold yourself in this extreme position with your feet quiet. Notice how much tension there is in your body, your feet, legs, torso, and neck. Come back to the center and relax. Now lean backward and notice again the degree of tension in your whole body, especially up the front of your thighs and torso. Come back to the center and feel the freedom and ease of being in balance—I like to call this being in *pure balance* (fig. 5.17). Take time to imagine the significance of this contrast on a horse. You only tipped a little bit. If you are not balanced over your stirrups with your center directly over your feet, you are tense. You have to be tense in order not to tip over or fall off your horse. This is true whether you are in a deep, upright seat, or a half-seat—both of which I will discuss next.

Seat Positions on the Horse

I'm going to break from doing pure groundwork at this point in the session to explain the different seats you can use in Centered Riding because you need to simulate, or imagine these possible positions in many of the exercises you do off the horse as well as on. There are three (figs. 5.18 A–C):

1. The *deep*, upright seat. It is a called a three-point seat position, with both seat bones and legs

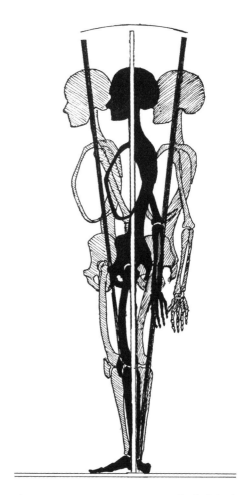

5.17 The "Teeter-Totter" exercise. Rock slightly forward from your feet, balance in the middle, rock slightly back, and come back to "pure balance."

touching the saddle. This seat gives the rider the most complete contact possible with the horse's back, and therefore the most intimate control of his movements. It is used extensively for schooling and riding on the flat, and in dressage work.

2. The *half-seat.* Also known as the two-point or jumping seat, and ridden in a forward-angle position. Here, your weight is balanced over your stirrups with your seat bones not touching the saddle at all. It is a strong, adjustable seat, used in the trot and canter, efficient for cross-country riding, and very useful when working with a

<u>5.18 A–C</u> *(A) The deep seat*   *(B) The half-seat*   *(C) The light seat*

young horse who is not yet strong enough to carry a rider's full weight directly on his back. A galloping seat is an accentuated half-seat with a shorter stirrup so the hip and knee angles become even more acute.

3. The *light* seat. This is a slightly forward seat with the rider's body weight just barely off the saddle and useful for schooling on the flat as well as cross-country riding. It is an amalgamation of the half-seat and the deep seat, thus giving the horse a little less direct weight to carry on his back.

Feet in the Sand

Now, in order to find your balance, stand quietly again, feet not more than shoulder-width apart and become aware of the soles of your feet. Pretend that you are standing on slightly damp sand and making an imprint with your foot—not a deep hole, just a mark on the sand. The sand is firm and pleasant, not too hot or cold. Leave an imprint of each foot, each separate toe, big toes, second toes, third toes, fourth toes, little toes, all equal. The ball of your foot, the outside rim of your foot, and your whole heel from the edge to the center, all leave their imprint. The sand fills up the arch of your foot. You have made a perfect imprint of your foot in the sand. Do the same with the other foot so that both feet feel as if they have a total warm connection with the sand. Notice how completely *grounded* you feel.

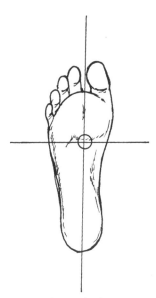

_5.19_ This is the location
of the "Bubbling Spring."

_5.20_ Palpating the bottom of the foot on the "Bubbling Spring."

The Bubbling Spring

Now think about the balance point of the foot. If you were a tightrope walker, you would be very conscious of the balance line down the length of the foot (fig. 5.19). This line extends from between the big and second toe to just inside the middle of the heel. Another balance line crosses the width just at the back edge of the ball of the foot. The intersection of these two lines is the foot's balance point. To find this spot more exactly, sit down and palpate the bottom of your foot with your fingers as shown in figure 5.20. You will find the point of intersection about two to three inches behind the big joint of the second toe in a soft part of the foot. Play with this spot for a bit, and you will find it very pleasant. In acupuncture, this spot is called the "Bubbling Spring."

In my martial arts class, we were taught to let energy come up from the ground through the _Bubbling Spring_ or release it down into the ground through that point. Stand again and open your feet so that they make an imprint on the imaginary sand, and think about the _Bubbling Spring_. Imagine energy from the ground coming up through your legs and into your body.

As you stand there, become aware of how your center balances over your feet, over their _Bubbling Springs_. As you find your center, feel the energy surging back and forth through your body below

5.21 Energy effervescing up through the body from the "Bubbling Spring."

your navel. There is a Chinese proverb that says, "When the chi (energy) starts at your center, goes down through the hips and knees and out through the *Bubbling Spring,* this spirit of lightness comes up through the *Bubbling Spring,* the knees and hips and when it reaches the top of your head, all dullness vanishes (fig. 5.21)."

There are receptors in the bottoms of your feet that trigger an automatic reflex throughout your body, which in turn, enables you to stand upright without tension and effort. You will find that the *building blocks* of your body will stack up automatically now, as you stand centered with your feet "open and receiving." Your balance is easy and you should feel a definite connection with the ground. In addition, when you sit with your pelvis squarely balanced on your seat bones, either on a chair or on a horse, another set of receptors is activated in your seat. As a re-

sult, your body will again stack itself up, and become balanced automatically. It can be a great relief when you allow this reflex action to do the balancing work for you. Balance is dynamic, it is never static; your body must allow for all minute adjustments in order to maintain equilibrium.

The Sled

There is a close relationship between being *centered* and *grounded,* and the reflex actions that trigger upright balance. First, imagine yourself sitting on a small sled, and somebody coming along behind you and pushing your shoulders to try to make you and your sled slide forward. Your upper body will actually be shoved forward before the sled starts to move. Your seat will then move with the sled, and as it picks up speed, your shoulders will actually be left behind. If the person behind you pushes the sled only, your upper body will fall back because your bottom will be taken out from under you (fig. 5.22).

Now, imagine instead that the person behind you places his hands across your lower back just behind your center and pushes in that spot. This time, the sled moves forward easily, carrying you with it in balance without flopping you forward or back (fig. 5.23). Since you are *grounded,* sitting solidly on the sled, initiating move-

5.22 Pushing a person on her shoulders, above her center, gives her a jerky start and she falls backward.

5.23 Pushing a person from behind her center gives her a smooth start and she stays balanced.

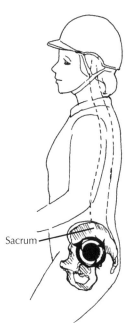

5.24 A side view of the torso and pelvis showing your center as a rotating, floating "ball," spinning gently backward.

Sacrum

ment from your center, you become more stable. Your balanced seat on the sled triggers the upright reflexes and if you *center* and *let your spine lengthen,* you will become powerful in your stability. Through your awareness work, you can now allow your body to become balanced.

Center and Grow

Picture the *ball* in your center suspended inside the *bowl* of your pelvis. Let it float there and gently rotate backward, softly touching, but not attached to the top of your sacrum (fig. 5.24). (I'll discuss this anatomy in detail on p. 49.) From this center, you can grow in all directions, but chiefly down and up. You must first grow down and become *grounded* before you can grow up. It is helpful to think of the directive as *"ground, center, and grow."* And, imagine that you are a growing *spruce tree.* A tree cannot *make* itself grow; it can only *allow* itself to grow. So, *allow* your torso, the trunk of the tree, to grow up while your legs, the roots of the tree, grow down. It's okay to repeat this directive as often as you want, then let it go, as trying to constantly maintain this "growing" feeling will cause you to become rigid.

Another way to understand how your body can grow is by imagining a *bungee cord* attached to the middle of the top of your head just above your ears (fig. 5.25). If this bungee cord is pulled up from the *front* part of the top of your head, it will pull your face up, jutting your chin out, and shortening the back of your neck and hollowing your lower back (all of which are undesirable and make for stiffness). And, if this bungee cord is pulled from

5.25 Imagine hanging from a "bungee cord." The nice thing about a bungee cord is that it has resilient strength and stretches both ways.

the *back* part of the top of your head, your chin will jam into your chest forcing you to look at the ground, and again creating stiffness. However, if it is pulled from *above,* just above your ears, your head and torso will stretch up, while the elasticity of the cord will allow your legs to drop down. Using either the *bungee cord* or the *spruce tree* images along with the image of the *ball* in your center, you can begin to utilize the concept of *center and grow.*

Clear Intent and the Unbendable Arm

To add to your new understanding and help improve communication with your horse, you can use the concept of *clear intent.* In the practice of the martial arts, strength can become effortless. Centered Riding not only teaches relaxation and softness, but this sort of effortless strength as well. In order to experience it, try this simple exercise—the *Unbendable Arm.* You will need a partner. With your thumb up, extend one arm a bit forward of sideways. Make a fist and keep your arm straight. Let your partner stand behind your outstretched arm, and put one hand under your wrist with the other hand on top of your elbow. She should now attempt to bend your arm, softly at first, but building up to real force. Whether or not your partner succeeds in bending your arm is not important, but take note of the type of resistance you offer. Your partner will probably feel a lot of effort

<u>5.26 A & B</u> *The "Unbendable Arm."*
(A) Jineen is resisting. Note her clenched fists, jaw, and belly. (B) With Jineen's "grounding" and "clear intent" her arm will remain straight. The slight bend of her elbow allows her arm to be resilient; it's not a sign of weakness.

on your part, as you are likely using tight, resistant muscles (fig. 5.26 A).

This type of resistance is frequently the result of anxiety. In this case, it is anxiety about letting your arm bend. What would happen if you replaced your stiff resistance with a *clear intent* that your arm will not bend? Try standing calmly centered, conscious of your *Four Basics—soft eyes, centering, breathing,* and *building blocks.* Sense that your feet are clearly connected with the ground. Using the same arm as before, give it a good shake from the shoulder to bring some awareness into it.

Extend it again, but this time let the elbow be very slightly bent, the fingers softly open. Position your hand with the thumb side on top, so that when your partner tries to bend your arm, she will not be able to damage your elbow (fig. 5.26 B).

This time, before your partner puts any pressure on your arm, you must make a decision. Decide absolutely that your arm will not bend. Don't make this decision by screwing up your eyes and holding your breath, but rather center yourself and make the decision from your center. Since you are not a light bulb that stays on when you flip the switch, you will need to make this decision repeatedly. Maintain *clear intent* that your arm will remain straight. You will not have to work and struggle to keep the arm straight–you simply have this *clear intent*.

Again, starting gently, your partner should steadily increase the force on your arm unless she feels you waver. If you do waver, she must not decrease her efforts, but must stop increasing the pressure until she feels new energy surging through your arm. Then she can continue building the effort to her full strength.

If you lose your *soft eyes,* or change your quiet *breathing* and *centering,* your arm will bend. It helps not to watch your arm, but to look around at the room, or talk to your friends. Realize it is fun, and smile. Your arm may feel springy but resilient to your partner, and you may be surprised by the amount of effort she uses while you feel as if you are doing no work. The true test is if you can keep your fingers soft and flexible while your partner works at bending your arm.

The *Unbendable Arm* is not as miraculous as it may seem. When you become anxious or fearful, you use extra muscles that actually interfere rather than help. They get in the way of the muscles that were originally intended to do the job. With your *clear intent,* you have allowed your body to decide which muscles to use.

Try this same *Unbendable Arm* exercise again with a slightly different focus. Adding to your *clear intent,* imagine that your arm is a *fire hose* (fig. 5.27). The pressure is tremendous, shooting the water a long way out, through the walls of the room, out into space. Let your "*fire-hose arm*" send the water through in pulsations of energy. Fire hoses with water rushing through them are springy but do not collapse. When you keep in your mind the pulsating image of water pouring through the hose, your partner will feel surges of energy passing through your arm and it will be remarkably strong. The texture of the *Unbendable*

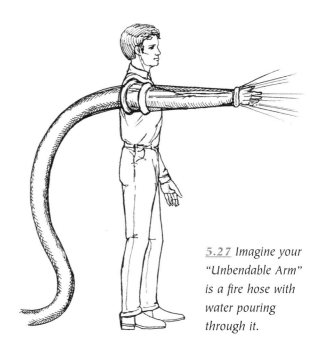

5.27 Imagine your "Unbendable Arm" is a fire hose with water pouring through it.

Arm should be soft and resilient, without tension, and the contrast between how your arm feels now and the resistant tightness of the first effort I described will be very evident to your partner.

The *Unbendable Arm* exercise will help you understand the availability of the kind of strength and energy that comes through *clear intent.* You now realize how strength comes from elastic energy, not rigidity. I refer to this strength in my teaching as "*Unbendable Arm* energy." It can be used in countless ways, on or with a horse, using either *clear intent,* or with the image of the *fire hose.* Horses clearly understand this effortless language and instinctively, even profoundly, respect it.

Now take a little walk, keeping in mind your new understanding of your anatomy, as well as the sensations you have acquired from doing your groundwork. With a relaxed head and neck, *soft eyes*, and easy *breathing,* walk, allowing your pelvis to move easily around the *ball* in your center. You will find that your lower back moves softly, and you will realize that your pelvic bones can move in many directions without disturbing the quiet, rotating stability of the *ball*. Release your hip joints and knees, and let your *bungee cord* take you forward and upward. As you walk, you will feel that your body is working more efficiently without effort.

The Balance Beam and the Wiggly Barrel

There are additional experiments that explain centered balance. Instructor and trainer, Michel Vermeulin[1], has a potent way to show you how much you depend on your horse's barrel to maintain your balance. He has you sit on a balance beam, or a two-by-six-inch plank, laid between two upright barrels or supports. You are allowed a sweater or pad to sit on. Since your feet cannot touch the ground you have no grip and must depend totally on balance both sideways, and forward and back. Clearly, you need your *Four Basics* and *grounding* to make this possible (fig. 5.28).

Robin Brueckmann has her students straddle a 50-gallon drum lying on its side, which for most of us prevents our feet from touching the ground. This wiggly barrel gives you amazing feedback on the need for, and how to use, your Centered Riding *Basics* and *grounding*.

5.28 When you sit like this—on a plank or a balance beam—and your feet cannot touch the ground, you have to rely solely on centered balance without thigh support to keep you upright.

ON THE HORSE

You should now be ready to take your new awareness onto your horse. However, you must first be sure you are sitting on a saddle that fits you *and* your horse. An ill-fitting saddle will not only be unbalanced on the horse's back, but will cause discomfort as well, making it difficult for both of you to learn. I used to think a horse that would not stand still was just a fidgety nuisance in need of discipline. Now I realize that most of these horses are indicating that they are uncomfortable. Several years ago, I worked with a small, stocky mare that would not, or could not, stay still for even a few seconds. She was steadier when working, but still moved with tension. After we carefully padded the saddle so that it no longer pinched the sides of her spine—especially in the area just behind the shoulders—she became perfectly quiet, stood stock still with her ears flopping, and worked happily in a relaxed fashion. She was comfortable.

Now when I travel to teach clinics, I bring two or three excellent saddle pads, as well as several smaller pieces of padding. Before I start the class, I make sure every horse is comfortable. In the majority of my classes, I find that I must use at least one of these pads.

A saddle correctly balanced on the horse's back has the lowest part of the seat in the center of the saddle, close to the pommel. If the lowest part is too far back, the rider will have to constantly struggle to keep her center over her feet. If it is too

---

1 Michel Vermeulen. Graduated from Haras du Pin, the French National Stud school for trainers, and from Saumur, the French Cavalry school, home of the famous Cadre Noir, at the head of his class. In Europe and the US, he has trained many successful horses and riders in all phases of riding.

far forward, it causes discomfort to the rider's crotch. Saddles can also be too narrow and painfully pinch the horse at and just below his withers, and along each side of his spine. Fortunately, there is a large variety of pads available to help with balance and fitting problems.

For a saddle, which is balanced but pinches the horse, a fairly thick pad can afford some temporary relief. This sort of pad is also very useful in promoting the comfort of the horse simply as additional protection from the bumping of the rider.

Pads, of course, are not the final answer. The real solution is a balanced saddle that fits the horse, but the pad can temporarily alleviate discomfort during a lesson so the horse and rider can learn properly. This is an example of the importance of awareness—in this case, awareness of your horse's needs.

For this initial session in developing awareness on your horse, you will need a helper. Take some time to just sit on your horse at the halt with your feet out of the stirrups. Your helper can hold your horse if necessary. As you sit on your comfortable horse in your balanced saddle, make sure your seat bones are in the deepest part of it just behind the pommel. In order to make sure your seat bones are not too far back, without your stirrups push your legs out in front of the saddle so that your lower legs hang ahead of the flaps. Now slide or wiggle yourself forward a little and then let your legs hang down again in the normal position. Your seat bones should now be in the proper part of the saddle.

The Rocking Chair

With your feet in your stirrups, try the *Teeter-Totter* exercise you learned in your awareness work on the ground, only this time do the *Teeter-Totter* on your seat bones instead of your feet. Seat bones are shaped a little like the rockers of a *rocking chair*, and you would like your "chair"—your upper body—to balance over the middle of the rockers (fig. 5.29). Many riders habitually lean either too far back or

too far forward. The *Teeter-Totter* exercise will help you to find this middle point of balance.

If you tend to lean too far back, onto the *back* of your seat bone "rockers," at first try tipping too far forward, onto the *front* of the rockers. This position will cause some of your muscles to tighten to prevent you from falling over. Lean too far back, and once more, your muscles will tighten your

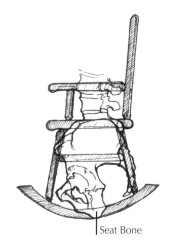

Seat Bone

5.29 From a side view, seat bones are similar to the rockers of a rocking chair.

legs. Lean too far forward again, and then come very slowly upright, stopping when you feel that no muscles are needed to keep you perpendicular on your horse. This position is the perfect balance point and gives you *pure balance* (figs. 5.30 A–C).

If your tendency is to lean too far forward, do the exercise above in the opposite direction.

Finding your correct balance point through a position opposite from your tendency causes you to move your body through unfamiliar territory. In other words, if you tend to lean backward and try to correct yourself simply by straightening up, you will come forward through familiar territory and will probably stop in familiar territory before you come to the correct perpendicular point of balance.

Your new corrected *pure balance* point may feel strange at first, but you will gradually begin to sense how wonderfully right this position feels compared to your old, familiar, but incorrect one. Now that you have found the balance point, think about how effortless this position feels. Move to your familiar backward or forward position and notice how much more effort is needed. Not only

5.30 A–C *Learning balance and relaxation.*

(A) *When Cynthia leans too far forward, she grips with her legs and holds her breath.*

(B) *She has the same problems when she leans too far back.*

(C) *Now that she has found "pure balance" she can sit effortlessly, though the picture shows some tension in her upper body probably caused by self-consciousness.*

is it hard work to be out of balance, but also from the extra effort involved in simply hanging on, your legs are not readily available for the use of aids. If, at any time, you find yourself losing your balance, and we all do, try the *Teeter-Totter* at first physically, and later just mentally, to bring yourself back in balance.

Now that you have found yourself balanced, you may discover that you don't dare to move. "I'll lose it all if I move!" you may think. Luckily, this is a dilemma easily resolved.

Keeping Your Pure Balance

With your fingers, find the hollow at the top of your sternum (breastbone) where your collarbones attach in the center of your upper chest (sterno-clavicular joint). (See figs. 5.5 and 6.7.) Remove your fingers and move that spot left and right, back and forth. It might help to imagine that there is a *searchlight beam* emanating from that spot. Swing that beam back and forth ahead of you. What happened to your shoulder girdle (shoulder blades and collarbones) and your sternum? Because they are attached at that spot, they followed your movement. What happened to your rib cage? Did it move? Of course it did, because all those ribs, except the floating ones at the very bottom, are attached to the sternum on one end and the thoracic vertebrae on the other. If the sternum rotates back and forth, so must the ribs and the thoracic vertebrae to which they are attached.

In short, by rotating that one little spot high up on your chest, you have freely rotated your whole upper body. What part of your skeleton allows all this free movement? It is the lumbar spine, the five big vertebrae between your rib cage and your pelvis, which allows the torso to bend and rotate.

With this in mind, sit balanced on your horse and swing that hollow spot around one way and then the other. You will probably need someone to hold your horse at this point. With limp arms, swing your upper body around, back and forth

several times. Allow your arms to flap against your body as they swing out, then curl around against your back and front as you twist (fig. 5.31 A–C). As you twist back and forth, remember that *searchlight beam*. Let your head and eyes follow that beam as you look behind, right and left.

Now sit quietly again. With your arms hanging softly, lift the tips of your shoulders straight up, push them back, and let them drop freely. Repeat this motion several times, and gradually allow the shoulders to move independently in any direction as you speed up the whole movement.

Sit quietly once more, and *center* yourself. Now begin to do a *shake out* of your upper body so it shakes the shoulders and makes your arms rattle. You can now alternate this shaking with your shoulder rotation and the upper-body twisting. Finally, simply lie down on your horse's neck with your head resting on the side, and your arms and legs hanging loose and limp. Have a rest, breathe freely, and when you sit up again, give yourself one more good shake.

How do you feel now? Have you lost any of your inner balance and poise? You might be surprised to find that your balance has actually improved because these exercises have afforded you some relaxation and freedom of movement. You should no longer feel worried about losing your hard-won balance when you move off.

Before you ride off in your newly balanced position, dangle your legs, without stirrups, down your horse's sides. Shake out first one leg then the other, and then both at once. If you are very tight in your hips or have arthritis, do only what is comfortable. Do not be brave and try to work through pain. Working in pain irritates and often damages whatever is hurting. It is better to do less and gradually build up to the increased motion as your body becomes accustomed to it. Centered Riding almost always helps alleviate stiffness and pain, not by the "grin-and-bear it" method, but by education and the resulting ease of movement. ∾

5.31 A–C Keeping your "pure balance."

The rider is doing one complete rotation of her torso swinging her arms as shown. She could have allowed her head and neck to go more freely with the rotation.

WHAT ARE THE ESSENTIALS OF Learning Balancing and Relaxation?

ON THE GROUND

- ► Check for tight places in your body—the *elastic suit.*
- ► *Shake Out* like *beads on a string* to release all joints.
- ► Seat positions: the *deep seat, half-seat,* and the *light seat.*
- ► *Finding Your Sun; Feet in the Sand; Teeter-Totter; Bubbling Spring; Sled; ground-center-grow; bungee cord; clear intent.*
- ► The *Unbendable Arm* for soft power. Imagine it as a fire hose.

ON THE HORSE

- ► Saddle must fit and balance on the horse correctly.
- ► The *rocking chair* to find *pure balance.*
- ► The *searchlight beam* for easy rotation of your upper body.
- ► *Shake Out* your legs.

WHAT ARE THE RESULTS?

- ► Freedom of movement without losing balance.
- ► New awareness.

6

The Following Seat

Now that you have a sense of balance when the horse is in motion, you are ready to coordinate this into what I call the *following seat.* I'm going to introduce you in this chapter to the movement of your horse's body, with special emphasis on his back. You will become more aware of how your body—in all its different parts—can coordinate with the horse's movement so that, first you do not interfere with it, and secondly, can use this coordination in order to tell him what you want him to do. (In other words, you follow him using a *following seat.*) With this, your directives will be clear to him so he will obey them willingly.

ON THE GROUND

Skeletal Anatomy

In order to use your body with maximum skill, you need to have an understanding of where the bones of your skeleton are, and how they articulate. I tell my students to "ride with their bones," so the muscles will be able to do their parts easily. But, in order to "ride with your bones" you need to understand your skeletal anatomy. And, in order to understand your skeletal anatomy, you will need patience and perseverance! There is a lot of information here to absorb, but rest assured that it will be worth the time and trouble in the end. Do not get discouraged!

PELVIS AND LUMBAR AREA

Take a moment to think about the anatomy of the torso. I'll start with the pelvis. There are three parts: the sacrum, and the two illia, which connect at the pubic arch. The sacrum, which is formed by the last five spinal vertebrae fused together, forms the back of the pelvis, with the illia forming the two sides, wrapping around to the front where they attach at the pubis. These bones are so firmly attached to each other by ligaments that they seem to form one solid piece shaped somewhat like a *bowl.*

The sockets of your hip joints lie on both sides of the pelvis, as I explained on page 33. The balls at the end of your femurs (thighbones) fit into these sockets, and it is at these points that your legs support not only your pelvis, but also your entire upper body (fig. 6.1). The pelvis hangs on the hip joints much like a hammock supported by your legs. The dense, heavy bone at the bottom of the pelvis helps to stabilize it. Your hip joints not only allow you to be erect, but along with the joints in your knees and ankles, allow you immense flexibility.

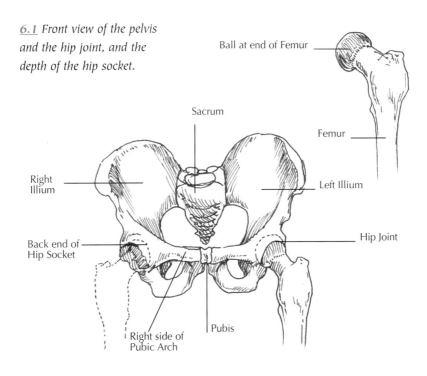

<u>6.1</u> *Front view of the pelvis and the hip joint, and the depth of the hip socket.*

Ball at end of Femur

Sacrum

Femur

Right Illium

Left Illium

Hip Joint

Back end of Hip Socket

Right side of Pubic Arch

Pubis

FRONT VIEW

The weight of your torso coming down from the spine through your sacrum lands somewhat behind the upward support and thrust of your legs. This construction allows a slight shock-absorbing quality in your pelvic region. In addition, the vertebrae of the lower back that make up the lumbar spine have a slight forward curve, which also provides some shock absorption (fig. 6.2 A). However, if this curve becomes too pronounced—if you hold yourself in a sway-backed posture (lordosis)—the lumbosacral joint is placed directly above the hip joint. This position (a very common one) eliminates nature's intended shock absorber, and will cause jarring and pain (figs. 6.2 B and 6.3). This shock-absorbing system continues throughout the length of your spine, with the forward curve of the lumbar spine, a backward curve in the thoracic (rib cage) area, and another forward curve in the cervical (neck) area. These are all moderate curves, which provide a cushioning effect for your back. If any of the curves are too pronounced or too straight, your back will suffer stress and work inefficiently. If, instead of forward, you pushed your lumbar spine into a roached, or slumped position you will have a different problem—one that can be harder to overcome (fig. 6.2 C): the pelvis tucks under, putting you on the back of your seat-bone *rocking chair rockers* (p. 44), and tends to lock as the slightly forward curve of the supporting cushion of the spine is lost. Correct positioning of your back, starting with your pelvis, is important for your balance, resilience, and comfort (fig. 6.2 A).

It is interesting to note that your center of gravity is in the same area as your center, though they are not the same thing. However, this location of your center of gravity in your pelvic area, explains why you need to have your center over your feet, or your feet under your center, in order to be

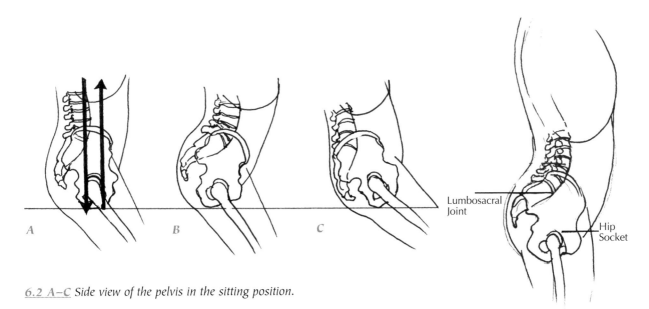

Lumbosacral
Joint

Hip
Socket

<u>6.2 A–C</u> *Side view of the pelvis in the sitting position.*

(A) The pelvis balanced ideally. This allows the upward thrust (up arrow) of your seat bones, or legs if you are standing. The weight of your body goes down (down arrow) through your lumbar spine and seat bones, or legs. When the downward thrust of your weight is slightly behind the upward thrust of your seat bones, or legs, you will have shock absorption in the pelvic region. (B) Lordosis—the top of the pelvis is locked forward. (C) The pelvis is locked backward in a roached, or slumped position.

<u>6.3</u> *This side view of a standing pelvis locked forward (in lordosis) is an uncomfortable position assumed by many riders.*

in balance. While you are standing upright, feet somewhat apart, bend your three leg joints–the hips, knees, and ankles. This position is similar to the *half-seat* on your horse (fig. 6.4). Notice that your center remains over your feet. If it did not, you would fall over. Move back and forth between a *deep,* upright seat, and a half-seat, and notice how your three joints adjust and coordinate to give you a soft balance while in motion. You will notice when you bend your joints into your half-seat that your hip joints move back the same distance as your knees move forward. The movement is distributed equally between the joints (fig. 6.5).

The muscle attachment between the pelvis and the rib cage are important to your posture. The psoas muscles run from the front of the lumbar spine across the front of the pelvis and attach to the upper inner femur. The diaphragm goes across the torso at the bottom of the rib cage, which it cups up into with a big root attaching it to the lumbar spine. The fibers of the root of the diaphragm intermingle with those of the top of the psoas (figs. 6.6 A & B). This means that breathing with the diaphragm can help engage the psoas muscles, which is very important in seat, balance, and posture.

<u>6.5</u> *Centered balance in the deep seat. As Lucy brings her hips forward into the deep seat she should allow her knees to come more forward as Cynthia (in red) has done.*

<u>6.4</u> *Centered balance in the half-seat. Lucy (wearing blue) is well-grounded with energy going forward through her knees. She is also showing good flexion of ankles, knees, and hips. Cynthia shows tension in her lower back resulting in some stiffness in the rest of her body.*

RIB CAGE

Above your pelvic and lumbar area, your rib cage consists of 12 pairs of ribs with one end of each rib attached to one of your 12 thoracic vertebrae (figs. 6.7 A–C). These attachments allow some limited hinge-like motion. However, this is a part of our bodies where tension can severely limit the available mobility. The ability to lift and expand the rib cage at those hinges is very important in breathing. The front of the ribs (except the bottom two "floating" pairs), are attached by cartilage to the sternum. Cartilage is moveable, giving the front of the ribs more mobility than the back. As a result, many people use only the front of the rib cage to allow expansion of the lungs. In fact, allowing both front and back to move makes breathing more efficient.

SHOULDER GIRDLE

The balance and carriage of your shoulder girdle above your rib cage are also important. Your shoulder girdle consists of your shoulder blades (scapulae) in back, and collarbones (clavicles) in front. Shoulders are only attached to the skeleton where the collarbones meet the top of your sternum in the front. As you did in Session One, try putting your fingers at the top of your sternum where your collarbones meet (sterno-clavicular joint) and move your shoulders around with big motions to get acquainted with that joint. Your shoulder blades in the back are not attached to your skeleton at all; they are supported by your muscles only, (just as your horse's are, by the way). The whole shoulder girdle is supported by your rib cage, as well as by muscles from your head and

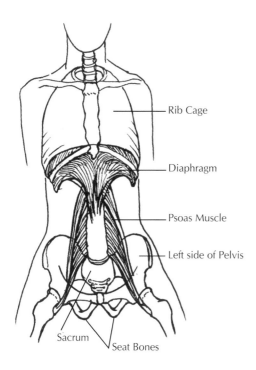

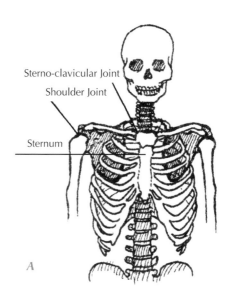

Rib Cage

Diaphragm

Psoas Muscle

Left side of Pelvis

Sacrum

Seat Bones

A

Sterno-clavicular Joint

Shoulder Joint

Sternum

A

FRONT TOP VIEW

Shoulder Blade

Collarbone

B

6.6 A & B *The diaphragm muscle and the psoas muscle shown from front and side views. Note the way they are attached to the lower spine, and how the psoas muscle is attached to the femur as well.*

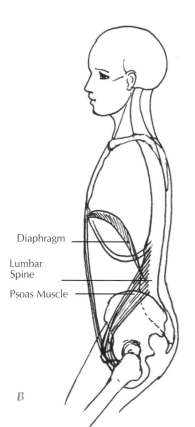

Diaphragm

Lumbar
Spine

Psoas Muscle

B

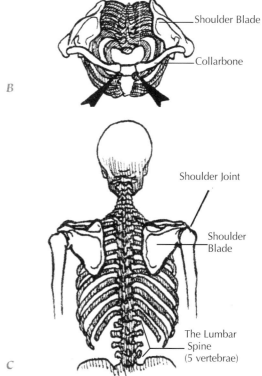

Shoulder Joint

Shoulder
Blade

The Lumbar
Spine
(5 vertebrae)

C

6.7 A–C *The shoulder girdle (shoulder blades and collarbones) and the rib cage.*

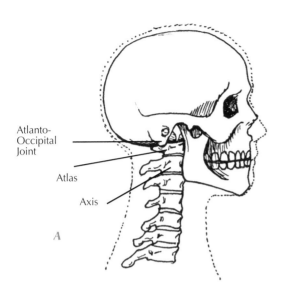

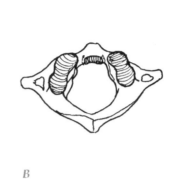

Atlanto-
Occipital
Joint

Atlas

Axis

A

B

6.8 A & B

(A) The head and neck side view indicating the location of the atlanto-occipital joint, which you cannot see in the human skeleton because it is deep in the skull between the ears. (B) A top view of the atlas.

neck, and can be very mobile unless you allow tension to lock up this area.

Freeing the Head and Neck

Above your shoulders, your neck supports your head, but unknown to many, one-half of your neck is actually *inside* your head. The point at which your head balances on the top vertebra of your spine (the atlas) is the atlanto-occipital joint (figs. 6.8 A & B). To discover this important spot, place a finger on the front cartilage of both ears and point the fingers toward each other. The atlanto-occipital joint lies directly between your two fingers, well forward under your skull, between your ears, and very near the hinge of your jaw. While continuing to hold your fingers on your ears, "bobble" your head so your face moves slightly down and up. To measure the distance from the back of your neck to the atlanto-occipital point, or "bobble spot," put your thumb in your ear and your index finger on the back of your neck. You will notice that the distance between your thumb and finger is quite far—about 3 inches or more, which means the spine is attached to the head further forward than we often imagine.

If you habitually carry your head and neck in a forward position, do this little easy *wobble-bobble* of your face up and down for a bit, with your fingers on your ears, and you will find that, without your consciously aligning them, that your head and neck will come up and back more directly over your torso. Now take your fingers away from your ears and feel the new balance of your head. It should feel effortless compared to your old head carriage.

THE SLIPPERY SPOT

This bobble spot feels like a tiny slide—a *slippery spot*. There are actually two spots, though they feel like one. The top of your atlas has two areas that remind me of tiny, parallel, shallow bathtubs (fig. 6.8 B). These hold the two prominences of the occipital bone, the supporting points of the skull. It feels as if these little slippery spots let these prominences slide somewhat forward and back on the atlas. This means that when the bottom of the skull slides a little back, the top of the skull goes that same little bit forward.

6.9 Lucy is feeling the "slippery spot" between her thumbs, which are on the front cartilage of her ears.

To sense this little slide motion, try putting your thumbs in your ears and your fingers on top of your head as if you were holding the rim of a wheel. The hub of the wheel is above the level of your eyes, halfway between the atlanto-occipital joint between your ears, and the top of your head. Now bobble your head slightly so that your chin drops slightly. As your thumbs move back a tiny bit to follow this motion, your fingers move forward an equal amount. This little wobble between the atlas and the skull is the "yes" nod of the head. The "no" motion is just under it between the atlas and the axis, the second vertebra of the neck (figs. 6.8 and 6.9).

It helps to realize that the front of the skull is heavier than the back. In fact, the entire skeleton is heavier in front than in the back. Therefore, we have a series of interlocking muscles from the back of the neck all down the spine to keep us in balance. Since we tend to overdo most things, tension in the back of the neck is very common. To get

away from this try the little *wobble-bobble* again. You will discover a lightness and freedom in moving your head that results in the release of tight areas in the rest of your body. As a result, some people like to call this spot the "magical joint." Each time you allow this tiny sliding motion, letting your face momentarily drop rather than lifting your chin, you will feel a wave of softness at the back of your neck that travels down your back and allows your neck, shoulders, and back muscles to feel long and wide. You will also notice that your head will feel as if it has lightened, as if it is floating a bit forward and up into space. This is only a momentary sensation. It isn't a feeling you can maintain, but now that you have found this release, you can repeat it anytime you want—standing around, riding a horse, or driving a car.

Lengthening the Spine and Widening Your Body

Every time you free your head and neck, as you have just done, your back will get long and wide. This allows the sacrum, the back of the pelvis, to drop down. And this movement, in turn, brings the pubic arch (the front of the pelvis) up as it engages the abdominal muscles allowing the hip joints and legs greater freedom, and the legs to drop down. This action is commonly called the "pelvic tilt," but it is usually achieved by pulling the front of the pelvis up with the abdominal muscles rather than releasing the back of it down. Try it both ways. The release method seems effortless while the pull-up method puts tension in the body from the lower abdomen into the lower back. You will also find that this tension has the undesirable effect of tightening the hip joints. Release and lengthen the back, and the pelvic tilt simply happens. When teaching this, for short, I simply tell a student, "Lengthen your spine."

A student of mine, who is also an instructor, wrote me not long ago that "lengthening the spine,

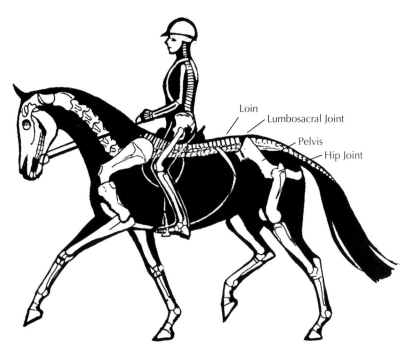

Loin
Lumbosacral Joint
Pelvis
Hip Joint

_6.10_ *A well-balanced horse and rider as described in the text.*

and the magical spot at the base of the skull, continue to be keys for teaching" and, of course, for riding also. I also like the phrase "magical joint" for the connection of the spine to the skull. The delicate motion in that magical joint is vitally important for releasing tension so the head and body can come into balance.

Engage Yourself

Take a moment to think of what happens when you have your horse balanced (fig. 6.10). His neck is soft and slightly arched and his head hangs easily from the poll where his spine connects to his skull. This release at his poll allows his back to be long and wide—long from poll to tail, and wide through the rib cage and loin. He can curl his pelvis and loin, bascule at the lumbosacral joint, and step more forward under his body with his hind legs, because his hip joints are free. He has what we often call "engaged himself." He is prepared for new, or greater movement with energy.

When he is engaged and therefore truly balancing himself, he is free to use his body and legs with maximum efficiency and brilliance.

Now compare what these exercises have been doing to your own body. You have rebalanced yourself. Your neck is soft, your head poised lightly, your back is long and wide with the pelvis engaged under you, and your legs and arms are totally free. You too, can be efficient and brilliant. This means you can use the words engage and engagement interchangeably between horse and rider. When, with intent, you ask your horse to engage himself, you can feel it in your own body and know he is having the same sensation.

All the above in this chapter may seem like a long list of things to do in order to attain this feel. With practice, however, the process can quickly be shortened. *Ground-center-grow* can encompass the whole process, allowing you to have a *following seat.* Grounding gives you a sense of the sacrum and legs growing down to connect with the earth, while from your center you grow up through your long, wide back, and your soft neck and balanced head. Presto! Your pelvic area becomes engaged and you are ready for whatever may come next.

ON THE HORSE

Discovering Your Body While Mounted

FOLLOWING YOUR HORSE'S BODY

At this point, your helper can either lead you at a walk, or longe you with long side reins on the horse. In either case, he should let the horse walk freely at his own rhythm, neither holding him back nor hauling him along. For the moment, ride without stirrups. You can hold the reins on the buckle, or not hold the reins at all. Try closing your eyes as your horse walks. You should find it pleasant to do this exercise with your eyes closed. However, if this is scary for you in any way, leave your eyes open until you become more comfortable with the sensation. Your awareness will be more profound with your eyes closed, but do not close them if it makes you feel precarious or anxious (fig. 6.11).

Try putting one arm up over your head with the thumb toward the horse's tail, elbow pointed forward, and fingers pointing softly to the sky (fig. 6.12). Notice the increased receptiveness of your body to the horse's motion. Do the same with the other arm.

Think about softly stacking your body above your moving pelvis. Remember those receptors around your seat bones, which allow your body to balance easily one part above another (see p. 39). Let them go to work. Feel that your midriff will stack over your pelvis, your ribs will stack over your midriff, your shoulders will hang over your ribs from your head and neck, and your stacking reflexes will go on up through your neck to the base of your skull between the ears and out through the head. Allow the motion of the horse to ripple up through your body.

It is not always easy to simply hang your shoulders above your ribs, as shoulders have a tendency to tighten, especially in moments of stress. It is a common problem to find yourself riding with round shoulders, head forward, the back of your rib cage bulging, and your center hanging forward through your belly. Tight shoulders can cause your carefully stacked body to come tumbling out of balance.

To cure this problem, try imagining the *bungee cord* being pulled straight up out of the top of your head (see p. 40). Imagine it pulling you up like a puppet, and feel the upward surge of energy

6.11 *Jineen is following the horse's body but she could be sitting more deeply in the saddle. This will happen when she closes her eyes and relaxes into the exercise.*

6.12 *Jineen is sitting much deeper in this photo because her arm and hand are raised high over her head causing that side to soften. This allows her to feel the motion of the horse more clearly.*

6.13 Imagine you are a giraffe with a graceful curve of the neck, instead of a turtle that has difficulty extending its neck.

through your whole body. As the cord gently pulls and releases, let your shoulders open and your sternum rise. As the *bungee cord* continues to pull, let your center settle down, and roll back over your seat bones instead of hanging out in front.

Don't let yourself be a turtle. Be a giraffe instead (fig. 6.13). The turtle draws its head in, but the giraffe, with all its dignity, lets its neck get longer as he quietly approaches a tree. His back, neck, and poll reach up and he delicately takes a nibble from the leaves at the top of the tree. Imagine that you have giraffe shoulders hanging from that long neck. A giraffe moves as if there was oil between his shoulder blades and ribs. Let your own shoulder blades be as oiled and free in movement as a giraffe's. If you find you still have a tendency to collapse the front of your body and tighten your shoulders, think of both the *bungee cord* and the giraffe.

When you are comfortably balanced, your horse will probably have a relaxed, free walk. You are not going to ask anything of him. You are going to experience the subtleties of the motion of his back. Turn your awareness to the two sides of the horse's body. When he is in motion, the horse's two sides never do the same thing. One side is

always moving a little forward and up, when the other side is moving down and back. If you are following the motion of your horse, the two sides of your body will be moving in different directions. You should follow each side individually through all its movements.

Now notice what effect your horse is having on your seat bones. Where is he moving them? Is he moving them forward and back? Is he moving them up and down? Does he move them sideways? He moves them in all these directions, alternately. When one seat bone moves forward, the other is sliding back. When one is going up, the other is going down. Notice that your pelvis, with its *bowl* shape (see p. 49), is now experiencing a rather pleasant wobble. Let that bowl balance over the seat bones and softly move as it follows the horse's back. Your lower back will have to be released just enough to allow for this. It isn't a big motion but just a gentle movement as if you were sitting on undulating water. The *ball* in your center can float quietly within the *bowl*. The back of a young, not yet muscled horse has a lot of motion. As the horse becomes more correctly muscled his back comes up under the saddle and through the loin, making him much more stable and easy to sit on.

Backward Pedaling

Now become aware of your hip joints. Put your fingers on them if you want (fig. 6.14). Remember where they are—on either side of your pelvis, low down, and halfway back. Notice how the motion of the horse gives a rotary motion to the leg in the socket. It is a backward rotation and because of the alternating motion of the horse's sides, it feels as if you are *pedaling a bicycle backward*. This rotary motion moves the entire thigh including the knee, so the knee too will pedal slightly backward. Notice in which direction, or combination of directions, your knee is pointing. They include out, forward, and down, as your thigh lies on your horse. The horse's back moves less than his sides especially as

6.14 *This rider is pointing over the top of, and beyond her greater trochanter deep into the hip socket.*

6.15 *When the* left *hind foot comes off the ground at the walk, the horse's belly swings to the* right *over the foot that's on the ground.*

6.16 *When the* right *hind foot comes off the ground, the belly swings* left *over the foot that's on the ground.*

he becomes better muscled, so it becomes increasingly important as your horse advances that the hip joint remain free enough to let the thigh move independently of your quiet pelvis.

Once you are aware of the motion of the knee, notice what is happening to your lower legs. They are pushed by your horse's barrel, first to one side and then to the other. When the horse puts one hind foot on the ground for support, he puts his belly—a substantial weight—over it, and that side of

his back stabilizes. As he moves into the next step, the belly moves across over the other foot for support and as the first foot comes off the ground and swings forward in the air, that side of the back activates (figs. 6.15 and 6.16). Your lower leg can "follow" his belly in and under on one side, and then in and under on the other side.

This "following" with alternate legs is purely an exercise in becoming aware of the feel of the belly, back, and hind-leg motions of the horse. You

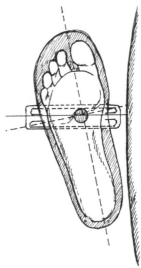

6.18 The stirrup must be at a right angle to the horse's side and your foot should be placed on it as shown. This spot marked is the "Bubbling Spring." The base of the little toe is near the outside edge of the stirrup and the foot should be angled slightly outward.

6.17 A foot placed correctly in a stirrup. It would also be acceptable with the stirrup placed one-stirrup's width forward under the foot.

should not ride this way as it will tend to make your horse waddle. When your leg follows your horse's barrel in and under, starting the moment the hind foot comes off the ground you can affect the motion of the hind leg as it is in the air. You cannot influence a horse's leg that is on the ground and carrying weight. So you will find the horse is giving you the timing for your lower leg aids through the motion of his body. At this point in your experience, however, just follow, and do not encourage the sideways motion of his belly. Accept all the horse's motion.

Grounding Your Feet

Now come to a halt and ask your helper to place your foot so that the stirrup is under the *Bubbling Spring* point of your foot (see p. 38). The outside edge of the stirrup iron should be aligned with, but not touching, the base of your little toe. The bottom of the stirrup should be perpendicular to the horse's body. Your toes will be slightly turned

out, so the bottom of the stirrup iron will cross your foot diagonally just behind the ball of your foot. Your foot will lie parallel to the ground, resting easily, not pressing on the stirrup. To avoid pressing too hard on the stirrup, it is important to allow your ankles and knees to softly flex. In this way, your feet will remain under your center, and essentially horizontal to the ground, as your horse moves (figs. 6.17 and 6.18).

Now ask your helper to slap the soles of your feet rapidly, giving special attention to the balance point of your foot—the *Bubbling Spring* where the stirrup lies. To do this she will need both hands. Her hands will alternately slap the sole of the foot: ball-stirrup-heel-stirrup-ball-stirrup-heel-stirrup and so on, as shown in the photo sequence (figs. 6.19 A–D). This way the *Bubbling Spring* receives double stimulation. You will become more aware of the soles of your feet and you will feel grounded.

Being aware of your feet in order to ensure their *grounding* is essential to the establishment of balance and fluidity on your horse. During a lesson with my student, Saundra, I asked her, "Where are your feet?" They were in the right place, under her center, but she had no conscious awareness of them.

"Where are my feet? I don't know. Down there, somewhere. I never thought about them much."

"We need," I said, "to wake up your awareness of your feet as a part of you; in fact, as your bottom *building block*."

So, we went to work. At the halt, I manipulated her ankles and feet, slowly and gently turning the soles outward and inward, and the toes up and then down. I got her to wiggle her toes inside her boots and rotate her own ankles as I had been doing.

"Become aware of the soft soles of your feet," I said as I slapped the soles of her boots with my hands. We talked about the *Bubbling Spring*, and I put her feet in the stirrups so that the bottom of the iron crossed under that spot. I slapped the bottom of the stirrup, and she was delighted.

"I have never felt my feet like that before!" She wiggled her toes some more to enhance the feeling. She did some work at the walk and then picked up the trot. For some time I asked her to think of nothing but her feet as she rode.

"Search for the feeling of your soft soles on the bottom of the stirrup," I told her. "Wiggle your toes again and feel each toe carrying its share of the weight. Allow your legs to be long and find the sensation of the soles of your feet resting on the warm, soft dirt of the arena. Allow yourself to be grounded. Don't push on the ground but let the ground carry your weight softly as you rise to the trot. If you push down, you try to put more weight on the ground than you actually have. Just let your weight "be" on the ground. The ground won't let you go through it, so it pushes up against you. Take that upward energy and allow it to travel up through the *Bubbling Spring* of your foot and on up through your center."

By this time, Saundra was herself a *Bubbling Spring* of ecstasy. She had found her feet and it was a brand new feeling.

"Do your feet now feel connected to the ground as you ride?" I asked.

"Yes."

6.19 A–D The hand sequence for "slapping feet":

(A) Left hand on the ball of the foot.

(B) Right hand on the stirrup.

(C) Right hand under the heel.

(D) Left hand under the stirrup

"Do your feet connect with your center?"

"Yes."

"And do you now find that your center, your feet, and the ground are all connected and in communication?"

"Yes, yes, yes!" Saundra replied with enthusiasm, as she discovered the difference this revelation made to her riding. She was more stable and capable and was able to ride with more authority.

Dropping the Knees

You will discover these improvements as well and you may find that because of the new depth of your seat, your stirrups will feel too short. You now have a choice depending on the type of riding you wish to do. If you want a longer stirrup, but do not like stretching down for it, this is your chance to drop your stirrups somewhat but not too much. Your legs can be soft and longer, but your foot should still rest easily on your stirrup for gentle support.

If you like a shorter stirrup, which many people do, keep your stirrup the same length and let your knee hang down. As you do this, you will feel the front of your knee below your kneecap looking at the ground. The knee will move a bit forward as it drops, your lower leg will move back, and your foot will rest softly in the stirrup directly under your seat bones. Let your knee in front of the stirrup leather feel as heavy as your heel behind your stirrup leather.

Notice now as you walk that the knee has to flex alternately with each stride, right and left. The back of the joint of each knee distinctly closes as your thigh and knee are pushed down, forward, and up. Let the knees move freely. This gives you a very deep, strong seat. The foot is held in place while resting lightly on the stirrup, and though it can follow the horse's belly in and under, it cannot drop way down with each stride. The action of the knee angle closing and opening slightly with each stride, coordinated with the soft movement of the

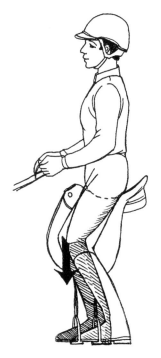

6.20 Knee dropping: note the drop feels as though it descends from the top of your boot.

hip joints and ankles, absorbs the difference in the amount of vertical motion between your seat bones and feet (fig. 6.20).

At this point, it should be clear that your "seat" on the horse is not just your pelvis on his back, but the coordination of your balanced pelvis and your hip joints, thighs, knees, ankles, and feet. All these parts working in harmony constitute your seat.

Influencing the Horse's Movement

Now you can begin influencing the horse's movement. As his body moves your seat bones alternately forward and up, then down and back, with each step, allow yourself to realize that the seat bones are moving in a circular pattern. To make this pattern clearer, drop your arms to your sides and shadow the movement of your seat bones with your hands (fig. 6.21). You will discover that you are making alternate circles with your hands, six inches to a foot in diameter—forward, up, back, and down. Notice that your hands are moving as if they were slowly spinning a wheel backward, or as if

6.21 Two riders mimicking the movement of their "backward-pedaling" seat bones as if they are doing the "following seat" on the horse.

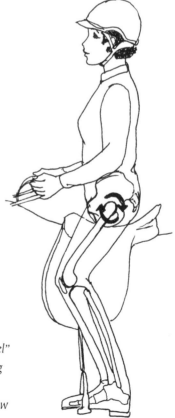

6.22 In every gait, "feel" your hip joint "pedaling backward" to some degree, in order to follow the horse's two sides.

they were pedaling backward on a bicycle. Keep your hands circling for a moment while allowing your seat to follow the alternating thrusts of the horse's body. Now notice that because the sides of the horse move more than his back, your hip joint is absorbing the difference and it is the hip joints that are the backward-pedaling leaders coordinating the pedaling movement of your seat bones and legs (fig. 6.22).

Where does the directive for this motion come from—you or the horse? The horse creates the motion, but you, the rider, enhance or inhibit it according to what you do. Note the stride of

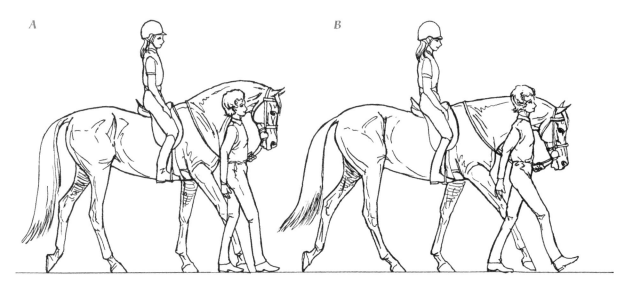

6.23 A & B The "pianissimo-crescendo" exercise. The horse should be on a loose rein with a person beside who has been instructed not to influence the horse. When the rider "thinks" pianissimo, the horse shortens his stride (A), and when she thinks crescendo, his stride lengthens (B).

your horse if you easily follow his body. It is long and free. Now try driving with your seat bones, push with them. What happens to his stride? It becomes shorter and stiff.

You can use the concept of your *backward pedaling* to change the length of your horse's stride. The musical term, *pianissimo* might help you understand this idea. When music is *pianissimo*, it is quieter, but it maintains its rhythm. Similarly, as you walk your horse, try decreasing the motion with which you follow the pulsations of your horse's back and sides. Without losing his rhythm, subdue, but do not stop, the pedaling of your seat. Stay soft, do not stiffen, and keep breathing. This is riding *pianissimo*. Notice how the horse's stride becomes shorter without changing rhythm.

The opposite of *pianissimo* is *crescendo*. In *crescendo,* music increases in volume without changing rhythm. Try this image with your *backward-pedaling hip joints*. Expand the pedaling cir-

cles while maintaining the same rhythm. You will feel your horse step further under you with longer strides (figs. 6.23 A & B). The concepts of *pianissimo* and *crescendo* combine well with the image of your *backward-pedaling hip joints* and, by visualizing smaller or larger circles, can be used at any gait to decrease or increase your horse's stride. As always first practice at a walk, so that you can slowly become familiar with the concepts and sensations.

To increase your understanding of the *pianissimo-crescendo* exercise, you can try doing it incorrectly. For instance, experiment doing it with hard eyes, or while holding your breath. Try it while locking your neck and head, or move in a different rhythm from your horse. The result will be that your horse will produce stiff strides lacking in rhythm. To compare, try the exercise again correctly. The easy rhythm of his strides will show you that you really need all the *Four Basics*, all the time.

What changes have happened to you and your horse during this time of being led? You are aware that your balance with your center over your feet is correct and easy. You have become increasingly conscious of what the horse's body is doing to your entire body, from the bottom of your feet to the top of your head. Notice how you are using *grounding* and the *Four Basics—soft eyes, breathing, centering,* and *building blocks.* Is your horse moving more freely with better rhythm in his motion? Is he stepping through more deeply with his hind legs?

Two Seats at the Trot

So far, all your *following seat* work has been done at the walk. Now it's time to pick up the trot. Later on in this book I will be discussing trot exercises ridden in three different seat positions, but here we are only concerned with two—the *half-seat* and the *rising trot.*

The *rising trot* (also known as *posting*) is a seat in the trot where the rider comes completely out of the saddle on every other stride of the horse. It is the most comfortable of all the trotting positions for both horse and rider.

Before you pick up a trot, you will need to find your balance in the *half-seat.* While standing still on your horse, find a position where you can slide your weight down onto your stirrups so your seat comes off the saddle an inch or so. You will be in the half-seat. Your knees and hip joints will be flexed and your torso will be slanted forward. When balanced in the half-seat, your center will be over your stirrups and feet. If you dropped a *plumb line* from your center through your foot, your knees would be ahead of that line, your hip joints

would be behind it, and your head and shoulders ahead of it. (A plumb line is a length of string with a weight on the end. Used by builders and surveyors, it always hangs down perpendicularly.) The tip of your toe will be under the tip of your knee. Rise up and down a few times as if doing a rising trot. Then practice some rising trot at the walk until balance is easy.

After resting, pick up the trot in the half-seat position, off the horse's back but not rising up and down. Let your joints absorb the horse's motion. If you want to, rest your knuckles on the horse's neck in front of his withers to help you balance at first. When comfortable, start rising to the trot in that balance and then begin going back and forth between the half-seat and the rising trot. I call this the *Two Seats* exercise. It is good to switch seats every five or six strides so you become comfortable and secure in each seat, and can fluidly switch from one to the other.

You have probably been carrying your torso at approximately a 45-degree angle. You can take on a somewhat more upright position by allowing your knees to flex more forward, your hips to come more under you, your shoulders to come up, and your hip joints to be more open. Conversely, you can flex your joints more deeply, which will lower your torso to a more horizontal position. You can do the exercise of *Two Seats* at rising trot and half-seat in any of these positions. This exercise using the various positions will substantially improve your balance and stability.

WHAT ARE THE ESSENTIALS OF The Following Seat?

ON THE GROUND

▶ Learn your skeletal anatomy to understand the articulation of joints.

▶ Ride with your bones.

▶ Discover the shock-absorbing quality of your pelvic region.

▶ Find the *slippery spot* between your ears.

▶ *Lengthen your spine* and *widen your body*.

▶ *Engage* yourself the same way your horse engages himself.

ON THE HORSE

▶ Be led with your eyes closed to discover your horse's body.

▶ *Let your neck lengthen,* and your shoulders become free.

▶ Find how the horse's back and sides move your pelvis, hip joints, and thighs.

▶ *Pedal your hip joints backward.*

▶ Find the *Bubbling Spring* with your foot in the stirrup.

▶ Feel the *ball* floating in your center.

▶ Ride *pianissimo* and *crescendo*.

▶ *Drop your knees.*

▶ Ride *Two Seats at the Trot*—half-seat and rising.

WHAT ARE THE RESULTS?

▶ A foundation to correctly absorb all that Centered Riding has to offer.

▶ A well-grounded, secure, stable seat.

▶ A horse moving in balance and rhythm.

7

The Horse Is Your Mirror—
His Body Reflects Yours

L et's take a moment to expand your awareness by increasing your understanding of your horse's body, and how it relates to your own. It can be interesting to do a riding exercise I call *Comparable Parts* to help you discover just how your horse's anatomy and movement correspond to your own. I will tell you about this exercise in detail when you are back on your horse in the second part of this chapter, but first you need to do more exercises on the ground where you pretend to be a horse. It is helpful to know the bony structure—the skeletal parts and joints—of both the human and the horse. I can completely understand that you may be thinking, "Oh dear, this sounds so boring," but believe me, a thorough knowledge of anatomy will be very helpful as you progress through Centered Riding.

ON THE GROUND

Comparable Anatomy

You are already aware of your own skeletal anatomy and how the bones articulate. Your horse's skeleton is surprisingly similar. Remember that the *slippery spot* (the atlanto-occipital joint) between your ears is the point at which your spine and skull connect. The horse's spine connects with his skull just below his poll, very near the top of his head. Your head is balanced above your *slippery spot;* your horse's head hangs below his. Your jaw, as well as your horse's jaw, is attached on either side near this area at the temporal mandibular joint. Your tongue, and your horse's, is attached near the *slippery spot* with roots extending into the

throat. The horse's ears are set just above the point of his jaw attachment (fig. 7.1).

This area of jaw, tongue, poll, and ears is complex and important in that tension in any component will affect the rest of the body in both horse and rider. When your horse "gives in his jaw," "flexes his poll," and "chews on his bit," he relaxes his jaw and tongue, softly mouths the bit, and frequently swallows. This relaxation has several immediate effects upon the horse's body. He lengthens the topline of his neck, raising it slightly just in front of the withers, lengthens and widens his back, engages his pelvis, and he frees his legs at the hip joints, for more powerful and fluid movement. When you "give in the jaw" at your *slippery spot*, your body will react in a very similar way.

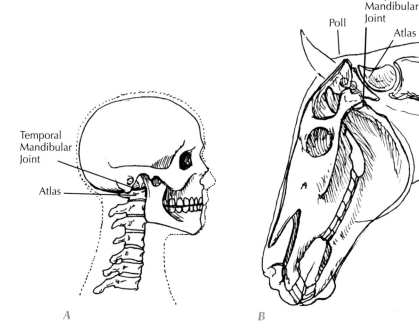

7.1 A & B
(A) The area at which the human's spine supports his skull. The temporal mandibular joint, from which the jaw hangs, hides the atlanto-occipital joint, which is the actual support point.
(B) The comparable place where the horse's spine supports his skull.

Temporal Mandibular Joint

Atlas

Poll

Temporal Mandibular Joint

Atlas

A

B

Both you and your horse have cervical vertebrae in the neck (fig. 7.2). The horse's withers compare to what we sometimes call in our bodies, "the widow's hump," the slightly prominent vertebrae at the base of your neck. As with your shoulder blades, the horse's shoulder blades are not attached to his skeleton except by muscle. Unlike your shoulder blades, however, which lie flat across the back of your ribs, the horse's shoulder blades extend down his ribs on either side. A veterinarian friend of mine had difficulty freeing her own shoulder blades because she was visualizing them extending down her sides as they do in all four-legged animals. When she discovered that they actually lay across her back, she was able to free her shoulder blades more easily.

The configuration of your ribs and your horse's is similar, with your diaphragm at the bottom of your rib cage and your horse's at the back of his rib cage. By now, you are aware of the location and shape of your pelvis. That of your horse is less evident. The point of his hip corre-

sponds to the top of the side of your pelvis. The point of his buttocks is the same as your seat bone, and his croup is the same as your sacrum.

Your horse's hip joints are about two-thirds of the way back from the point of his hip toward the point of his buttocks. This may surprise you, but his pelvis is long compared to your somewhat bowl-shaped pelvis. From the hip joint, his femur is buried in muscle and extends to his stifle, which is comparable to your knee. His gaskin is the same as the tibia of your lower leg, and his hock corresponds to your ankle and heel. His cannon bone matches the long bone on the top of your foot, and the first knuckle of your toes is the same as his fetlock. Your toes are comparable to his pastern and coffin bones.

Similarly, the anatomy of your horse's front legs matches that of your own. The point of the horse's shoulder compares to yours, as does the upper arm (humerus). Though the horse's elbow is closer to the mass of his torso than yours, it is a comparable joint. His forearm is the same as yours,

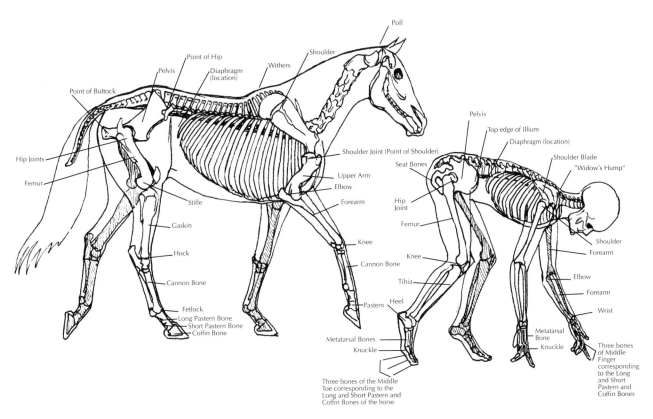

_7.2_ _"Comparable Parts" shared by horse and rider. It's interesting to see how the bones of the horse compare to ours—the exception being that the horse has no collarbones._

and his knee is the same joint as your wrist. His cannon bone compares to the long bone in your hand, which extends from your wrist to the first knuckle of your middle finger. The knuckle is the same as his fetlock, and the bones of your finger are his first and second pastern bones. The last bone in your finger compares to the coffin bone in the horse's foot.

Now as you do some exercises on the ground with a partner (either one of you can play the horse), keep in mind how your anatomy compares to your horse's anatomy. First, shake yourself like a St Bernard coming out of a river (I call it the _Shaggy Dog Shake_), take a few moments to review _lengthening the spine and widening your_ _body–freeing your back_ (see p. 55), and establish _grounding_. Remember the feeling of _center and grow_, thus softening your neck and "poll" (between your ears) to allow your head to float and your back to lengthen and widen. This allows you to _drop your sacrum_ and free the hip joints, which let the pubic arch come up a little and the legs go downward toward the ground.

Dancing Hands

This first exercise, _Dancing Hands_, will clearly illustrate the title of this chapter. Your partner will mirror you. I developed the exercise from one used in the martial arts called "Push Hands," and it helps you to communicate with _use of self._ You will need

7.3 A—E Some possibilities for fluid movement doing "Dancing Hands."

to stand facing your partner as shown in the first photo (figs. 7.3 A–E). Each of you should place your feet as if on opposite corners of a square. Touch the palms of your right hands together. Allow them to feel as if they are held together by soft magnets. Now decide which one of you is to be the leader and which one is to be the follower. Taking care not to move too fast nor knock the "following" partner out of balance, the leader should move his arm and hand smoothly in any direction. She should use *clear intent* before she actually moves her hand to allow for communication to the following partner. The movements can be small at first and then become more daring as you discover how your magnet hands begin to move together as shown in the photo sequence. The leader can move her hand forward and back, from side to side, in a circle, and even behind herself, or her partner. The follower must allow her hand to move effortlessly along with the leader's hand wherever it goes. The follower must be totally attentive, re-

ceptive, and supple. Any stiffening in either partner will block the flow of communication between your two hands. Your feet should not move out of place, but all the joints above them, ankles, knees, hips, shoulders, elbows, and wrists, can move and coordinate wherever is needed to keep the body in balance. This exercise requires the *Four Basics* from each partner: *centering, breathing, soft eyes,* and *building blocks* together with secure *grounding.*

When you and your partner are able to do this exercise smoothly, try changing roles, try it with your left hands, or even with both hands (figs. 7.4 A & B). Finally, do the exercise with both of you leading. This is a fascinating experiment, which requires complete concentration on your *use of self* and softness. The trick is to have *clear intent* of your movement before you start and then, keeping the intent clear, to follow through with the movement. A quick decision to change direction will not succeed. You will find, remarkably, that you and your partner will be moving in unison, and each of

you will not only *think*, but will *know* that you were the leader! Doesn't this sensation compare wonderfully to your relationship with your horse when you are riding in harmony? Don't you feel that he is leading as much as you are?

Fingers under the Armpits

To continue to develop sensitivity with your knowledge of *Comparable Parts* and the awareness that you and your horse reflect each other, try another exercise that I call *Fingers under the Armpits*. To start, your partner will pretend to be the horse. This exercise will not only help you understand how your horse's use of his body is reflected in your own *use of self* but also, like *Dancing Hands*, will help you experience communication through *use of self*.

Stand behind your partner and place two or three fingers on either side of her rib cage below the armpits, a little like your legs around your horse's sides as shown in the photo (figs. 7.5 A & B). You will be asking her to move, turn, and halt without actually pushing her around. Neither one of you can talk–your only connection with each other is through your fingers. The "horse partner" must not use her imagination, or try to guess what you want, but must move only when your directives are clear. This experiment works the best if the horse partner can keep her eyes closed. To do this, she must be able to trust you not to run her into anything!

7.4 A & B The "Dancing Hands" exercise being done with both hands. This can be done with one person leading, or even with both people leading at the same time.

There is really only one way to use your fingers to communicate clearly with your partner. Pushy, demanding fingers create resistance both in horses and people, and light fingers, without *clear intent*, will be ineffective. So, you will need to develop *light* fingers directed by a *clear intent*.

First, think exactly what you want your horse partner to do. If you want her to move forward, you must realize that she has to put all her weight on one foot in order to move the other forward. To move her right foot forward, she will have to put weight on her left. Through your own *use of self* and an understanding of *comparable body parts*, you can tell her which leg should step forward. To do this, *breathe, center and grow* as you put your weight on your own left foot. You are using only your *clear intent* and your own body to communicate with your horse partner. Your connecting fingers have not moved.

My friend, Lucy Bump[1], who is a specialist at teaching this exercise, explains, "When I do the rider's part of *Fingers*, I think about just letting my fingers float (not pushing or squeezing). I *center and grow*, and *ground* myself, and do myself what I want my horse partner to do. My intent and the movement of my body from my center are what transmit my messages to my horse through my floating fingers. Sometimes you must wait for your horse partner to respond, or even repeat it."

Perhaps your horse partner is "green" and did

---

1 Lucile Bump. Centered Riding Level IV Senior Instructor and clinician. Owner of Southmowing Stables, a center for Centered Riding, in Guilford, Vermont.

The "Fingers under the Armpits" exercise: 7.5 to 7.8

7.5 A & B Lucy is asking Cynthia (the "horse") to shift her weight onto her left foot so she can move her right foot forward (A). In the next picture Cynthia understands and obeys Lucy's lightly fingered instructions (B).

not hear you. You will need to train her to hear and understand the message. Rebalance yourself, *breathe, center and grow,* and shift your weight again. If she still doesn't hear you, don't give up. You must use the same repetitive process you follow with your real horse. Suddenly, it will become clear to her—she will shift her weight to the left, and you are off. If you ask your partner, she will tell you that she did not feel any perceptible change in your fingers, but that it simply became obvious that she should shift her weight and move into a walk. Your *clear intent* caused changes in your body, which allowed your partner to interpret your request.

Continue with the exercise, experimenting with turning, halting, or backing up. For each new movement, you will need a new *clear intent* and the same system of body language. When you have been successful with this exercise, try directing your horse partner without *centering,*

grounding, and *breathing,* and without your body language. Simply put your fingers on, and start walking. Notice how unbalanced and awkward the movement becomes as you drag your partner along with crude signals. Finally, complete this exercise by exchanging places with your partner and becoming the horse. You need to experience receiving the directives as well as initiating them. Think how fluidly and effortlessly you will be able to communicate with your real horse using the principles of this exercise.

How Does the Horse Feel?

Here are some additional exercises you can try to further clarify your understanding of how your own body, and *use of self,* can facilitate communication with your horse. You will need to get down on all fours so you can pretend to be a horse, but there is one big difference between you and him. Your horse, or any four-legged animal, has eyes set in his head so he looks forward while allowing his neck to be long and soft as his head *hangs* from his poll. Because you stand up on two legs your head *balances* on the top of your neck. When you are on all fours with your neck long, you will be looking at the floor, not ahead. So, nature moved your eyes from the top to the front of your head, which means that in order to feel like a horse when you are on all fours you will need to imagine that your eyes are on the top of your head looking forward. Do a bit of *Teeter-Totter* on all fours to determine where your best balance is. It is easy to have too much weight on the forehand. If you *center and grow*–horizontally, this time–you will bring your weight more back in your body as the pelvis tips to give you more engagement. Then check your lateral balance. Do you tend to carry more weight on one leg or on one hand than the other? See if you can even yourself out. Allow your weight to siphon out of the heavy hand or leg over into the light one. See if your *Teeter-Totter* doesn't feel more fluid and easy.

You are now ready for your partner. She will be on her feet while you are on your hands and knees. Have her put her hands on your back over the lower part of your shoulder blades as shown in the photo (fig. 7.6). Her palms should be flat, her fingers pointing forward. If you were carrying a saddle, this is where it would lie. Your partner will learn as much from this exercise as you. Her job is to let her hands totally follow your back, while you walk freely using your body fully. The motion of your back will cause her hands to make a figure-of-eight on your back. When you have been walking like this for a bit, have your partner, without warning, stop following your motion and keep her hands rigid on your back. What is your immediate reaction? You will probably want to stop. Try having your partner alternately follow, and stop following your motion in order to understand the effect of her hands on your back. You will probably feel that her following hands will en-

7.6 *The "rider's" hands on the "horse's" back allow the rider to feel exactly how much motion there is when the "horse" crawls.*

hance the motion of your back, and her rigid hands will restrict it.

Have your partner put her fingers around your body so that the palm of her hand is flat on your back, and the fingers point down your sides, on your ribs as shown in the photo (fig. 7.7). In this position, her fingers simulate a rider's legs. After you find a nice swinging walk let her, again without warning, squeeze and hold with her fingers. What is your reaction? Again, you will want to stop. This

_7.7_ This photo shows the position of the "rider's" hands simulating a rider's legs on the sides of a horse.

Now have your partner experiment by using her body *incorrectly* for a few strides, and then *correctly*. Let her try to hold her breath, harden her eyes, let herself be out of rhythm with your motion, tighten her jaw, or stiffen her hip joints. Notice how uncomfortable she can make you and how your body reacts with resistances, all of which reduce your efficiency. Let her direct you through circles and serpentines. See how you dislike being pushed around, but how willing you are to cooperate with a directive that is in rhythm with your movement. Directive aids out of rhythm cause frustration.

Switch places with your partner, so you can try being the "rider." Note how clear your partner's reactions are to you as a rider, and now that you know how the horse feels, imagine how much easier it will be for you to give organized, sensitive aids.

In a similar but more dramatic exercise, you are the horse again and let your partner, standing up straight, straddle you as shown in the photo (fig. 7.8). She will walk as you move under her, following her directives. Again, only move if her legs make it completely clear to you what she wants. Do not respond to confusing or unclear signals. What makes you want to move off? You will probably find that you respond better to her *center-and-grow* directions, and following legs, than to squeezing, tight legs. Can you turn if she stiffens, or locks her inside leg? No. She must soften the inside leg, letting her knee point in the direction she wants you to go, and using it in rhythm for you to move forward and around it. You will also need her outside leg's steady support. Experiment with turns, lateral work, and pirouettes. In fact, the more movements you explore with this exercise, the more clear and fascinating the whole communication with your horse becomes. Don't forget to have your partner try a few movements incorrectly such as simply holding her breath. You must, of course, also try being the rider. You can work out endless

reaction may puzzle you, because you probably think that if you squeeze your legs, you push your "horse" forward. To understand this apparent discrepancy, try walking on again and have your partner follow your body motion with her hands in rhythm as your legs would follow your horse's belly. Notice how comfortable and how easy it is for you to move forward through this following motion.

7.8 The "rider" is straddling the "horse" using her legs as directives as to where to go.

problems by being first the horse and then the rider.

When my students work with these exercises, I frequently hear such reactions as, "Now I understand why I have been having trouble doing circles," or, "This will allow me to ride my horse with more sensitive aids rather than just strength." Doing these exercises on the ground, pretending to be a horse and reacting to a rider as a horse

would, can open up a whole new relationship with your horse.

You will become increasingly aware that the more you follow the motion and rhythm of your horse's body, the more willing and able he will be to use his body freely and effectively when you ask. As you progress, you can combine this knowledge and awareness with the ability to use carefully timed aids in a correct rhythm with your horse. You will be able to ask for increased balance at all gaits, in all your work.

ON THE HORSE

Finding New Awareness

On your horse, start at a walk, and as your horse moves, simply become aware of a few parts of your body. Using the new awareness of the *slippery spot* between your ears, find your head balance and allow your head to have a soft *wobble-bobble*, which moves your face slightly down and up to normal with each stride. Though this motion should be very small, it has a quite different effect on your body below than if you lock your head on top of your neck. Rather than becoming rigid, your body can follow the horse's motion.

Be aware of the top of your head, then of the bottom of your seat bones. Shift your awareness back and forth between these two areas, taking time to fully sense these parts of your body. Now add your center to your points of awareness. Feel your head, center, and seat bones. Next, add the flat soles of your feet (fig. 7.9). Move your awareness back and forth from your head, to your center, to your seat bones, to the soles of your feet, and back to your seat bones, center, and head. Two to three mental trips down and up your body will give you a surprising sense of balance and unity without your making conscious adjustments.

You can experiment in exploring your body by conducting a running conversation with it. "Hello,

7.9 Feel your head, center, seat bones, and soles of your feet stacked up as the stars are in this drawing.

neck. I am just checking in. You're a little tense. Don't worry. I'll be back."

Simply make a note of what you find, then leave the neck, and go quickly to the next spot, and the next, throughout your body. Keep re-exploring your body in any sequence that is comfortable for you. Take a moment to feel how aware you have become of your entire body, and then drop your awareness into some of the individual spots again. Be sure to include any areas that were tight the first time and note any changes. Do these spots still feel the same or worse, or have these tight spots become more free and mobile? You will probably find increased freedom and mobility in these areas, even though you feel you did nothing to cause this change.

Despite the fact that you felt you did nothing to alleviate your tightness, your new awareness is actually responsible for the improvement. Each time you drop awareness into a part of your body, you drop a bit of energy there, too. If you use that bit of energy to make a conscious correction, you

use up that energy. If, instead, you simply become aware of a tight spot and then mentally depart that particular spot, leaving the energy there, the body will make its own correction more efficiently than you consciously could. The body is an enormously complex machine with millions of interrelated parts. To lift your arm do you consciously think, "I must release the muscles under my arm and tighten the muscles on the top of my arm and do the opposite to let my arm down again?" Of course not. In addition, these muscles interact with others in complex ways. A task that is impossible for us to consciously coordinate is actually easy and automatic for the body, if we simply *allow* it to work. We have here another example of the value of *aware and allow*. We become *aware*, and then *allow* the correction to take place. Your awareness becomes a directive, not a forced directive, but an *allowed* directive.

Comparable Parts Exercise

Let's expand this exercise by including your horse's body in your awareness. This is the exercise I call *Comparable Parts*. Refer to the drawings at the beginning of this chapter. Put your awareness in your "poll" where your neck and head connect between your ears (see fig. 7.1), and then in your horse's poll. Now continue onto other parts of your body, and your horse's body. Become aware of your elbow and his, your ribs and his, your hip joint and his, your knee and his stifle, your ankle and his hock, your toes and his pastern and foot, and your *breathing* and *soft eyes* and his. Keep mentally running through your body and your horse's body. Don't get stuck in any one place, but move quickly from one part to another, first on your body and then the horse's body. You will find that any part of your body that is tense will also be tense in the comparable part of your horse's body. What a can of worms this opens up! However, don't panic, because you can turn this can of worms into a useful bag of tricks. You will find that if you free your tense spot, your horse will free his comparable part. He is your mirror.

As you ride, if you feel that something does not feel quite right, it is best to check yourself first, then the horse. It is usually your problem, which is affecting the horse. However, sometimes the horse will have a problem that you will pick up from him. Since you are the thinking member of the team, it is up to you to lead the way by keeping your comparable part free as you work on helpful exercises or movements for your horse to free his part.

You can expand your understanding of *Comparable Parts* by watching other horses and riders. You will notice that a horse that continually goes on his forehand will have a rider that tends to be round-shouldered with head forward, and eyes looking down. This horse virtually cannot balance and come off his forehand until the rider centers herself, releases her body, balances her head, and allows the front of her shoulders and body to open up. It is unfair, as well as somewhat fruitless, to ask the horse to do something that the rider is not also doing. Tight hip joints in the rider mean tight hip joints, and therefore less engagement, in the horse. Holding your breath causes tension everywhere—in you and the horse. A tight tongue will give your horse a tight mouth, and so on. Conversely, when you *center and grow*, your horse will rebalance, become more engaged, and lighter on the forehand. His footfalls will also become lighter. A following seat will help you to have a supple lower back, which will help your horse to have the same.

I was once working through this exercise of *Comparable Parts* with one of my students who had a nice horse, not a fancy one, but well trained. With this exercise, once a student catches onto the system, I keep quiet, offering no input or comments, as the student discovers the results for herself. Sue was working her horse while those of us who were watching remarked quietly among ourselves that we had never before seen this horse go

with such freedom and lightness. Finally, Sue began to respond as well. She had been totally in her right brain and when she paused to discuss the exercise, it took her a few minutes to be able to communicate with words. I asked her a couple of times what had happened out there. She finally said, "I am going to let my horse "sell" me—get rid of me!"

When I asked why, she replied, "All these years I have been trying to loosen up his right hip. It wasn't his hip, it was mine. When I let my hip go, he let his go!" His new freedom of movement was such a radical change that he was muscle lame the next day. Sue spent much of the same day asleep. For both horse and rider, the change in the application of energy caused dramatic readjustments in their bodies.

You will find that this session both on the ground and on the horse will help you locate the cause of problems and resistances in your horse. The first thing to ask is, "Am I doing something with my body that makes it difficult for my horse's comparable part, or is he, because of sore muscles or badly fitting tack, or some other reason, uncomfortable? Are my aids clear, or is he confused? Am I asking for a task that he is physically or mentally not ready for?" Any of these problems are good reasons for your horse not to cooperate. If none of these reasons seems to apply, then maybe he is just being naughty, in which case you will need to indicate clearly that such behavior is not acceptable. Make sure before and during the quick correction, that you are centered, in balance, and *breathing*, and that your intent is clear. As soon as he cooperates, reward him well with praise.

Through your new consciousness of *Comparable Parts* in you and your horse, you will find that this exercise in exploration has improved your overall balance and coordination. You can now become aware of your body as a united whole as you work in harmony with your horse.

WHAT ARE THE ESSENTIALS OF The Horse is Your Mirror— His Body Actions Reflect Yours?

ON THE GROUND

- ► The similarity of your horse's skeleton to your own.
- ► Directions with *clear intent,* not force.
- ► The feeling of *ground-center-grow*.
- ► *Dancing Hands* with a partner.
- ► *Fingers under the Armpits* exercises. They help you discover what your horse feels about your directives, as well as teach you to be sensitive.
- ► Always perform as both *"rider"* and *"horse"* for full understanding.

ON THE HORSE

- ► Explore your body.
- ► *Comparable Parts:* for example, your horse will be tight where you are tight.
- ► Do not dwell on one part—move on quickly.
- ► When solving a problem check yourself first, before checking the horse.

WHAT ARE THE RESULTS?

- ► Understanding why you need sensitivity, not strength.
- ► Awareness of your body as a united whole, and the body of the horse.
- ► Harmony through improved balance and coordination.

8

Raise the Horse's Back through Transitions

Y ou have been discovering through Centered Riding methods how to sense and follow the movement of your horse's body, and how your own body movements and your *clear intent* can influence the way he will use himself. Now you can use your newly learned skill to actually *improve* your horse's abilities as well. Every discipline of equestrian sport, whether it be reining, dressage, cutting, jumping, or endurance riding, requires the horse to be strong and balanced, and well muscled. Good musculature enables the horse to raise his back, which, in turn, gives him the ability to engage and activate his hindquarters—his pelvis and hind legs more—effectively. Riders in every discipline use exercises involving transitions, circles, and turns to build this good musculature. The exact aids vary with the discipline, but the basic intent is the same.

When correct musculature of the horse's body is developed through proper training, he will have a good topline and bottom line, as well as be evenly developed on both sides. We have all seen horses with upside-down necks, and weak backs and quarters. Frequently, this is not so much a conformational problem as a muscle-development problem, and with proper training can be cured or substantially helped (figs. 8.1 A & B). In this session, I am going to discuss how transition exercises help the horse, and I will address circles and turns in the next session in Chapter 9.

Center of Gravity

This seems a good moment to tell you about the horse's *center of gravity*, the balance point of his body, in the area of the girth. His *center of control and energy*, however, is below his spine at the back of his loin just below the lumbosacral joint (fig. 8.2). Similarly, our center of control and energy is in our lower back just in front of our lumbosacral joint. Because we stand vertically, in contrast to the horizontal horse, our center of gravity is not near our shoulder blades but rather is in the same area as our center of control and energy. As a result, when we put our center of gravity over our feet for balance, we also find our center of control in the same spot.

The location of the center of gravity, in both rider and horse, changes at times. When you are startled or frightened your center of gravity rises above its desired depth as it does in times of tension, or apprehension. In either case, it makes you less grounded. The center of gravity of a startled or actively engaged horse moves slightly back as he tips his pelvis down to bring his hind feet more nearly under his center of gravity. Since all movements of your body immediately affect your horse, and thus how he uses and develops his body, you will need to increase your body awareness.

8.1 A & B A well-muscled horse (A). A poorly muscled horse (B).

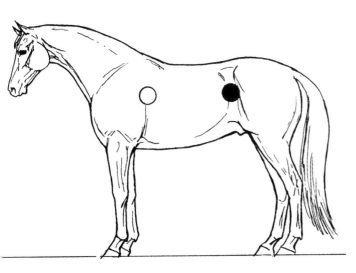

8.2 The horse's center of gravity is indicated by the clear circle. His center of energy and control is shown by the black circle.

ON THE GROUND

Further Understanding of Breathing

Let's start by using your breath more effectively—we can call it *power breathing.* Stand balanced with soft hip joints flexed slightly back and knees flexed slightly forward. This is actually a position of strength. Put one hand on your belly, quietly *center* yourself, and note that on your in-breaths you tend to lengthen through your body and grow a bit while your stomach softly expands. Ray Mulry, in his book *In The Zone,* calls this "soft-stomach" breathing. It enhances release of tension, and "opening" and lengthening the body. Walk around and enjoy the comfort and peace that comes with this quality of *in-breathing.*

Now, stand with the flexion in your hip and knee joints—your position of strength. As you crouch a little deeper by closing the hip and knee

joints take an in-breath, then use an out-breath as you come up, which you will find engages your psoas and stomach muscles, and becomes a power breath. Ray Mulry says, "Exhale into the exertion." Go down with the in-breath and up with the out-breath several times. Then practice these *in-out breaths* without going up and down. Notice how your body is responding. You will probably find that your body opens upward on the in-breath, and that your psoas and stomach muscles engage on the out-breath, and the "exhale into the exertion" will give you a sense of *grounding,* balance, power, and lightness. It tends to lower your center of gravity. These are the components of the *center-and-grow* rebalances you will use when on your horse.

Walk around again, and before each time you stop, go, or turn, use an *in-out breath* to help rebalance yourself. You can adjust the intensity of the in-out breath from a strong burst of exhale *power breath* to a very delicate one—it's almost just a suggestion—and anything in between. Experiment with this. Does it change the quality of your turn or stop? How would your horse like this if you used this technique before you used your seat, legs, and hands?

Experience What the Horse Feels

You can experiment with some exercises that will give you a sense from the horse's viewpoint of how different positions, postures, and motion affect his comfort and ability to move. At the same time, it will give you a clear sense of what your body must do, what muscles you should use in addition to your breathing to affect the horse, and what muscles he will use in response.

First, get down on your hands and knees. Find a balance with your hands below your shoulders, and your knees below your hip joints. Now gently engage your center, and allowing your hip joints to slightly close and open, rock back a tiny bit and then back again to balance. Notice how this pelvic rocking motion tends to fill your lower back across the loin. This puts you in a position for balanced, fluid, forward motion.

Notice that your shoulders are also part of the rocking motion and since they are not carrying a lot of weight, they are free for forward movement. Shift your balance forward, putting weight on your shoulders and hands, and you will no longer be able to move forward; your hands will seem to be stuck to the ground. This is how your horse feels when he is too much on his forehand.

Refine this experiment further by *centering* and allowing your neck to lengthen, and the *slippery spot*—the "magical joint"—to soften. This softening is the same as when your horse relaxes at the poll and jaw. He gently moves the bit in his mouth as you soften your hands to receive it, saying thank you. Though this moment of softening is not a sensation you can keep or save in either yourself or your horse, you can ask for it again at any time, as often as you want.

Remember, we ask our horse to do what you have just been doing—to lengthen his neck and engage his hind end so he can raise his back for more efficient movement. To understand this better, focus your awareness on your own torso and lower back each time you allow this lengthening of your neck. Notice how this lengthening enhances the feelings you just had when you engaged and rocked your pelvis enabling you to move forward easily. With practice, you can direct your neck to lengthen, which can trigger the sensation of rolling the *ball* backward in the pelvis (see p. 40) while engaging your lower body, allowing your back to fill, and freeing your legs for activity (see p. 55). An *in-out breath* at the same time will make this even clearer. Similarly, as you become familiar with these sensations, you will also be able to lengthen your neck by starting at the other end—your lower body. For some people, one sequence is easier than the other. Use whichever one works best for you.

Transitions

Try some transitions. First, stay on your hands and knees and initiate the tiny rocking motion you did earlier. When you are rocked back, do an up transition—move forward for a couple of steps. Notice how easy it is to move forward from this position with your "hind legs" pushing first. Your rocked-back position is the same as a horse with his hind legs engaged. Conversely, if you rock forward putting your weight on your hands and shoulders, it is almost impossible to move forward. Try minimizing the motion as you rock back and forth until you can rock back simply by rolling the *ball* back in your pelvis and lengthening your neck. When you can do this with *in-out breaths,* you are performing a rebalance!

Try a down transition. While walking on all fours, try your rebalance by rolling the *ball* backward in your pelvis and allowing your neck to lengthen. Let your legs stop, first one, and then the other. The weight on your hands will remain light. Now try the transition using your hands as brakes. Notice how jarring and uncomfortable this feels, just as when your horse stops on his forehand with rigid legs.

There are many ways a horse and rider can perform awkward and not athletic transitions. To experience these uncomfortable sensations, try your transitions with your head too high, too low, or with your back hollowed, and again with it arched too high. You will begin to really appreciate how essential it is to have the back, and weight-carrying hind end of your horse, developed and engaged in order to maneuver him efficiently.

This first-hand knowledge of how your horse feels will help you find the best way to communicate with him. You will increasingly find that knowledge of *Comparable Parts* and an improved *use of self* will enhance the quality of your communication.

ON THE HORSE

Why are rebalancing and self-carriage important? A riderless horse in a relaxed mood carries most of his weight on his forehand, and for casually moving and clumping around that is adequate. When something stimulating happens, feed time at the other end of the pasture, for instance, he will bring his hind feet forward under his rounding back, lighten his forehand, and take off with spring and energy to the food area. In effect, he rebalances himself for the new activity.

A rider on a horse's back increases the tendency for the horse to be heavy on his forehand so when you start to work your horse and improve his musculature, you will need to help him reorganize his balance as he moves by using various exercises that put him in situations where a change of balance is the easiest way for him to go. He will engage his haunches as he brings his hind legs more forward, raises his back, and lightens his forehand.

You did something remarkably like this with your own body when you practiced *ground-center-grow* earlier. You improved your *use of self*. You rebalanced. Now, on your horse, you will enhance the rebalancing that helps his self-carriage if you simultaneously rebalance yourself. Since, as in so much of this work, you can get, but not keep the rebalance, you will need to repeat it often (or, not so often) depending on the ability of your horse. The resulting improved carriage of your horse is something he will be able to increasingly maintain, as he grows stronger. So, after each rebalancing you should say (by ceasing your aids), "Thank you. Now carry yourself without my help for a bit." It might be three strides, or ten, or twenty, before you need to do the next rebalancing with your horse.

Ride a Square

In this session, you will be able to practice some rebalancing. Start it with a very useful exercise to encourage your horse to use his back and hind end,

and lengthen his neck. On your horse at the walk, and using your following seat, review your *Four Basics*, and *grounding*. Explore your body to check for imbalances and tensions. When you and your horse are comfortable together, start to walk a square. A good size for your square is 20 meters (about 60 feet) on each side. This square must have definite corners that you should ride through as right-angled turns, not as curves. In order to navigate a proper corner, your horse will actually have to do either a turn on the forehand, or a turn on the haunches. Do not concern yourself at this point with making tidy and exact turns on the forehand or haunches. Simply allow the horse to have his weight on his forehand to move his haunches around the corner, or on his haunches to move his forehand around. If you are riding in an arena, start your square away from the rail to allow your horse room to maneuver the corners (fig. 8.3).

Keep a light contact on the reins, but do not use them as directives as this is a lesson in your body awareness and activity and your horse's response, not on the use of the reins. Before each corner, establish *clear intent* of your new direction, as you did with your partner in the *Dancing Hands* exercise. You will discover how responsive your horse is to your *clear intent* and body language to turn without rein aids. Mary, a student of mine, was long lining her horse, King, when she noticed how sensitive he was to her body language. After repeated transitions to canter, he began to make the transition to canter when she simply thought about it. King was responding to the subtle changes in her body, even through the long lines.

Ground-Center-Grow Rebalances

Now, as you ride your square to the right, do some rebalances before and after each corner by *centering* yourself, rolling the *ball* backward in your pelvis to engage it, and allowing your legs to lengthen down while your torso and neck

8.3 *"Riding the Square." The horse does a turn on the forehand, or a turn on the haunches, to get around the square. Note that the line of travel should be well away from the fence so the horse cannot collide with it.*

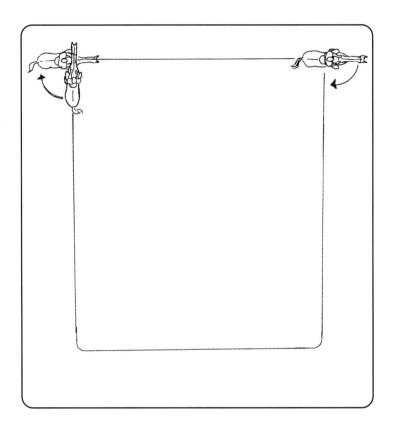

lengthen up through the *slippery spot* between your ears with *in-out breaths.* Do a rebalance quickly–a split-second spine *ground-center-grow–* and release. If a rebalance takes too long, it locks you up and prevents your horse from responding. As you walk through your square, notice what effect the repeated rebalances have on your own body. You will find that appropriate words to describe your sensations would be "lengthened," "softened," "energized," and "balanced." In effect, you will find that when you rebalance, you engage your pelvic area.

Continue the exercise and now notice how your horse's body responds to these rebalances. You will find yourself using the same descriptive words for his response. He softens through his body, his stride lengthens, and he engages his quarters around his center. By improving his way of going, you are developing the correct muscles

and thus improving his conformation. A dividend of the rebalancing before and after your corners, or, in fact, at any time, is an increase in the sensitivity of your seat to receive the motion of the horse. Through the rebalancing, you are inviting your horse's back to come up and fill your wide, receptive seat.

Add a Full Transition

This is a good point to begin to think about up-and-down transitions because repeated transitions are an excellent way to improve a horse's musculature and balance. Let's add to the *Ride a Square* exercise. Instead of continuing around the turn, do a downward transition to a full halt at each corner. To do this, you need to do a preliminary rebalance to alert the horse to the change. Center yourself, engage your pelvis by rolling the *ball* backward, and let your seat bones become grounded in rhythm with the walk, first one then the other. Each seat bone should become grounded exactly when your horse's hind foot steps down on that side, causing your pelvis to roll under. At the moment of your transition to halt, your four-beat walk changes from a one-two-three-four rhythm to one-halt, two-halt. This sequence will give you a halt from engaged hind legs rather than stopping on stiff front legs. If you *breathe in-out* one or more times during the transition and then breathe normally as the horse stands at the halt, you will reduce the tensions that are so often involved in transitions of any kind.

Remember the *Unbendable Arm* exercise? Your halt transition can be made even more effective by allowing the combined sensations of your horse's hind foot stepping and your seat bone becoming grounded, to fill your hand on that side. At this moment, do not draw your hand back but give it the quality of the *Unbendable Arm* (see p. 41).

Now that you have halted, use your right leg one or more times to move your horse's haunches around his forehand so you will be facing down the next side (fig. 8.4). Your hands keep the front feet in place but do not be too particular at this point doing what is, in effect, a "turn on the forehand." Accuracy can come later. Before you move off into the walk, prepare your horse with a *ground-center-grow* rebalance (discussed above), being careful to *breathe in-out*.

Do you remember your *backward-pedaling* seat bones (see p. 62)? This upward transition to walk is similar to the down transition to halt, but instead of *grounding* your seat bones as I just explained, you pedal them backward. So, rebalance and pedal your seat bones backward as you use both legs to tell your horse to move off toward the next corner of your square. When you reach this corner, repeat the halt, and the turn-and-walk sequence. As soon as you are comfortable with this exercise, take a break by trotting around the ring a bit. Notice how your horse's trot is lighter and

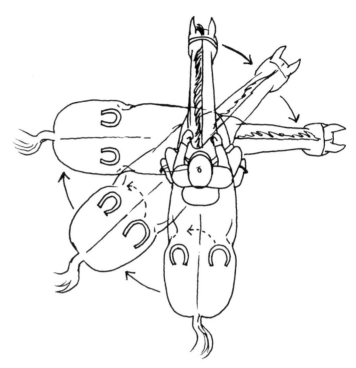

8.4 A quarter-turn on the forehand. The front feet should stay on the same spot, but do not be too concerned with accuracy since the point of the exercise is to activate the horse's hind legs.

more balanced. He is more engaged and his back is fuller up under your receiving seat. You may repeat this exercise if needed.

Now you can try the same exercise, but instead of asking your horse to move his haunches to cause him to face the next corner of the square, ask him to move his forehand one-quarter turn around his haunches to cause him to face the next corner of the square (fig. 8.5). Again, not being too particular, close both legs behind the girth to stabilize the haunches and move both hands to the left to direct the forehand to the left. Later when perfected, this will be "a quarter-turn left on the haunches." After you feel comfortable with the exercise, trot or even canter around the ring once or twice.

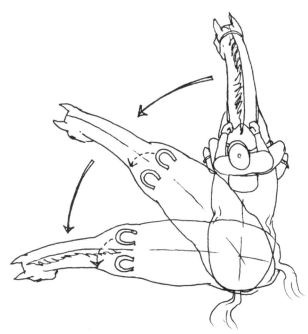

8.5 A quarter-turn on the haunches. The hind feet should stay on the same spot. This exercise strengthens his hind legs, which ultimately helps him raise his back, and lighten his forehand.

In the final part of this exercise, after you have asked your horse to turn on his haunches in the corner of the square, pick up a trot. If your horse is balanced enough to move immediately forward off your light legs with an upward feeling (which is being "in front of your legs"), continue to trot around the whole arena to reward him. Repeat this exercise several times.

As your horse trots off, you will again notice an improvement in the quality and balance of his trot. He is beginning to develop better use of his mus-cles toward raising his back. Remember that good musculature in your horse is developed over a period of time and through many repetitions. Be careful not to ask too much of your horse until his muscles have been developed sufficiently for the job. As you both learn and develop, you will find that your centeredness and awareness are helping you to be more comfortable and less confusing to your horse. As a result, he will be able to develop the proper musculature, and in turn, make it easier for you to learn.

WHAT ARE THE ESSENTIALS OF Raise the Horse's Back through Transitions?

ON THE GROUND

- ▶ Center of gravity: yours is low, near your center. Your horse is further forward near the girth.

- ▶ *In-out breaths* engage your stomach and psoas muscles. "Exhale into the exertion."

- ▶ On your hands and knees: experiment with transitions. Notice they are easier when your weight is back in your pelvis rather than on your hands (as they are for your horse, too).

- ▶ To transfer the weight back, *lengthen your neck* and roll the *ball* backward in your pelvis.

ON THE HORSE

- ▶ A rider on top makes a horse heavy on the forehand, so he needs rebalancing.

- ▶ *Ride a Square* with *ground-center-grow* rebalances before each corner. Ride the corners with quarter turns on the forehand, or haunches. Add full halts.

- ▶ Use the *Unbendable Arm* in transitions.

- ▶ Reward regularly by allowing your horse to trot around the whole arena.

WHAT ARE THE RESULTS?

- ▶ Horse becomes lighter on his forehand, responds quickly to upward transitions (is "in front of your leg"), and has improved quality of balance.

9

Develop the Horse's Muscles through Circles and Turns

I n this session, you will consider adding circles and turns to the transitions you have
been doing. These will further help develop the musculature of your horse so he can
raise his back. Before you start you may find it helpful to review the working of the hip
joint in Chapter 5, because the correct use, and release of the hip joints, are important
in influencing your horse in turns. This will become especially clear in the session *ON
THE HORSE* in this chapter.

ON THE GROUND

The Mechanics of the Hip Joint

Give yourself a *Shaggy Dog Shake.* Then stand
quietly while you find your inner balance: *center
yourself;* pull the *bungee cord* at the top of your
head; *free your back; drop your sacrum;* and *ground*
your feet.

As you stand, think about your hip joint. Remember that the only part of the hip joint that you
can actually feel with your fingers in the front of
your body (see p. 33) is the *edge* of the socket that
holds the ball at the end of the femur (fig. 9.1). This
edge that you feel bears no weight. The weight-
bearing part of the joint is back and up inside your
pelvis, behind this front edge. The center of the hip
socket, which sits like an inverted cup over the top

of the ball on the femur, is the crucial weight-
bearing spot. It is this weight-bearing spot that
needs to feel well-greased so that it can support the
body, as well as act as a flexible hinge. Explore with
your fingers and your imagination to locate this
spot. When you find it, your "knowing" its position
can change or enhance the relationship between
your body and legs. You will discover that your
weight is distributed evenly all over the bottom of
your feet.

In contrast, if you concentrate on only the part
of the hip joint that you can feel with your fingers,
you will probably find your weight on the balls of
your feet. Your upper body will have moved forward an inch or so to balance over the front of the
joint. Some people, fearful of over-balancing forward, push the pelvis back over their heels instead.

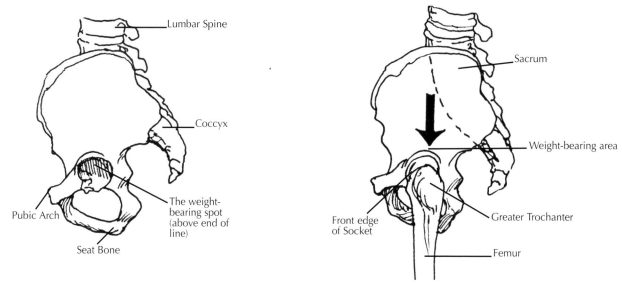

<u>9.1</u> *Details of the pelvic area showing the weight-bearing portion of the hip socket.*

When you find the true center of the weight-bearing spot in your hip joint, you will again find your weight spread across your entire foot. In addition, you will be able to drop a *plumb line* from your ear through your shoulder, center, hip joint, seat bone, and ankle, whether you are standing on your feet or sitting in the saddle.

Now that you have located the center of the hip joint, you can try an exercise to understand the importance of the freedom of this joint. It is best to do this demonstration with the help of a partner. While standing, locate the front of your hip joints by placing the tips of your fingers on them. Now have your partner put her fingers there, being sure that she is really finding the crease of the bend (fig. 9.2). Remember your *Four Basics.* Have your partner give a soft short push and then release. Have her do this several times. What is your reaction?

If you stiffen, you will be pushed off balance. If you soften and "give," and let the hip joints fold, you will stay balanced. Note what happens to the rest of your body when you allow your hips to

yield to your partner's push. Your ankles and knees will flex, your pelvis will move back, and your torso will slant slightly forward from the hip joints. As soon as your partner releases the pressure, you will bounce upright again. As you repeat this exercise, the movement will become very fluid, and the directives from your partner's fingers can become very light.

Try doing the same exercise without your *Four Basics.* Hold your breath, or use hard eyes. Tighten your toes, then lock your jaw, or try carrying more weight on one leg than the other. You will find that all the fluidness of motion has gone. Your partner's push receives only resistance. This contrast of trying an exercise both correctly, and incorrectly is useful in learning a new technique and forming correct habits.

Remember when you were being led on your horse, you allowed him to move your hip joints forward and up, then fold and drop them down (Session Two—*The Following Seat).* The following ground exercises should give you the same feeling.

9.2 I am touching both of Lucy's hip joints to encourage her to "fold" her hip joints around my fingertips.

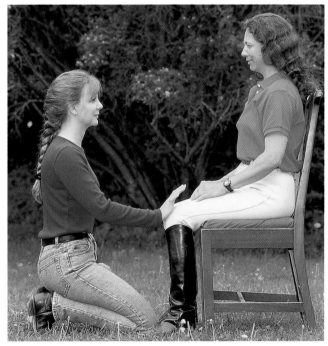

Bumping Knees

Before we start with *Bumping Knees,* once again locate your hip joint. Sit in a hard chair. Have your partner kneel in front of you, and using the heel of her hand, bump the end of your knee (figs. 9.3 A & B). You should be able to sense this bump in your hip socket at the head of your femur. Take

9.3 A & B Jineen bumps the front of Cynthia's knee to help Cynthia be fully aware of the sensation of the head of the femur deep in the hip socket.

time to clearly find and feel this sensation in each hip socket, as it will help you to precisely locate your hip joint. You need to know exactly where this joint is in order to maintain the stability of your pelvis on your horse while your leg, separate from the pelvis, can move as needed.

Now sit on the front edge of the chair. Keep your weight even on your seat bones and find your balance point—both in an upright position and in a forward, half-seat position. Remember, your seat bones are shaped somewhat like the rockers of a rocking chair. You can sit on the middle of the rocker in the upright position or further forward on the rocker in the half-seat. If you have trouble keeping even weight on your two seat bones, try putting your arm on your *heavy* side up over your head, fingers pointing to the sky and thumb pointing back. Allow that side to lengthen while the weight goes diagonally through you onto the *light* seat bone. Now do the *Teeter-Totter* in your chair and carefully note how the new softness in your hip joints keeps you in balance. Try the *Teeter-Totter* with hard eyes, then tight toes, and then a locked jaw. Do the *Teeter-Totter* with more weight on one seat bone, and notice that the hip joint on that side becomes more tense.

Deep Centering for Turning

Now that you have discovered how to keep your hip joints free, you will need to understand another concept, which will not only help you turn your horse, but will help you understand all your body parts and their freedom—or lack of it. This is the concept of *deep centering.*

Sit balanced and centered again on your chair, where I'm going to ask you to rotate and look over your shoulder. Find your center by imagining the *ball,* quiet and deep in your pelvis (see p. 40). Make sure your head and neck are free, your back is long and wide, and your hip joints soft. Now initiate a turn from the bottom of your torso, but instead of moving your pelvis around your center, allow the

9.4 Jineen "rotates" the "ball" in her pelvis, which results in her torso, head, and neck rotating to the right. Note that she has allowed her left shoulder to stay too far back.

ball to rotate within your pelvis (fig. 9.4). Sometimes, people imagine they are holding the *ball* in the palm of their hand and turning it. Other people find it is easier to initiate the turn by imagining they are holding the *ball* from over the top with the tips of their fingers on the *ball's* "equator."

Be sure that you allow the *ball* to rotate around the central point in the pelvis without rolling from side to side. Allow the rotation of the *ball* in your center to turn your torso and head. Be sure that the power (the engine) for the turn is initiated by this handholding of the *ball* inside the pelvis, and not by moving your shoulders or head. Your upper body should simply be carried along, with your neck free, and your back long and wide, hip joints soft. This is the concept of *deep centering* for turns.

At first, keep the *ball* rotation small and slow, being sure to keep your weight evenly on your seat bones. Be sensitive to any points of resistance in your body. If you find a sticky spot, stop and breathe softly and regularly. Think of breathing into that spot. It can help to actually put your hand on that sticky spot and then breathe into it. The tight spot should release, so that your rotation can continue smoothly beyond that point.

Still on your chair, square up again, give yourself a *Shaggy Dog Shake*, and make the same rotation to look over your shoulder *without* centering. Notice how crude this turn feels in comparison to the one you initiated through *deep centering*. When you use your *deep centering*, the thought seems to be all that is needed to make the turn.

Return to the image of the *ball* deep in your center, and try the same turning exercise with one arm up over your head, thumb back. Turn both ways while keeping your neck free and your sacrum heavy. Put the other arm up and repeat the turns. It will probably be easier for you with one arm than the other. It will also be easier for you to hold the arm up on the side toward which you are turning. Give the other, tighter side more practice, but be sure to do the exercise on both sides. Notice how effortless, yet how clear, your turns become. Remember the value of *clear intent*. Decide where you want to go and keep your *clear intent* throughout the turn.

Deep centering will teach you a lot about your body parts and their freedom, or lack of it. It will

also allow you to coax your body into new, suppler movements, and can be used effectively in many riding movements. Before you practice *deep centering* on your horse, using it as part of your turning aids (and to free up his tight spots), spend some time experimenting with it on yourself, both sitting on a chair, and when walking. Feel the turns really emanate from your center without disturbing your pelvis or your weight on your two seat bones, and without allowing your shoulders to "drag" you around instead. Always lead from the bottom up–from the *ball* in your pelvis. You will find how effortless a turn can be if it comes from your center.

Now that you have established your deep-centered turns with even weight on both your seat bones, keep in mind that it can be advantageous in many cases to briefly weight one seat bone more than the other. However, it is important to be able to keep *equal* weight on both seat bones through various movements *before* you try using *independent* seat bones to communicate with your horse.

Square Dancing

You can now try other exercises to enhance this communication. With the help of a partner, do *Square Dancing* (with or without music) to continue to improve your ability to turn your horse effectively.

As before, doing previous exercises on the ground, first give yourself a *Shaggy Dog Shake*, and establish your inner balance. You will be the leader of your dancing pair, so stand with your partner on your right. Put your right hand around your partner's waist, stretch your left hand in front of your body, and hold your partner's left hand (fig. 9.5 A). Your partner can either put her right hand on your right hand, on her own hip, or leave it free.

Before you start, both you and your partner should find your centers, establish your *grounding* and let your bodies lengthen up through your heads. Using the body language you learned with

9.5 A–E "Square Dancing." This experiment demonstrates how important it is for your real horse to receive the support of both your hands and legs.

(A) "Square Dancing" pose showing Jineen's (the rider) right hand around Cynthia's waist, and her left hand holding Cynthia's left hand, since Cynthia needs support from both Jineen's hands to keep her comfortably balanced.
(B) & (C) Jineen supports Cynthia with both hands (seen from the front and back views) as they move off into the dance circle.

your improved *use of self* while doing the *Fingers under the Armpits* exercise (see p. 71), alert your partner that you are about to move. Give a signal to rebalance by *grounding, centering and growing,* and *breathing in-out,* then step off into the beginning of the dance. You move in a circle about 10 or 15 feet in diameter. Go at a vigorous walk or skipping pace, and notice how your partner tends to swing away from you. Keep her secure with

your right arm and hand (figs. 9.5 B & C). Now pick up a little extra speed and make a smaller circle, about 6 feet across, and then go back to the bigger one. You will notice that you had to hold your partner a little more strongly in the smaller circle. Make another small circle and this time take your outside right hand off her side (fig. 9.5 D). You will find that she will swing way out without the support of your hand.

(D) Cynthia is swinging away because she has lost the support of Jineen's outside (right) hand.
(E) Cynthia is feeling insecure on the circle without the support of either of Jineen's hands.

Bring her back again and put your arm around her once more. Pick up speed on your circle, and this time let go of your inside left hand. She won't spin out as far, but she will definitely feel insecure about negotiating the circle. The outside (right) arm alone does not quite provide enough support. The touch in the left hand, though quite light, makes a big difference. She needs both your hands.

Return to the starting position, with both arms in the correct position on your partner. Give her your rebalance signal, move off and into a pirouette around your inside leg, and then go on again. A little farther along, do another rebalance, and another pirouette. With both hands in position, all should go smoothly. Now try two more pirouettes, first letting go with your outside hand, and on the next pirouette letting go with your inside one. In both cases, your partner will swing wide and feel insecure, and the pirouettes will be awkward.

You will find that not only is this exercise great fun when skipping to music, but quite enlightening. You will notice how your body-language re-balance signals are very helpful to your partner, just as they will be to your horse. This exercise shows you the importance of the inside and outside aids when turning, and helps you to understand what it feels like to be the horse. He needs the support of both of your hands, and both of your legs.

For a different experience, you should also try switching places with your partner, letting her be the leader.

Clear Intent with Two Plumb Lines

Let's add *clear intent* to the *Square Dancing* exercise. Here's an exercise to help with *clear intent*. First, imagine the *plumb line* hanging down through the middle of your body. Start by imagining it being pulled upward out of the top of your head. Now imagine it hanging down inside your head between your ears, down through your neck, and your rib cage just in front of your spine, through the middle of your diaphragm, and through your center at the front of your fourth and fifth lumbar vertebrae. Let the plumb line continue hanging down between your hip joints and down to your feet at the balance point of the *Bubbling Spring*.

Now imagine another plumb line hanging a foot or two in front of you. Make a decision that you are going to walk "through" that imaginary plumb line. This causes you to center yourself even though it always remains ahead of you. Let your body lengthen by pulling the *bungee cord* on top of your head. Use your *Four Basics* and start walking, always keeping one plumb line just ahead of you. Your *clear intent* is to walk through it (fig. 9.6).

Notice how your *clear intent* helps you to move forward positively—either around a turn, straight

9.6 This drawing shows one plumb line running through the person's body, and another plumb line just ahead of her. You have the feeling of walking "through" this second plumb line although it always remains ahead of you.

ahead, or doing other movements. You walk with ease and poise. Now try the *Square Dancing* exercise adding the image of the plumb line, and the concept of *clear intent*. You will find that the "dancing circles"—doing turns with your partner—become even smoother, as well as easier. Although, I'm specifically discussing exercises for turns and circles in this chapter, you can use this image of the plumb line in many situations on a horse.

The Capsule

To enlarge your understanding of the ways in which you can use your *clear intent* and deep centered energy try an entertaining exercise called the *Capsule*. You will need a group of people. I have done this exercise with as few as five people and as many as 350. You will need to move around in a small area, the size needed depends on the number of people. Half of a small riding arena was fine for the crowd. A 10-foot square or circle will work fine for five people.

Have everyone in the group stand comfortably, with feet slightly apart, and prepare for the exercise in the usual way. Allow your head to balance over your center, and your center over your feet.

Imagine a gentle traction on that *bungee cord* which pulls upward out of the middle of your head, and allow your body to get longer and wider. Let the soles of your feet spread out, and really feel the floor. Now let your center to begin to expand in all directions. Do your remember your *elastic suit*? (See p. 30.) Allow it to stretch in all directions: up, down, sideways, and backward.

Now imagine the *capsule*. Surround yourself with it and let it become your personal space. Allow yourself, as well as your center, to expand until you totally fill the capsule and feel how it envelops your energy and warmth as your energy bounces against its inside (fig. 9.7).

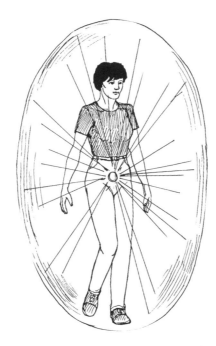

9.7 Imagine yourself in a "capsule" with energy from your center radiating against the sides and filling it up.

Now everyone should start walking, first in the same direction, and then in any direction. Keep weaving around, changing direction, maybe even turning around and going the other way. Weave in and out among the others in the group but keep the group cohesive. While continuing to constantly turn and change direction as they please, have everybody stay fairly close together rather than all spreading out.

Keep your eyes soft, your body centered, and sense the ever-evolving spaces opening up before you as you move around. You will find that you don't have to worry about colliding with other people because your resilient personal *capsule* will protect you. Your capsule will simply glance off their capsules. Your *soft eyes* see everything. Be aware of the sound, smell, and temperature. Be aware of your center and your *breathing*. Notice your easy balance as you move.

Now start increasing the pace. Spaces will keep evolving before you even at this quicker tempo. Keep the group compact, everybody moving about and changing direction. No one collides with anyone else. Keep building the speed of the pace, and then, using a bit more space, let the motion become a dance. Skip and dance, let your arms and body actively sway. Tip, bend, move, and twist in the joy of the dance. Feel the freedom of your body in the *capsule* as you dance. Feel the pulsating and whirling energy shared by the dancing group. Maintain this exhilarating feeling of group motion (fig. 9.8).

Now slow the pace by degrees back to a walk, and very gradually glide to a halt. Close your eyes for a minute. Feel your expanded centeredness and calm. Notice how light you feel while at the same time you are extraordinarily grounded. You can test yourself when you are in a crowd of strangers. Experiment with your *capsule* and you will find it easier to move around.

During this imaginary *Capsule* exercise, you succeeded in balancing internal and external awareness. This new expanded awareness can give you better control in several ways when you ride. Not only can you keep your internal awareness of yourself while at the same time being aware of your horse, but you will also find that riding in groups no longer has to feel like trying to catch a train in Grand Central Station.

You can use this feeling of being in a *capsule* in many ways. There is safety within it. I once taught a girl who had a bad experience at a show.

9.8 Every one in this group is in their own resilient, personal "capsule," protecting them from bumping into another. This works equally well when in a crowded riding ring.

Her employer had asked her to jump a rather lively Morgan in competition, and she agreed, even though she was insecure about jumping. I saw her the next day, and she was still quite frightened. We talked about it, and I suggested that she build a *capsule* of safety around herself. She could build the capsule around the horse as well as herself, and as long as she was centered and within that capsule, using her *soft eyes* and *breathing* she would feel confident and safe. After she built her imaginary capsule, she had an excellent ride, when under other circumstances she could have had a very tense and unhappy hour.

Now you can take your new understanding of the dynamics of circles and turns which you discovered through the *Square Dancing* exercises, and put them into practice on your horse along with the concept of *clear intent*. Using your imaginary *capsule*, you will be able to enhance your awareness, so turning your horse can become effortless, as well as energetic.

ON THE HORSE

The work you have just done on the ground can now be put into use as you get on your horse. Your newly expanded knowledge of your hip joint and finding equal weight on your seat bones, will greatly enhance your abilities to do turns and circles. The *Square Dancing* and the *Capsule* exercises will help your turning work, and keep you centered as well.

Balanced Body Rotations

As always, when you first get on, take time to find your *Four Basics*, inner awareness, and balance. Pick up your reins, allowing them to remain long, and without your stirrups walk off using your *following seat*. Breathe rhythmically and allow your following seat to establish itself quietly and steadily on your horse's back. Trust yourself and him. If he jigs and jogs, quickly and quietly *ground* yourself, and bring him back (with the reins if necessary), and then drop the reins again to the buckle and resume walking. He will soon learn that there is no necessity of doing anything but walk, and since horses are essentially lazy animals, he will be happy to do so. Notice that from your previous work on the ground and on the horse you are more aware of your softly following hip joints and lower back. Now put your feet in your stirrups on the *Bubbling Spring's* balance point (see fig. 5.19). Just rest them there, don't push. Let the stirrups carry the weight of your legs and feet. Think about the soles of your feet and become aware of their connection with the ground as your horse's belly moves your knees and lower legs as he walks along.

Check your balance. Do you have equal weight on each seat bone? If not, you may need to put one arm over your head for a moment to make the adjustment. When the seat bones are equal, check that the weight of your feet in the stirrups is also equal. Many people put more weight in one stirrup than the other. Take all the time you need to find that even, secure feeling.

Unevenness on your seat bones or in your stirrups usually comes from tightness in the torso or the legs. Remember that simply becoming aware of the tight spots can alleviate the tension. Use the *deep centering* exercise you practiced on the chair (see p. 94). If your right leg is your tighter leg, imagine emptying it, allowing it to be long and light. Usually, it is the hip joint and thigh that need emptying the most, though the knee may also need attention. Often, when you empty and loosen those spots, the lower leg will take care of itself.

Coordinated Use of Your Center and Legs

Now find the *ball* deep in your pelvis, and rotate to the left using *deep centering.* You will find it helpful to raise your left arm, thumb back, over your head as you did in the ground exercise on earlier in this chapter (see p. 95). Remember the turn is a small,

floating rotation of the torso. Don't force it. As you turn left, notice the automatic movement of the outside right leg. If you leave the hip joint and thigh soft, the leg will slide a little back and lie flat around the horse's side. This will *ground* this outside, right foot, releasing a little weight into it, thus helping your horse to balance. The sole of your foot will feel connected to the ground as if with a magnet. What a wonderful outside aid!

Rebalance Your Center

Still walking on your horse, turn left again allowing the new motion of your right leg, but this time pay attention to what your inside left leg is doing. It, too, releases at the hip joint, drops down deeper into the stirrup, and becomes available as an inside aid on the turn. This gives a very clear body-language aid to the horse, and influences the weight of your seat bone more subtly than if you were to just "press" your foot down on the stirrup. When you apply careful use of your weight, you must keep your torso upright. Do this by simply *allowing* one side to become longer, if needed. But, if you *lean* to one side, you will put your horse off balance. Again, raising one arm over your head will help keep you upright.

In fast work, such as cutting or barrel racing, the torso must adjust to stay over the horse's center of gravity. The horse will tilt more than your body, and you will remain close to, but not exactly on, the perpendicular (fig. 9.9).

Check your legs. They should feel even. You may have to remember, over and over, to *allow* your legs to be empty and free. You can retrain a more recalcitrant leg by repeating the *deep-centering* rotating exercise, turning away from the tight leg more frequently than the other.

It might be helpful at this point to imagine a letter "X" in your body. One line of the letter X will go from the tip of one shoulder to the opposite seat bone, and the other will go from the tip of the other shoulder to its opposite seat bone. The lines

_9.9_ In fast work, such as cutting or barrel racing, the torso must adjust to stay over the horse's center of gravity. The horse will tilt more than your body, and you will remain close to, but not exactly on the vertical as Martha Josey is demonstrating so well.

of the X will cross each other slightly below the middle of an ordinary letter X because your shoulders are wider than your seat bones. Your job is to keep the two lines of the X the same length. This means that if you drop your shoulder as you turn your horse, you will cause that line of

the X to shorten. However, you can rotate your body like a barber pole or a pepper grinder, keeping your shoulders horizontal, without changing the length of the X's lines.

Now that you are more even, do you notice any difference in your horse's stride? A little rebalancing can make a lot of difference to a horse. Think of this. If you carry a pack on your back that is heavier on one side than the other, you will have to adjust your stride to it. You are the pack on the horse's back and he must adjust to you.

Serpentines and Imaginary Circles

Maintaining your balance and the levelness in your seat and feet while still walking straight ahead on your horse, play with the *deep-centering* rotation exercise. Keep it a very small rotation, just a few degrees, one way, and the other. Your pelvis should maintain the *following seat* with your soft hip joints gently *pedaling backward* (see p. 58). Don't let them lock as you rotate. Keep searching for any tight spots and work them out, one at a time (see p. 76). By now, your head and neck should also be free and balanced.

When you are comfortable doing the *deep-centering* turns, incorporate them into the turns of a serpentine. Make your loops comfortably big. Don't worry about making exact loops yet. Simply keep the loops open–not too tight. As you walk the serpentine, rotate your torso slightly in the direction you are going so your shoulders, head, and eyes are directed ahead at the track you are following. Don't overdo the rotation. Your *soft eyes* will not need to rotate more than your body. For a clearer sensation, put your inside arm up over your head changing arms for each loop (fig. 9.10). Providing you keep *allowing* the motion of the *following seat* and keep your *pure balance*– forward, back, and lateral–your horse will hear you. If he becomes inattentive, give him a tap with your lower legs or with your whip, to say to him, "Wake up. I am up here talking to you." Once you have his attention, he will hear your delicate aids.

Think again about the imaginary circles your seat bones and hip joints *pedaled backward* as you practiced the *following seat*. These circles, or *"wheels,"* will become different in size as you begin to turn your horse. You can visualize the inside

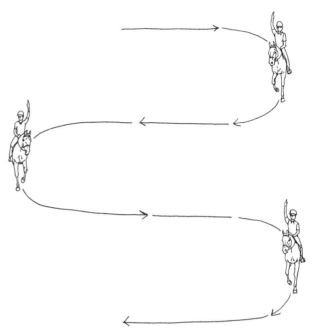

9.10 *Incorporating your deep centering turns into a serpentine will help your horse be balanced and rhythmical. If your raise your inside hand over your head at each turn it helps you sink into your deep center.*

wheel becoming larger, while the outside wheel becomes smaller. The inside wheel enlarges because this is the side on which you need the most energy. The inside aid produces most of the forward energy in a turn as well as suggesting the bend, while the outside aid simply keeps the horse from swinging or bulging out of the turn, and helps him balance. You may feel that the inside wheel becomes so large as it produces more energy that it comes up almost into your armpit and goes down inside your leg to your knee. It might help to imagine these *wheels* moving in oil.

Some people find that these *wheels* do not feel really round, but rather are oblong and move more like a continuous belt in a factory. Use whichever image is clearer to you. The idea of pedaling backward so that the bottom of the imaginary wheel moves forward as it follows the horse's back is more important than the shape or size of it.

Now as you make your serpentine loops, combine your *pedaling-backward wheels*, large and small, with a small rotation of your upper body. Be especially careful to keep the weight equal on your two feet and two seat bones, though your outside foot will need more *grounding* (see p. 101). You will find that you are making your loops without using your reins, just body-language aids, and the resulting placement of the legs. Later, you will combine these body aids with rein and leg aids for accuracy, but for now note that your horse is bending around the turns from his poll to his tail with only your body aids.

You have now improved the lines of communication. Enjoy the fluidness, energy, and quality of movement that you are sharing. Doing circles and turns, you can pick up a trot on a long rein and begin incorporating what you have learned at the walk into the trot. Remember to keep your body level and balanced while you allow your horse to move you.

Further Images for Turning and Circling

To do more with turns, and now some circles, review the coordinated use of your center and legs that you have just practiced. Riders tend to think that their usable legs start at their knees. They really start at your newly located hip joints. Try imagining that your legs are hanging from your ears. Your hip joint will soften and you will allow your whole leg to move properly.

Think of a cushion of air high up under your thigh, between the thigh and the saddle. Let your outside leg slide over that air cushion as you allow it to move slightly back from the hip joint. This tiny motion will place your outside leg in the correct position, just a little back, while you still leave the needed contact weight on your seat bone.

Imagining this cushion of air will help avoid a common tendency to sit down and back on your inside seat bone when bending your horse rapidly

round a corner. Think of how a skater balances as she pushes off into a left circle. She puts her left foot squarely under her center of gravity, she pushes off with a strong right foot, and she lengthens from her center, forward and up over that well placed inside skate. If for any moment she were to settle or lean back in any way, she would fall. As you ride a turn, feel that you are skating the turn in centered control.

Let's play with another new image for turns and circles. Imagine the two rails of a railroad track stretching out in front of you. Look down the tracks. They extend parallel out ahead of you for a long way. Somewhere out there they turn, and when a train comes along, it bends through the turn. Which track will take the brunt of the weight of the train as it goes through the turn—the inside track or the outside track? Due to centrifugal force it is the outside track that takes the weight just as your outside hand did in the *Square Dancing* exercise. But, what happens to the train if, as it goes through the turn, the outside track spreads too far away and buckles? There is a train wreck. What happens, if through the turn, the outside track remains in place, but the inside track disintegrates, or gets too far apart from the outside track? There is another train wreck. To get that train through the bend, you have to have a solid outside track, and both tracks have to stay the same distance apart. Though the outside track is going to have to be the more supportive of the two, the train will need the direction and balance provided by the inside track. The point of this analogy is to remind you again of the importance of your outside aids on a turn, which alter depending on your speed.

So now, look out above your horse's ears down those railroad tracks and ride turns and circles out through the tracks, first at the walk, then at the trot. You will need to include *centering and growing*, picturing *Square Dancing* for effective leg and hand aids, and the *ball* deep in your pelvis to direct the rotation of your body. Your pelvis will want to turn slightly. *Allow* it to do so, but do not force it. Let your *backward-pedaling wheels* and circles rotate freely. Drop your *plumb line* out in front and let your *clear intent* help you ride through it as you go down the railroad tracks (fig. 9.11).

"Feeling" in Your Riding

Riding with this combination of awareness and imagery, not only improves communication with your horse, but also increases the shared energy between you. You are now adding "feeling" to your repertoire. You can ride with accuracy. Notice also that your *clear intent* and your *capsule* are important parts of this enjoyable whole. This *clear intent* will prove very effective in more advanced work, especially when combined with a body practiced in the coordinated use of leg aids in the balanced body rotation and the leg and hand aids you learned in *Square Dancing*. Use these images when doing circles and turns in slow, simple movements, until they are a part of you. Eventually, when you plan a circle, the "feelings," or images are there intact for immediate use. They will no longer have to be processed each time you need them. You are building the coordination and the muscle memory you will need for more advanced work.

9.11 Keep "soft eyes" and look ahead to keep your horse secure and balanced as he moves forward through the confines of the railroad tracks.

Develop the Horse's Muscles through Circles and Turns?

ON THE GROUND

▶ Mobility of your hip joints, and the depth of the hip sockets. *Bumping Knees.*

▶ *Deep centering* and turning to feel turns coming from deep in your center.

▶ *Square Dancing* to appreciate the different responsibilities of the inside and outside reins when turning.

▶ *Two plumb lines,* and *clear intent* to help you move positively.

▶ The *Capsule* to balance internal and external awareness.

ON THE HORSE

▶ Balance must be equal on both sides of the horse.

▶ Your shoulders and legs position themselves when you turn from your center with *clear intent.*

▶ Imagining an X through your body helps your balance.

▶ When turning, balance yourself like a skater circling on the ice.

▶ Look ahead down the *railroad tracks.*

WHAT ARE THE RESULTS?

▶ Increased "feeling" in your riding.

▶ A feeling of deep stability in your mobility.

▶ Additional awareness of the importance of *centering.*

10

SESSION SIX

Gain Extra Stability from Riding in Three Seats at the Trot

By this time I am sure you have become aware of how important it is to your horse's ease of motion for you to be in balance, as well as fluid in your movements, at all times. You have already been working on ways to achieve this fluidity and balance, but let's see if you can find some other viable ways to help your horse. The more stable you are in your own balance and movement, the easier it is for your horse and the happier he will be. In this session, I'm going to help you find extra stability by practicing what I call *Three Seats at the Trot*. For this you will do what may seem to be some unrelated exercises on the ground, but they all will feed into your being able to feel the sensations from, and then actually doing, *Three Seats* repetitively.

ON THE GROUND

Feeling the Inside and Outside of Your Legs

Standing on the ground, settle yourself and make a mental check of your body as you have done in previous groundwork. Picture your hip joints, then imagine your hips as they widen out to the greater trochanters. Now place your hands on the inside of your upper thighs and run them down the inside of your legs to your ankles (fig. 10.1). Do this, two or three times. The combination of imagining the width of your hips and sliding your hands down the inside of your legs, helps your hips to release and open.

For contrast, start the same way, but put your hands down the *outside* of your legs (fig. 10.2). Notice how very different this feels and how the freedom in your hip joints is lost. Also, for comparison, instead of using your hands, visualize alternating going down the inside and outside of your legs.

Now, try this interesting conceptual exercise while walking along. Before you start, pull the imaginary *bungee cord* on the top of your head, and find

10.1 *The girls are "Sliding Hands" down the* inside *of the legs. Jineen's (on the left) toes should be turned slightly more outward.*

10.2 *"Sliding Hands" down the* outside *of the legs. Jineen's toes are fine in this picture.*

your balance. Now walk, and once more mentally travel outward from your hip joints down the inside of your legs. You can walk right along at any speed you feel like. Keep repeating the routine in your imagination. You will find the new freedom in your hips comfortable and your feet feeling more correctly balanced. Wouldn't this be a good image to use when wrapping your legs around your horse?

Stop, turn around, and walk back again, but this time, imagine your hands going down the outside of your legs. Imagine this repeatedly. How does it feel? It's awkward, isn't it? You are waddling from side to side. Try doing three or four strides first one way and then the other, going back and forth from inside the legs to outside the legs. Notice the purity of the walk when you mentally travel down the inside of the legs, and the awkwardness of movement when you go down the outside of the legs. If you watch others doing this exercise, it is easy to tell which way they are thinking.

One way of entertaining yourself when you have to wait in an airport—and what does one do in an airport except wait—is to watch the people walking by. It's pretty funny. Some people walk extremely well, and it is a pleasure to watch them, but there are many people who roll awkwardly along on the outside of their legs.

To experiment a little more with these concepts, become aware of the *plumb line* that hangs down through your center. As you did earlier, then imagine another one that hangs straight down in front of you (see fig. 9.6) Keep that plumb line in front of you and walk forward while mentally moving down the inside of your legs. Have some fun with this exercise and try walking backward, first down the inside of your legs, and then down the outside. The difference between the two is even more pronounced. Focusing on your *two plumb lines*, walk forward again and feel how this exercise has improved your fluidity of movement.

Three Seats at the Trot

For continued improvement of your balance, let's try some modification of your position on the horse. These trot exercises, done in three different positions—*rising trot, half-seat,* and *sitting trot* (in the deep seat), will stabilize your balance. In all your riding at the trot, using these three seats interchangeably will be useful both in improving your stability and effectiveness, as well as giving you a start in learning the modification of positions on the horse.

I have already explained the advantages of practicing the rising trot and half-seat alternately in *Two Seats at the Trot* (see p. 65). Now I want to add the third position—the *sitting trot*—introducing it in stages instead of simply telling you to, "sit to your trot," which can have you bumping painfully on your horse's back.

The first stage will be learning what I call *Monkey* and *Reverse Monkey* (as adapted from the Alexander Technique). I will also introduce you to the *Horse Stance,* used in Eastern martial arts. These exercises will lead you into the sliding, dropping motion that your seat bones will need in order to follow the two sides of the horse's back in the sitting trot.

Exercises to Help the Sitting Trot

MONKEY/REVERSE MONKEY

Let's start the *Three Seats at the Trot* exercises by learning *Monkey* and *Reverse Monkey*. Some people like to call it the *close-open-close* exercise. Find your hip joints again, and bend forward from them, keeping your back straight and your head and neck a continuation of your back. Bend down slightly and come up again. Next time, bend down, touch the backs of your knees with your fingers, then let your knees flex forward and your hip joints close, and flex back. Look down at the ground and let your arms hang straight down. Your center is directly over your feet. If a plumb line goes from your center to your feet, your shoulders will be ahead of it and your pelvis behind it. You will find that this is a strong, balanced position. You are now in the *closed* position called *Monkey* because that is what it looks like (fig. 10.3). Come upright somewhat, then drop down to *Monkey* several times until you can really feel that the hip joints and the knees have to open and close to bend and unbend equally.

Drop down to *Monkey* position once again and then think about bringing your sacrum, and therefore your pelvis, forward. Try putting one hand on your sacrum so you can feel it as it moves. Notice that as your pelvis comes forward, your shoulders go up and back, and your knees go forward and down. Returning to an upright position out of the *Monkey* position is very much like moving from a half-seat to an upright, deep seat. If you think of taking your pelvis and knees forward, your shoulders will move back over your center and feet as a result. Your center stays in the same place throughout (fig. 10.4).

You will find that this is a more balanced way to go from a half-seat to a deep seat than by simply drawing your shoulders up and back. Try shifting to upright while thinking of moving only your shoulders into an upright position and you will notice that you tend to lock your knees and not allow

10.3 In the "Monkey" exercise, this is the closed hip angle.

10.4 Coming back into an upright, deep seat from "Monkey" with their hips forward and opening, Cynthia (right) is in a true deep seat, while Jineen is not quite there.

the pelvis to move. As a result, you will fall backward because both your pelvis and your center are no longer over your feet. If, when you change seats, you concentrate on bringing your pelvis forward and allowing your knees to flex and come forward, your pelvis will come over your feet and the shoulders will take care of themselves. Therefore, when you move your shoulders, remember that your hip joints, knees, and ankles must coordinate with them to maintain your balance.

To even more clearly understand how your basic balance remains the same in every seat, let's try the "open" or *Reverse Monkey* (fig. 10.5). From your *Monkey* position, shift first to an upright po-sition and then continue beyond upright until the fronts of your hip joints are fully stretched. It should feel as if you wanted to lead with the fronts of your hips. Your knees will actually still be leading, but your hip joints will be well forward. Try to keep the pubic arch up and your back flat without hollowing it. This time look straight ahead. If you kept your neck and head parallel to your back in this position, you would find yourself awkwardly looking up. So, allow yourself to look straight ahead. This is *Reverse Monkey*.

To go back to *Monkey* you have to flex those hip joints, knees, and ankles again. Notice that the pelvis moves with the torso rather than the legs.

The hip joints, knees, and ankles allow the changes of the angle between torso and legs. Go back and forth between *Monkey* and *Reverse Monkey*, always keeping your knees bent. Repeat it until you can do it smoothly and your balance is easy (fig. 10.6).

HORSE STANCE

Now, with your feet squarely beneath you, take the *Horse Stance*. To do this, you need to place your feet under your center about as far apart as they would be if you were sitting on a horse, and bend your knees and hips as if you were sitting upright in the saddle. Let your toes turn slightly out (fig. 10.7 A). What would happen if you were riding in this position and your horse suddenly disappeared out from under you? Would you land on your feet? If you were in this position, you would. And what would it feel like? Try jumping up and down in this position so that you feel the slap of the ground under your feet as you come down, and you really know that your feet are solid under you (fig. 10.7 B). This is how solidly balanced you should feel on your horse.

10.5 Here is "Reverse Monkey" with the open hip angle. Cynthia's (right) stance is excellent.

10.6 "Monkey/Reverse Monkey."

(A) "Monkey position": the hip angle is closed.
(B) The upright, balanced position: the hip angle is more open.
(C) "Reverse Monkey": the hip angle is fully open.

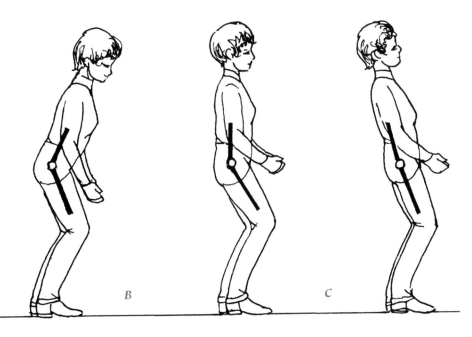

A   *B*   *C*

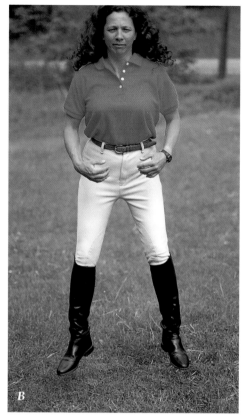

10.7 A & B Cynthia is in the "Horse Stance" with her toes turned out slightly, ready to jump up—feet off the ground (A). When she lands, she will feel a "slap" on the ground, and know that her feet are solidly under her (B).

You don't always have to be in an upright position to have this balanced, secure feeling. Pick up the *Monkey* position. Though the angulation of your body is more extreme than in the *Horse Stance*, this is also a very balanced position. Jump up and down in this position. You are just as solid on your feet in this position as in the more upright stance. You may have noticed that the *Monkey* position is similar to the half-seat, and the *Horse Stance* to the deep seat. You can now understand that you can be just as solid over your feet in the half-seat as you are in the upright, deep seat.

Go still deeper, bending your joints even more in the Monkey position, as if you are galloping, then straighten right up as if you are riding Western or dressage. In any of these positions, if you are in the correct balance and the horse disappears from under you, you will land on your feet. But if your feet are out ahead of you, what will happen? You will land with an uncomfortable bump on your rump. In any seat, the good, solid feeling of balance remains the same.

Two Sides of the Horse

Now that you have an understanding of a truly balanced seat, let's think more about the sitting trot. What is involved in the sitting trot? First, there is a lot of motion in the sitting trot. Many riders think that when you are sitting to the trot you must be very still, but in actual fact, the back and sides of the horse are active in the trot, and if you are to follow the horse's movement, you must be active too.

10.8 Cynthia and Jineen show how their seat bones will drop on each stride following the motion of the horse's back.

10.9 The girls are tracing circles backward with their hands. This prepares the rider to do "backward pedaling circles" as she drops a seat bone at the same time the horse's back drops on that side.

The trot is a diagonal gait. When one pair of diagonal feet are on the ground, one side of the horse's back is up, with the muscles on that side in use, driving the horse forward. In the next step, the other diagonal brings the other side of the back up. As a result, the horse's back will tip slightly from one side to the other. When you ride the trot, if you come down with your pelvis square, you will come down on the high side only, with full weight on those muscles that are in use. This is uncomfortable for the horse.

If, instead, you were to let the two sides of your pelvis, and therefore your seat bones, alternate going forward and up, *pedaling backward,* with the horse's back, you would distribute your weight evenly no matter which side of the back was up. This would be much more comfortable for the horse and for you as well.

To get a feeling for this, take the *Horse Stance* once again. Allow one seat bone to drop a little, and then switch and let the other seat bone drop. One side is always going up while the other side is going down. It is important to keep your pelvis in the middle and not let the motion go from side to side (fig. 10.8). You will notice that in order to allow your seat bones this sort of motion, your hip joints must be free to move. Each time your seat bone goes down, the hip joint on the same side drops and the knee flexes a little forward, and then the other side drops and that knee takes the flexion. Once again, we have alternate knees going with alternate seat bones.

Remember the *backward-pedaling circles* you developed while learning the *following seat* at the walk? You need to add that concept with the feeling of your dropping seat bones doing circles. So, once again take the *Horse Stance.* Put your hands beside, but not touching, your hips, and begin tracing backward circles in the air with your hands (fig. 10.9). When you have clearly established these hand circles, you can begin to let your seat bones do the *backward pedaling,* first one side, and then the other. To do this, you must be centered and allow the *ball* in your pelvis to

10.10 Counterclockwise "backward-pedaling" circles in the hip joints and seat bones.

roll. Keep the circles small at first until you become familiar with this motion of your hips and seat bones, and then let the circles get bigger and freer until you are exaggerating the motion (fig. 10.10). Play with these seat-bone circles until you feel really free in the hips.

This is more motion than you will need on your horse, but it's often useful to exaggerate a new movement when learning it, and you will be able to subdue the excess motion on your horse. Also, when you are actually sitting on your horse, your seat will not go from side to side as it tends to in this exercise on the ground, but will stay in the middle over the horse's spine. To experience how this might feel on your horse, try to keep your pelvis in the middle when doing your groundwork.

With the *Monkey* and *Reverse Monkey*, you have learned how to go from half-seat to deep seat, and with your *backward-pedaling circles*, you have learned how you can follow all the motion of the sitting trot.

Simulate Riding Three Seats in the Trot

Let's put these two exercises together to simulate moving from rising trot through half-seat to the deep seat at the sitting trot and back again. Take your *Horse Stance* and then put yourself in a half-seat position and flex your knees alternately as if following the two sides of the horse's body. Keeping your knees flexing alternately, gradually move your knees and pelvis forward and your torso upright into the deep seat position. Maintain the alternate flexing of the joints as you sit to the trot. You will find your seat bones *pedaling your bicycle backward* as you did earlier to absorb the motion of the horse's back.

Now rise to the trot a few times, allowing your torso a slightly more forward angulation before changing the angles of your hips, knees, and ankles as you shift into a half-seat. Then, still keeping your knees flexing, move back into a deep, upright position in a sitting trot. Do three or four imaginary horse strides in each seat, starting in the half-seat, then moving to the deep seat, and finally doing a rising trot. It may take you several strides to change from half- to deep seat, but once you are established in each new position, allow yourself the full three or four strides in that seat. To really enhance your understanding of the movement of the three seats, try this exercise on the trampoline. Keep the rhythm slow and the motion will feel much as it will on your horse.

If you keep in mind your *Four Basics* as well as your *two plumb lines*, and remember the *Monkey* and *Reverse Monkey* exercises, you will be able to stay in balance with your center directly over your feet in any of these seats.

ON THE HORSE

You have already ridden in *Two Seats at the Trot*–half-seat, and rising trot. Now it's time to add the sitting trot. Begin with some warm-up: walk in the *following seat*, progress through the rising trot and half-seat, remembering to *center and grow* throughout. After this warm-up, halt your horse and stand still for a moment.

Dropping Your Knees

As you did in the groundwork, mentally trace the shape of your legs from the sockets of your hip joints out to the greater trochanters, and then down the inside of your thighs to the knees. Notice the pleasant wide feel of your seat on the horse's back. If you need to, contrast this sensation with the tight feeling caused by either "mentally" running down the outside of your legs, or using your hands instead.

As you sit on your horse, add to the idea of the wide inside of your leg by picturing your femur as it travels down through the muscles of your leg toward your knee. Now imagine that the femur actually projects right through and beyond your kneecap. This mental image will help you release and drop your knee significantly. If you have your partner on the ground, have her place a finger in the air a quarter-inch in front of your kneecap, in line with your femur. Your mental journey from your deep inner hip joint out to the greater trochanter and down your extended femur will cause your knee to drop enough to touch her finger as shown (fig. 10.11).

The actual bend of your knee joint in this position is distinctly below your kneecap, at or just below the top of your boot. If you keep this in mind, you may find it easier to allow your lower leg to drop back against your horse in the correct position. As your femur drops down and forward, it is going to poke that kneecap down and forward as well. As a result, your lower leg will be gently pushed, or laid back against the horse's side at the bottom of the saddle. The point of your knee will be slightly in front of the tip of your toe and your lower leg four-to-six inches behind the girth. This position of the lower leg is the result of the release of the hip joint, and free movement of the knee. Be sure to try this positioning with both legs.

Notice that not only is your thigh directed forward and down, but it is also aimed out, depending

10.11 *Releasing her hip, Cynthia has dropped her knee down and forward a quarter-inch to touch my finger.*

on the width of your horse. This forward, down, and slightly outward placement of your thigh gives you the direction in which your knee should release. If you have trouble seeing this position of

10.12 I am helping Cynthia visualize the angle of her femur so she can understand the direction her knee is pointing.

knees to release, and your hips and buttocks will become immensely wide and mobile, and able to move with your horse.

Riding Three Seats in the Trot

Now you are ready to try your three seats in the trot. *Three Seats* is an exercise equally useful for English and Western riders—most Western riders rise to the trot at least some of the time. It can help to soften the knees and improve balance and riding in a half-seat in a Western saddle will have the same effect. By adding the third seat—the sitting trot, both the Western and the English rider can soften and deepen her sitting.

As you did in your ground exercise, you will go from half-seat, to the sitting trot in the deep seat, and then to rising trot—about five to seven strides in each seat (figs. 10.13 A–C). At first, it may take you several strides to allow your alternating knees to move forward from half-seat position to the deep seat of the sitting trot. Once you are there, start with only one or two strides of sitting trot before going to rising trot. This way you will not have time to stiffen up in the sitting trot and will feel only the pleasant elasticity of the *following seat*.

So now pick up a trot and take your half-seat position, being careful not to pinch your knees tight against the saddle. With your full weight on the stirrup, your pelvis will be slightly back and off the saddle. After you have trotted for a bit in your half-seat and have found a good rhythm, allow your knees to drop alternately forward until your pelvis is under you, and you are sitting on your horse's back with your knees still alternately flexing. The secret to sitting to the trot is to let your *hip joints and knees pedal backward alternately* following the horse's back. You've got it! You are doing it; you are sitting to the trot. Before you

your leg, get your helper on the ground to line up a riding whip with an imaginary line extending from your femur to show you where your knee is aimed (fig. 10.12).

Walk your horse forward, and as you follow your horse's motion, notice that you release your knee first on one side and then the other. Sometimes, I have fun telling people to shoot rubber *bullets* through their femur and out the kneecap. As you *shoot the bullets* and release your kneecap, your lower leg automatically comes against the horse's side and stimulates his hind leg. Play with this idea of *shooting bullets* through your femurs and out your kneecaps, but be very careful not to shove with your knees. If you find yourself pushing with your knees, you will notice that your hip joints and buttocks have tightened. Allow your

10.13 A–C "Three Seats at the Trot." Both riders are demonstrating the three positions to be ridden.

(A) The half-seat.

(B) The deep seat.

(C) The "up" of the rising trot.

stiffen in your excitement, change to rising trot. Repeat the progression again—half-seat, sitting, rising.

Have a good practice session using *Three Seats*, incorporating all these images so they become familiar. You will notice that your horse's trotting rhythm becomes the same in each seat and becomes very rhythmical with clear beats. His balance improves, and his back comes up. He steps more deeply under his body, softens at the poll, reaches onto the bit, and fills your hands. Notice how stable your lower legs and feet are beneath you, and how securely balanced you feel. You are *grounded*.

Keep the trot slow at first until you are comfortable with the motion in the sitting trot. You may find it useful to put one arm over your head to find your balance as you go through the changes from one seat to the other. Eventually, you will be able to do as many sitting strides comfortably. It is important, however, not to do more than seven strides in each seat as alternating between seats is of benefit to the exercise. Also, do no more sitting-trot strides than are comfortable to avoid stiffening and causing your horse's back to tighten and drop. The repetition itself is a wonderful exercise for stabilizing your balance with your feet under you in the same place for each seat. At all times, your lower leg should be in contact with the horse at the bottom of the saddle a little behind the girth. If you ride *Three Seats* correctly, your horse will maintain the same rhythm throughout as you will be consistently in balance, and he will be comfortable and content beneath you. The *Three Seats* exercise will continue to be useful to you as a warm-up in all phases of riding and in any discipline.

There are pitfalls in learning *Three Seats*. The most common one is in the transfer from half-seat to sitting. You are trotting along doing a nice half-seat with alternately flexing knees and ankles. You decide to sit so you stop letting the knees flex, lock them, and sit down. The locked knees take your lower leg forward ahead of the girth and you are no longer in balance or have a *following seat*. Instead, you have a bumping seat to which your horse objects by hollowing his back and raising his head. Also, if you change from half-seat to sitting trot by only bringing your shoulders up and back, and forgetting to bring your pelvis forward first, you will come down out of balance on the back of the saddle. No wonder many horses don't like the sitting trot any better than their riders do! Now, however, you know how to fix the problems and sitting trot can become fun.

Try some turns and changes of direction while practicing your *Three Seats*. Before each turn, remember to do a *ground-center-grow* rebalance. As you start your turn, try pointing or opening the inside knee a little in the direction you want to go. Think of *shooting the bullets* out of your kneecaps. If you want to go to the right, you shoot the inside bullet just a tiny bit further to the right than you would while traveling straight ahead. You will find that your horse follows the bullets around the bend. Many of the intricacies of using your body on the horse for a circle or turn, including the *grounding* of the outside leg and foot, are taken care of simply by pointing your knee to where you want to go. The rest of the body will follow with the correct motions and your horse will feel the changes and respond. Go ahead and have a good practice session using your *Three Seats*, and include circles and serpentines.

Correct Use of the Inside Leg at the Rising Trot

Long-time horsewoman and Centered Riding instructor, Susan Harris[1], talks of "the release of the

---

1 Susan Harris is an international clinician, instructor, author, and equine artist from upstate New York. She has trained horses and riders, judged, and competed in most riding disciplines, including dressage, eventing, hunters, jumpers, equitation, and Western pleasure and performance, for more than 30 years. She is a Centered Riding Senior Instructor, and author of *Horse Gaits, Balance and Movement; Grooming to Win;* and the *United States Pony Club Manuals*. She has also, with Peggy Brown, produced two videos: *Anatomy in Motion, The Visible Horse;* and *Anatomy in Motion, The Visible Rider*.

outside leg for following the motion more accurately at the posting trot," and explains it in the following discussion.

"Most riders are more aware of the two sides of their own and their horses' bodies while trotting in half-seat and sitting trot. Many riders are unaware of the alternate lifting motion when *rising* to the trot. They rise equally from both knees at once, resulting in a stiff, mechanical, 'jack-in-the-box' posting motion. This often leads to tight, pinching knees, and heels that slip up as the rider rises.

"The following is an exercise that helps the rider to feel the movement and free the two sides of her body (and her horse's body) in the posting trot. The exercise is simple: each time you rise, release your *outside* leg backward and downward a little as if *backward pedaling* (fig. 10.14). (Do nothing with the inside leg; just keep the knee soft and the foot *grounded*.) This motion is very small; you should not feel yourself rocking from side to side. You must release your kneecap in order to *pedal backward*. This makes the exercise valuable for riders who tend to pinch with their knees and tighten their thighs. It's important to post on the correct diagonal (rise when the horse's outside front and inside hind leg go forward) and release the outside leg back and down only at the moment when you rise.

"As you practice this exercise, you will probably notice that your horse moves with bigger, stronger strides, and you may feel his back round up under you (fig. 10.15). You may need to adjust your pedaling motion, using a tiny, soft motion for a light, sensitive horse, and pedaling strongly (like pedaling a bicycle uphill) for

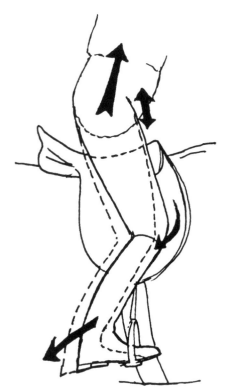

10.14 Each time you go up in the rising trot, release your outside leg downward and backward as shown as if "pedaling a bicycle backward." The small arrow in front indicates the hip joint being opened, and the other arrows show energy being sent up through the body, then down and back through the leg.

a sluggish horse. For comparison, stop pedaling, and rise equally from both legs at once, for a few strides. You will probably feel a difference in your horse's movement, and in your own flexibility and balance.

"What happens when you release your kneecap as you rise? First, this motion helps you follow the movement of the horse's back and barrel more accurately. Also, each time you *ground* your outside foot backward and downward, the motion creates a momentary stronger contact, like a rub, between the horse's barrel and the

10.15 *By releasing your outside leg and softening your inside knee at the rising trot you will increase the horse's roundness and engagement (raising his back).*

calf of your inside leg. This amounts to an automatic inside leg aid created by the motion of the horse's barrel. In other words, he puts the aid on himself. By releasing down and back as you rise (on the outside diagonal), this automatic inside leg aid occurs just as the inside hind leg pushes off the ground and swings forward. This asks for a longer stride with more engagement, which helps to raise the horse's back up. Another benefit is that you are repeatedly *grounding* your outside foot, which helps your balance (both lateral and front-to-back), and the horse's straightness. (There is more about straightness in the session on lateral work). Finally, *backward pedaling* emphasizes the rhythm, and helps you and your horse stay 'on the beat'.

"Why not give an inside leg aid as you rise? If you consciously squeeze or nudge with the inside leg as you rise, you will probably use your muscles too hard, too long, or slightly out of rhythm, and you may find it hard to keep your balance. The automatic inside leg aid created by *releasing the kneecap* is almost effortless. Like the *Unbendable Arm* effect, it allows your body to choose only those muscles it needs to apply the aid, resulting in a softer, more subtle aid that 'breathes' with the horse, and is accepted more easily even by touchy horses."

All of the images you have been using in your work at the trot, including *the backward-pedaling* circles (first learned in the *following seat* and progressively developing more vigor), *releasing your kneecap,* and *shooting the bullets,* can be used together and effectively in any gait. These images help to keep your seat open and fluid, offering no resistance to the horse, and enabling him to clearly feel very subtle aids. This clarity encourages him to obey, to use himself efficiently and with grace. When you also use your *Unbendable Arm* power, and *ground-center-grow* rebalancing with *in-out breaths*, you assume control without inefficient use of muscle. You will find that your horse's rhythm stays the same in each seat, and becomes very even and positive—his balance improves, his back comes up, he steps more deeply under his body, he softens at the poll, and he reaches into the bit and fills your hands. You really become a team. ⤳

WHAT ARE THE ESSENTIALS OF
Gain Extra Stability from Riding in Three Seats at the Trot?

ON THE GROUND

- Mentally going down the inside of your legs (versus the outside) gives you a feeling of width through the hips.
- *Monkey-Reverse Monkey* and the *Horse Stance* show the flexibility and balance needed when going from one seat to another—half-seat to sitting to rising.
- The sitting trot requires you to follow the two sides of the horse's body by *pedaling backward*.

ON THE HORSE

- Drop your knees so your lower legs embrace your horse. *Shoot bullets* from your kneecaps.
- Ride in *Three Seats at the Trot,* remembering to alternate between seats.
- Sitting trot from following the two sides of the horse's body while going from half-seat to sitting.
- Learn the correct timing for using the inside leg at the rising trot by stepping down and back on the outside leg on the "up" of the trot, and freeing the inside knee.

WHAT ARE THE RESULTS ?

- An open fluid seat, with added balance and stability.
- The horse's rhythm improves, his back comes up, and he steps more under his body.
- The horse develops a very steady rhythm with balanced, forward motion.

11

Discover Shared Energy

One of the great joys of riding is being able to share effortless motion with your horse. This session will give you some tools to achieve this goal. In the process you will do some mundane activities such as deep-knee bends and getting out of a chair, and discover how much easier they are to do when you use energy appropriately.

Which comes first—energy or balance? Energy requires balance. Balance produces the opportunity for energy. Balance, therefore, needs to come before energy. You have been learning a lot about balance, but what, exactly is energy? One definition in *Webster's Dictionary* says that energy is "internal or inherent power." Another says it is "power efficiently exerted."

Clearly, your ideal ride on your horse requires these sorts of energy. We all know that when we gallop across country on a horse, we are using energy. Energy can also be used in a more subtle, though equally effective way. Energy can come from within us, from our very core, from our center. From here, it flows outward in all directions. When you allow your body to lengthen, energy flows through your free neck and out your head. It flows out through your hands and knees and keeps your feet wonderfully grounded. Your energy can be directed as it is in the *Unbendable Arm* exercise, and it can rebound and be reused.

Energy produces impulsion in the horse. Impulsion is not "increased speed," it is "contained" energy. In fact, speed can be the enemy of impulsion as it is the enemy of balance. Balance is not helped by speed, because speed alone will put your horse on his forehand. However, speed's downside can be helped by balance, because a balanced horse is more able to bring his hind legs further forward under himself for a long, driving stride. If a horse moving at speed tends to lose his balance, his contained energy, or impulsion, which is dependent upon balance, can be compromised (fig. 11.1).

Impulsion can come from fear, and the resulting increase in adrenaline. This causes the horse to have an undesirable reaction, such as "fight, flight, or freeze." Conversely, good impulsion can come from balance as you discovered when you practiced frequent transitions, and from energy using *ground-center-grow* rebalances. Instead of tension, this sort of impulsion is full of buoyancy—lightness that enhances all your horse's movement. So, good impulsion comes from a combination of balance and energy, but remember, energy in turn is dependent on balance. If you or your horse is out of balance, your energy will be used up in recovering your balance. If you have balance, any energy you produce can be used to improve the movements of your own or your horse's body. Once you have gained balance with energy, you will have tremendous opportunities for improving your horse's movement.

You will also need *clear intent* if you are to put these opportunities into practice. It is through *clear intent* and *centering* that you channel your energy. For instance, your intent to release your head and allow your body to lengthen and widen, will produce the energy to do it. Your intent to do *ground-center-grow* rebalances with your horse will increase your horse's impulsion and buoyancy. Without *clear intent* and without balance, the effectiveness of your energy will be inhibited.

11.1 A & B A horse in rising trot showing energy and balance (A), and another with no impulsion (B).

ON THE GROUND

The Deep Knee Bend

How do we put all these conceptual ideas into practice? A good way to start is to study the *Deep Knee Bend* exercise as it relates to the rising trot.

First, let's examine how your body moves as you ride the trot. For the moment, I will discuss your dynamics while riding upright in a deep seat rather than a half-seat. On the ground, first do a *Shaggy Dog Shake*. Stand quietly for a few minutes and become actively aware of your feet—*Feet in the Sand,* and their center of balance at the *Bubbling Springs*. Keep your center deep and vital, and establish your inner balance.

Now contemplate what is involved in doing a *Deep Knee Bend*. Your center must stay balanced over your feet while your joints—ankles, knees, and hips—must adjust by flexing and moving. At this point, it becomes essential for you to understand the exact location of the knee joint. When your leg is straight, the bones of the lower leg—the tibia and fibula—articulate at the end of the femur. When your leg is bent, however, the kneecap covers the end of the femur. As a result, the point of articulation with the lower leg bones is beneath the end of

<u>11.2</u> *The location of the knee joint: note that the hinge for movement of the lower leg is between Jineen's fingers where she is pointing—beneath the end of the femur.*

knees to move forward and down as you bend them. Allow your knee below your kneecap (the top of your boot) to look at the ground.

With your center over your feet, bend your hip joints and your "low" knee joints equally. Let your knees go forward and slightly out, and your head forward and up. Descend slowly into a *Deep Knee Bend* keeping that balance and *letting energy go out of your knees and head.* (I'll explain how to do this in a minute in an exercise that involves getting in and out of a chair—the *Chair Exercise.*) Note that as you go down, your hips, knees, and ankles need to bend increasingly more acutely. Allow this to happen. Your heels may come off the floor. As you begin to come up, again with energy going out of your knees and head, keep the front of your body open and your head moving forward and up. Un-bend your knees and hips equally so your center always stays over your *Bubbling Springs.* Re-member to keep *breathing.*

Repeat the *Deep Knee Bend* slowly several times so you can sense how the different joints react as your body goes up and down. As you drop down, the knees move further forward, the hip joints go down and back, and the ankles bend acutely. As you come up, the knee joints come back again, and the hip joints move forward un-derneath you. As you go down *and* as you come up, keep allowing your head to go up and forward. You will notice that, as a result, you will feel ef-fortless, light, and balanced.

This *Deep Knee Bend* exercise is an exagger-ated version of the motion of the hip joints, knees, and ankles in the rising trot. It is important that your feet on the stirrups stay directly under your center. Also, as you come back down in the saddle, your knees must move forward in order for your hips to drop down in the correct alignment. It is a common tendency to lock the knees, keeping them from bending forward enough, and therefore forcing the hips too far back as they drop down to the saddle.

the femur. Sit on the edge of your chair with your knee flexed as if you are on your horse. Put your fingers on either side of your knee and swing your lower leg to find the point of articulation (fig. 11.2). You will probably discover that this point is lower than you had realized. This knowledge will give you a different sensation when you bend your knees, and you should find it easier to allow your

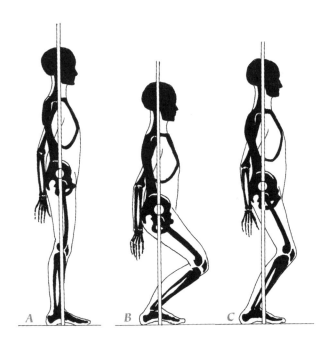

11.3 A–C The "Deep Knee Bend." These drawings clearly show the dynamics of the rising trot.

(A) Body in upright position with hips and center over the feet. (B) Hip, knee, and ankle joints closed for a Deep Knee Bend with hips and center still over the feet. (C) The same joints opened for the rise to standing, with the hips and center again over the feet.

over your toes as the torso comes down, and back as it goes up. This motion requires soft hips, knees, and ankles (figs. 11.3 A–C).

Chair Exercise

This exercise will help you appreciate how helpful a balanced position plus good use of energy can be. Sit in a chair with a hard, flat seat for the *Chair Exercise.* Sit near the front edge and put your feet directly below your knees. To get out of a chair from this position, you either must heave your body out over your feet or lean very far forward so that your center can be over your feet. Both methods are awkward, yet this is much like the old-fashioned "chair" seat on a horse—unfortunately, still seen today. Stand up and sit down a few times and notice how hard you come down on the chair (figs. 11.4 A & B). Those poor horses!

Now find how far back you must bring your feet to have them under your center. Try standing up and then sitting again from this balanced position. Breathe out as you move, or use the *in-out breath* when appropriate. You can easily transfer weight back and forth between your seat and your feet. When you put yourself in this balance on your horse, this ease of motion will be enhanced because he will produce some of the upward lift (figs. 11.5 A & B).

An easy way to reinforce the feeling of your feet under your body is to take a half-seat on your feet as if on your horse, and jump up and down in place several times. Let yourself really feel the slap of the soles of your feet each time you hit the ground. That is where your feet should be and feel when on your horse—below your center, making you safe, solid, and secure.

Try the exercise of getting out of a chair again. Notice that if you are sitting like a lump, even if you are balanced with your feet under you, getting up will take a real effort. On the other hand, when you release energy from your center forward and out through your head and knees, you will float up effortlessly.

To check your own position, stand sideways to a long mirror in the *Horse Stance* (your feet a horse's width apart, torso upright, knees and hips bent as if your feet were in stirrups, and toes and knees headed slightly outward). On the horse, this would be an upright, deep seat. Go up and down as if in a rising trot. Notice that your center and torso are moving straight up and down as if in a tube, with your head sliding up out of the tube. Notice again that your knees move forward out

11.4 A & B
If Jineen sits like this with her feet ahead of her under her knees, she can only get up by using a great deal of effort.

11.5 A & B
If she sits with her feet under her center, she can rise with ease.

11.6 Lucy is well-balanced with her center over her feet. At first, she may have felt that the front of her body was too far forward but she quickly got used to this new position.

Similarly, when you are riding, your horse will more easily spring into balance beneath you if you release energy through *ground-center-grow* rebalances, than if you simply apply the aids of push and receive.

ON THE HORSE

Shared Energy between Horse and Rider

When you are working with a living being, you run the risk of giving all your energy to your horse and ending up exhausted. You have learned through your practice of *Comparable Parts* that you can help your horse improve his mobility by releasing tight areas in your own body. One of my students, having just learned about *Comparable Parts*, had a wonderful session on her 18-year-old Connemara. However, she was exhausted after it, and found herself sleeping for the next 24 hours, while her old horse went out on the trail and bucked! She had (incorrectly) given *all* her energy to her horse in her releases and forgotten about herself.

When working with energy, you must receive as much as you give. I like the picture of two donkeys walking side-by-side up a narrow trail. Each one is bumping along in a self-sufficient manner, except that they lean a little against each other because of the narrowness of the trail. As a result, each donkey is simultaneously giving help to, and receiving help from the other. Using balance and energy correctly, you can have this sort of symbiotic relationship with your horse. You can finish each session feeling stimulated and satisfied rather than tired.

11.7 This rider is out of balance—her feet ahead of her center, not underneath—and the result is her coming down "splat," causing both her and her horse to be unhappy.

In this session on your horse you can further help the softening of your seat and joints by receiving the upward thrust of your horse's body. Settle yourself on your horse, put your feet in the stirrups, and proceed at the walk, remembering to use your soft, *following seat.*

Before you begin the rising trot, try an experiment. First, lock your knees tight against the saddle. Then for comparison, allow your knees to move freely forward and out as your horse walks. Think about what you did when you were floating up and down off that chair in the *Chair Exercise*. You didn't lock your knees then. Are you in a position on your horse where you could float off his back at a rising trot? As you learned from the *Chair Exercise*, this will require that your feet be far enough back and your seat far enough forward to have your feet under your center. When you first

try this position on your horse, you may feel that your feet are ridiculously far back, and the front of your upright body exaggeratedly far forward. Bear with these feelings until this alignment begins to feel more normal. It may be helpful to remember the imaginary *bungee cord*, which stretches your head forward and upward (fig. 11.6).

To test your balance, be sure that you can rise out of the saddle and come back down very softly— at the halt and the walk. If at any point you become unstable and have to come down "thump" or "splat" on the saddle, you are out of balance and it will be an effort to rise up again (fig. 11.7). Remember the way you did the *Chair Exercise*: balance yourself in the correct position, and then, using your *clear intent*, send energy from your center out through your head and knees. When you are in balance, you can come down deeply or

11.8 Lucy has that "balanced, floating feeling," though this pretty picture is slightly spoiled by her left shoulder being tight and her left hand dropped.

just lightly touch the saddle with your seat and, without effort, rise immediately up again.

Now pick up a rising trot and find that balanced, floating feeling (fig. 11.8). Keep your body aligned as it was at the walk, with your feet under your center. You will soon notice that you don't feel ridiculous anymore and that you are doing much less work. You are now balanced and stable enough to allow the horse to do much of the work for you.

In rising trot, you may find yourself stiffening in an effort to avoid causing the discomfort that would occur (to both you and your horse) if you were to bang down on the horse's back. As a result, you may not really let yourself sit deep into the saddle on the downbeat. This stiffening will in turn affect the up beat. Johann Reigler of the Spanish Riding School explains that in the rising trot, "you go down so you can go up, and you go up so you

can go down." The quality of the downbeat becomes crucial to the quality of the trot.

With this in mind, begin experimenting with softening your hip joints each time you come down, so you can feel as if you are coming down into soft cotton wool. Remember that your knees will need to go softly forward and out at the same time. Take care that your hip joints and seat bones descend vertically so you settle into the deepest part of the saddle, not back toward the cantle. This will allow you to come down solidly on the horse's back but so softly that it cannot bother him. The softness of your seat enveloping his back allows him to push a little more strongly off the ground with his hind leg to bounce you up again. In doing this, he will also send his own back up every stride. Continue letting yourself down with soft hip joints and knees onto the cotton wool and letting your horse send you up again.

If you have trouble letting your knees go forward as your hip joints drop straight down, stop for a moment. Have someone put two or three fingers on the front of your hip joint, and the fingers of her other hand on the back of your knee right in the angle of the bend. Your helper must think of her hand as gently guiding the hip downward while the hand at the knee helps send the knee forward. Rise up out of the saddle and try following the direction of her hands as you come down. When you become more at ease with this motion, you can practice the "up" beat. Have your helper move her hands so that she sends you up by pressing the front of your knee back and pushes your pelvis up with the other hand under the edge of your buttock. Next, she can alternate the hand positions so that she helps you with your alignment on both beats, one after another (figs. 11.9 A–D).

Try this at the walk and then at the trot. Your helper will find it quite easy to maintain the rhythm on the down and up beat if he runs in step with the horse's hind feet. Soon you will find that you can maintain your balance without your helper's clear directions.

The Effortless Trot

Another useful way to help maintain your balance is to imagine the front of your body as a plate glass window. This window goes straight up and down the front of your body from your hip joints all the way up your torso. Some people find this too rigid, but this concept is interesting because while your body receives the support and stability of the window, you are allowed great freedom because you can see through the glass and be totally conscious of everything around you.

You should now find yourself rising in balance on your own. Notice that you have essentially the same weight on your stirrups when you go up as when you come down. You are not pushing down on the stirrups to get yourself out of the saddle. Instead, you are letting the horse thrust you up. He happily does this now because his back is comfortable beneath you. Your legs hang quietly relaxed around his sides; instead of being tight and braced, they are available when you need them to apply aids.

When you find this quality of trot, the "effortless trot," you will feel your horse moving forward with more balance and buoyancy and with rounder steps. His back will fill your seat. If you lose your balance and stiffen your hips and knees he will drop immediately into an ordinary trot. You can turn his beautiful trot off and on by losing the soft, *plumb line* balance by only a few degrees, or regaining it again. As a very experienced and able horseman told me in Germany when he learned the effortless trot, "Why I could trot like that all day and not be tired!"

Through your balance, you have been able to increase your horse's impulsion and buoyancy, which also increased his energy. How do you control all this energy? You can channel it by riding figures, which cause your horse to keep himself in balance. If, for instance, your horse takes some of this new energy and begins to lose his balance and charge down the straight side of the arena, you can ride him in a circle. The circle will make him balance himself to keep from falling over and you will have used energy and balance to gain control without resorting to wrestling him into obedience.

When you can use your *clear intent* to direct the energy in your body and therefore your horse's body, you will find yourself riding more effectively and easily. Your energy becomes a *shared* energy. Once again, you are using transitions and circles to develop your horse's body and mind, his balance and energy. No matter how sophisticated you become in your work with your horse, the simple principles of the *Four Basics, grounding,* and *clear intent* with transitions and circles remain your constant for successful riding. ⚮

11.9 A–D An exercise to help you be aware of the direction of the movement of your hip and knee joints during the rising trot.

(A) The helper is indicating the start of the "down" motion. Her left fingers direct the hip downward, while her other hand directs the knee forward.
(B) She is showing the completion of the "down."
(C) The helper is indicating the start of the "up" motion. Her left hand presses the knee back, and her right hand sends the seat upward.
(D) This shows the completion of the "up."

WHAT ARE THE ESSENTIALS OF Discover Shared Energy?

ON THE GROUND

- ► Balance, energy, and impulsion interact.
- ► Practice *Deep Knee Bends* to feel effortless, light, and balanced.
- ► The *Chair Exercise* teaches you about your balance and good use of energy.

ON THE HORSE

- ► Use the *Chair Exercise* techniques for improved balance.
- ► Come down softly on your horse's back.
- ► When working with energy, receive as much as you give.
- ► Allow the horse's thrust to give you "the effortless trot."

WHAT ARE THE RESULTS?

- ► Effortless, brilliant movement as horse and rider share their energy.

12

Feel the Alternating Sides of the Horse's Body

In the last session, you learned about using energy so that whatever you do on your horse can be done with less effort. Now, I am going to explain how you can learn about feeling, receiving, and using the upward thrust of your horse's body. Use of a trampoline helps with the groundwork in this session. But if you don't have access to a trampoline you can still benefit from the ground exercises by visualizing as you do them how they would feel on a trampoline.

With your improved sense of balance and buoyancy, you can do some exercises that will help you understand the alternating motion of the two sides of your horse as well as your own body. The trampoline simulates the motion of the horse so you can learn to receive the upward lift and thrust of your horse's body without being on his back.

ON THE GROUND

Learn to Receive the Upward Bounce of the Trampoline

When you do exercises on the ground, you hit the ground with a jar, no matter how softly you come down. When you are on your horse, you don't feel the impact of the horse meeting the ground as much because your horse has some spring in his body. Working on a trampoline is somewhere in between. It gives you a slightly more realistic feeling of the horse's body, and it provides an interesting and fun way to learn the flexion of your joints necessary for balance and buoyancy. Also, a trampoline gives you a chance to experiment with, and improve the motions of your body, without the complication of the living, moving horse beneath you, or without causing discomfort to your horse as you learn. Because the motion you feel on the trampoline is quite similar to the motion on a horse, it will be easy to transfer what you learn in this exercise to your riding.

12.1 A & B Cynthia is "finding" her hip joints with her hands. It would be more precise if she had pointed to them with her fingertips the same way that Beth does in figure 5.9 (A). Cynthia is locating her greater trochanters (B).

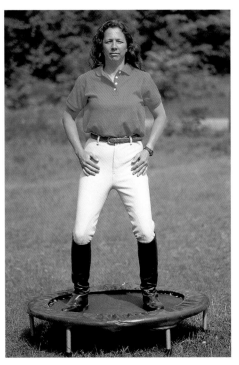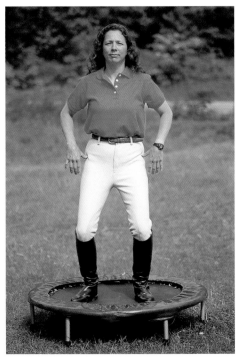

Stand quietly on your trampoline. Find your hip joints, remembering they are deep up inside your pelvis. Touch the front of them with your fingertips. Without taking your whole foot off the trampoline, flex one hip joint, knee, and ankle softly so that just your heel comes a little off the trampoline. Flex the other side, and then alternate from one side to the other. Now touch the sides of your hips at the greater trochanter and visualize the ball at the head of the femur sliding in the slippery socket of the hip joint, the actual hinge for movement of the thigh (figs. 12.1 A & B).

When your knees flex, they should point a little outward rather than straight ahead. Your lower back must be free enough to allow the pelvis to move a bit as the knees bend. Think of your trampoline as your horse's back. As you alternately flex each leg, one side of his back comes up a little, and then goes down. If you have no trampoline, simply imagine the trampoline's motion.

Keep transferring your weight from one foot to the other with these small joint flexions. Note as you work that all the joints of your leg–hip, knee, and ankle–become increasingly soft and mobile. You will also notice how much of the lift comes from the trampoline if you keep receiving its upward push and allow it to travel up through your body and out your head. As you continue to receive this motion, you will find your body and the top of your head moving softly up and down. Take a few moments to discover when the rhythm of your bounces is such that the thrust *up* feels equal to the drop *down*. With the wrong rhythm, the downbeat will feel heavier. It is common to work in too rapid a tempo at first. As you slow the rhythm, the up thrust of the trampoline will begin to feel stronger until the up and down become equal. This equalizing of the beats through finding the correct rhythm will also be true on your horse. Keeping your joints soft, especially the hips, and allowing yourself to receive the upward thrust are the keys to finding this rhythm.

To emphasize this point, try stiffening your hips as you continue to step downward with

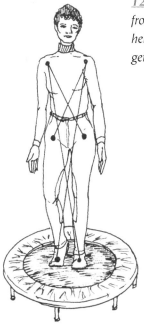

12.2 Imagining diagonal lines from point to point as you move helps free and even up your body, getting rid of tight spots.

your alternating feet. Two things become immediately apparent. First, it feels awkward and uncomfortable. You can't help but think, "Oh, the poor horse!" Second, you will notice that there is little or no up-and-down motion of your body. You are not able to receive the upward beat and the top of your head stays in the same place.

Return once more to correctly receiving the alternating lifts from the trampoline. Keep thinking of the rhythmical "up" with each bounce—through the center of your body, your neck, and head. Remember to find your *grounding* and receive the bounce into your feet through your *Bubbling Springs*. This is a good time to once again explore your body for tight spots and unevenness between your two sides. Breathe into those trouble spots and perhaps touch them with your hand. Allow them to empty and become full of space. Get your whole body involved. Imagine lines extending from your foot and hip on one side diagonally across to and out the shoulder on the opposite side. Bounce these diagonal lines back and forth. Be a little wild and have fun! (fig. 12.2).

To clarify the feeling of receiving the upward thrust, it can be helpful to work on the trampoline in the half-seat position. Try taking a stance on the trampoline as if you were riding in your half-seat. Start your stepping bounce and search for the right rhythm. As the strength of the "up" beat becomes more evident, bounce your way up from half-seat to an upright position. Use your hands alternately as if you were juggling balls. The same principles apply as when you are more upright. As long as you keep balanced, and centered over your feet, you can ride any seat successfully.

Improve Your Turning Techniques

The trampoline is useful for learning other techniques as well. One is the use of the hip joint, thigh, and knee in a turn. Up until now, you have only lifted your heels off the trampoline, leaving the toes touching lightly. Now you will need to lift your feet one at a time in a small walking-in-place motion. *Center* yourself and feel your *hip joints gently pedaling backward*. To turn right, rotate your right greater trochanter back so the ball at the end of your femur turns in its socket, and the whole thigh and knee rotate a little out as if opening a door. This motion invites your body to turn right, one step at a time. You might need two steps for a quarter turn, more for a complete 360-degree turn. With your opening, pointing knee it will become a light, balanced, stepping turn.

12.3 Work on the trampoline: learning to turn with your whole body involved, aids you enormously when turning your horse. It helps to put an arm over your head on the side you are turning toward.

Try turning one way and then the other way. One direction will probably be easier. Put one arm over your head when you turn in the more difficult direction (fig. 12.3). Do the exercise at a walk and then at a jog.

Add another component of the turn and include the shoulders and torso. First, stand still on the trampoline. Center yourself and take one hand and arm back, palm up and thumb leading, in the graceful sweep of a ballet dancer. Let your eyes follow the direction of your hand. Use an unhurried sweeping motion and practice it in both directions. Remember to breathe out as you move. This is a lovely exercise to open up the shoulders and the front of the body for any turn or lateral work. Now you can integrate the ballet arm and the opening hip and knee, one step at a time, in your trampoline turns.

Improve Your Halts

Next let's explore the full halt. You could just reduce your bounces and fade out the activity on the trampoline. This is a little vague and lacking in energy. Alternatively, you could stop both feet at once. This will certainly halt you abruptly, but notice that the trampoline continues to vibrate and you are not really still for several small bounces. On the other hand, you can smoothly and precisely stop all activity by softly *grounding* one foot and then the other to produce total stillness.

If you *ground* too hard or change the rhythm of your feet as you prepare to halt, you will not get the desired result. Establish a comfortable one-two, one-two rhythm and then, maintaining this rhythm, ground your center and one foot, then your center and the second foot. Breathe out softly. When the trampoline is still as you put the second foot down, you will know you have it right.

How does this activity on the trampoline translate to performing a halt on your horse? On the trampoline, your feet represent a *combination* of the horse's hind feet and your own seat bones in the saddle. The abrupt halt, which left the trampoline vibrating, is similar to pulling your horse to a halt with just your reins. Though he will probably stop, he will be leaning onto his forehand. Also, if you simply drop both your seat bones at

once, he may stop, but he won't be square. The reaction of his body is similar to the vibrating trampoline. Instead, you need to stop the hind end of the horse, his engine, one seat bone at a time, to achieve a balanced, motionless halt. Practice on the trampoline and then you can try it on your horse.

Besides increasing your awareness of the motion of alternate sides, this work on the trampoline will help you notice various other sensations. Your chest will feel lighter and freer. Let your shoulder blades slide around on your ribs. Feel as if you have dancing ribs and shoulders with your shoulder blades bouncing and sliding over your ribs. Don't *make* them dance, but rather let the motion of the trampoline cause this sensation. Feel the soft bobble of your head and the slight drop of your face with each bounce. Your whole body feels centered, light, elastic, and filled with energy.

ON THE HORSE

Now you can try putting into practice your new understanding of the alternating motion of the two sides of your horse's body. It is useful to do some of this work in the half-seat, so you must first reestablish your balance in this position, and take it one step further.

Further Details for Perfecting the Half-Seat

The half-seat is absolutely vital to the learning experience, and I take students back to it again and again. All my riders must know how to ride the half-seat regardless of the riding discipline they prefer. I have high-level dressage riders, saddle-seat riders, Western riders, and many others all learning the half-seat, and they all ride better as a result.

I remember my immense satisfaction when I was teaching several FEI dressage riders who tended to carry their feet too far forward. I short-

12.4 A good leg position: note the triangle-like shape of the lower leg formed by the vertical stirrup leather and the foot. Cynthia's heavy knee hangs in front of the stirrup leather balanced by the heel three to four inches behind the girth. The result is that the leg will hang snugly around the horse with the most contact just at the bottom of the saddle flap.

ened their stirrups and taught all of them the half-seat. They protested at first and then they loved it. When I came back the next day I found them in the arena warming up in the half-seat. Subsequently in their dressage work, using slightly shorter stirrups than they had originally, their balance improved and their lower legs became more effective.

Before you begin to use the half-seat exercises, do your warm up on your horse, being sure to use your *following seat.* Now halt your horse and think about the stability of your position. When you are riding in an upright, deep seat, your seat provides stability. When you shift into your half-seat, however, your seat is no longer in the saddle. Your new point of stability becomes your lower leg and foot.

As you sit with a deep seat, notice that your re-

leased, dropped knee is in front of your stirrup leather, your soft ankle is behind your stirrup leather, and your lower leg crosses the stirrup leather at an angle. Therefore, there is a sort of triangle formed by the completely vertical stirrup leather (perpendicular to the ground), the approximately horizontal bottom of your foot on the stirrup, and your lower leg (fig. 12.4).

When you let the leg hang with gravity without tensing your knee against the saddle, you will find that the inside of your lower leg will be snug against the horse, at the bottom of the saddle flap three-to-four inches behind the girth. It will be so snug that someone on the ground would have difficulty putting her fingers between your leg and the horse at that point. If, however, you pinch with your knee against the saddle, your lower leg will

12.5 Cynthia's tight knee takes the lower leg away from the horse's side and I can easily slip my hand under it.

be pushed away from the horse's side, as shown in the photograph (fig. 12.5).

Allowing your knees to be free and relaxed does not mean letting them flap outward. They should lie, headed essentially forward, lightly on the saddle, but not pressed muscularly against it. So now, with a helper holding your horse, take a

half-seat—well-grounded, with your seat just off the saddle, your weight in your stirrups, your lower leg against the horse's side—and see if, with both hands at once, you can reach your horse's ears (fig. 12.6 A). With your knees soft, this should be no trouble even though you are well beyond your point of balance. You feel stable. Now try it another way. This time, squeeze your knees tight against the saddle and see what happens when you try to reach those ears. You feel very wobbly (fig. 12.6 B). This precarious feeling should be sufficient proof that security does not lie in pinching with the knees, but rather in letting gravity and body weight drop your legs down against and around the sides of the horse.

Feeling the Balance between the Knee and Heel

To discover how truly grounded the correct, relaxed leg position can make you feel, you can try a little exercise with your helper. Before you start, notice that the weight of your knee balances the weight of your ankle and heel much as the weight of your shoulders balances the weight of your pelvis in the half-seat. Allow yourself the feeling that your lower leg is horizontal—your knee as low as your heel. Now have your helper, using the palms of her hands, alternately bump your leg gently upward first under the knee, then under the heel, back and forth. Note that the bumping spot under the bent knee is further back than the point of the knee (figs. 12.7 A & B). It is the weight-bearing point when you kneel on the ground. These repeated alternating bumps let you clearly feel the "depth" of your released knee. A few extra taps on the kneecap directed through your femur to the socket of your hip joint will give you the added feeling of exactly from where your heavy knee and leg hang. This is a wonderful exercise for increasing the balance and depth of your seat. You can take the feeling of this exercise into all your work. You are really *grounded*.

12.6 A & B

(A) *When her lower leg is stable, Cynthia has no difficulty reaching the horse's ears, even though she is well beyond her point of balance.* (B) *Cynthia has pinched her knee, her lower leg has come off the horse's side, and she is quite insecure.*

<u>12.7 A & B</u> *My left hand is bumping under Cynthia's knee, and my right is free* **(A)**. *Here, I'm bumping Cynthia's heel with my right hand, leaving my left hand free* **(B)**. *This exercise done back and forth increases the balance and depth of your seat.*

Now in your half-seat with your knees elastic, bounce a little. *Grounded* and with your point of stability established in your lower-leg triangle, you will feel solid. Notice that your essential body balance settles in a neat straight line from your center through your ankles and stirrups to the ground with your pelvis balanced behind it and your shoulders ahead of it (fig. 12.8).

Feeling the Two Sides of Your Horse
Go back to your deep seat and pick up a walk. As you walk, be conscious of the motion of your *following seat.* Remember how independently each of your thighs, hip joints, and knees, are moved by the two sides of the horse. Now shift into your half-seat again. You need to be only an inch or so out of the saddle with your center over your feet. Imagine dropping your center down between your feet to the ground. Feel the soles of your feet level and positively grounded. Begin to notice how clearly you can feel the two sides of the horse separately affecting the flexion of your feet and knees. One knee flexes slightly, and then the other does so as the horse's back alternately lifts and drops

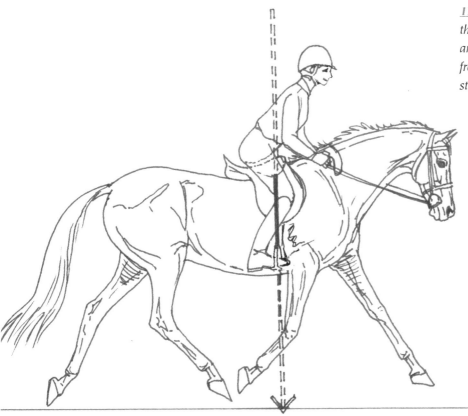

12.8 A side view of a rider in the half-seat. The vertical arrow shows the line of gravity from the center through the stirrup to the ground.

your stirrups under your feet. This is the same sensation you felt on the trampoline.

If you are not feeling this alternating push causing your knees to flex, but rather finding your pelvis pushed from side to side by your feet, then your knees are probably stiff. To get a clear understanding of this effect, halt your horse again, maintaining the half-seat. Put your hands on the horse's withers and push down so that a lot of your weight is on your hands. Now have a friend put her two hands under the stirrup and lift your foot a little up and down—or better yet have two friends, one under each foot, lifting alternately (figs. 12.9 A & B). Allow your hip and knee to flex as your foot is lifted. You will immediately notice that if you lock your knee or pinch it against the saddle, there is no flexion. The knee must be soft, closing and opening as your friend lifts and drops your foot. Now purposely stiffen your knee. Don't let it flex when your

friend lifts up your foot. You will feel that your pelvis is being pushed off the other side of the horse. Imagine what would happen to your balance on the trampoline if you kept your knees and hips stiff as you stepped from one foot to the other. You would find yourself swaying awkwardly from side to side just as you are on your horse.

Try walking your horse again in the half-seat with your weight still carried by your hands on the horse's withers. Let the motion of the horse close and open your knees as your friend did when you were standing still. Taking some of your weight on your hands makes it easier to feel the horse lift your feet alternately.

Alternating Lifts from the Horse's Sides

Now resume your half-seat with your weight once again in your feet and you will find that you can

_12.9 A & B_ _The rider is allowing her hips and knees to flex as the helpers lift her legs alternately (_**A**_). The helper on the right (in yellow) is using her body well to do this lifting, while the other girl is only using her arms (_**B**_)._

let the horse lift and drop one foot and then the other, as you absorb the motion in supple knees and hips while your pelvis stays level and squarely over your horse's spine. Now you can clearly feel the two sides of your horse, and yet you are able to stay balanced in the middle.

Take a break and walk for a bit in a deep seat. When you are ready, shift into a half-seat and pick up a trot. It is easier to feel the alternating upward thrust against your feet and knees at the trot than at the walk. You will also notice how similar this thrust is to the upward bounce of the trampoline.

Do a few circles and turns and try to keep the upward pulsations equal under each foot through the turns at the trot. Remember that your knees must alternately flex in order to follow the two sides of the horse. Finish this exercise by alternating between a few strides of half-seat and a few strides of rising trot. Ride about five strides of each, but don't get caught up in counting strides. Changing frequently from half-seat to rising trot and back again will allow you to find your security and rhythm without giving you time to get stiff or out of balance in either position. This work in the half-seat has probably made it easier for you to keep your feet beneath you in rising trot. Remember that riding in the half-seat is an effective way to find your *plumb line* balance when you feel uneven or insecure in the saddle.

Not only are you enjoying your improved stability and balance in your half-seat, but your horse is enjoying it as well as you make it easier for him to use his body. What about rebalancing your horse in your half-seat? In a deep seat, you were balancing your horse with *ground-center-grow* rebalances, *rolling the ball backward* in your pelvis, using your *in-out breaths*, and *lengthening your body* by tweaking the *bungee cord* at the top of your head. Your seat, however, was connected to your horse's back. Your lengthening went up through your head and down through your seat bones.

Rebalance in a Half-Seat Position

How do you do a rebalance in a half-seat—with your seat a little off your horse?

To answer this question, take your half-seat when your horse is at the halt. Though your center is still over your feet, your torso is slanted slightly forward. When you do the *ground-center-grow* rebalance in a half-seat, the *grounding* part is done as always—down through your feet to the ground. Your knees and heels drop down in a soft bounce, causing your calf to close around your horse. As you center yourself, the *ball* in your center rolls back making your tail drop a little as you send energy diagonally back and out through your sacrum, and forward and out through your head. As a result, the "grow" part of the rebalance is on a diagonal (fig. 12.10). Treat your body as if it were an *elastic band* or a *bungee cord*. Pull both ends of the cord for just a second then let it go. This momentary tweak causes your body to lengthen then come back to normal. A quick *in-out breath* during the tweak will help.

Balancing in your half-seat off the horse's back, now try several of these rebalances at the walk. Did you feel a quick little bump of weight in your stirrups on the *out* breath? This bump is a clear signal to your horse, and he will rebalance and engage his haunches.

Try these lengthening-body rebalances as you work your horse in the half-seat. Feel his balance and rhythm improve. If you are correctly allowing the lifts from the alternate sides of your horse, his rhythm should not change as you move from one seat to the other. If you find that it does change, explore your body to find what part you have locked or tightened—your jaw, your breathing, or your back, hips, knees, or toes? Regain your fluidness and balance, and your horse should have a steady rhythm.

12.10 A rebalance in the half-seat position is achieved by a momentary lengthen-and-release through the body. Think of a bungee cord on a diagonal going up and out of the top of your head, and down through your sacrum.

To expand this exercise, try working over cavaletti rails. You will need rails set on the ground, fixed so they cannot roll. At first use only one rail, then add rails until you are comfortably stepping through three. Rails set for walking should be 3 to 3 feet 6 inches apart, and spread to 4 to 5 feet apart for trotting, depending on the length of your horse's stride. First, walk over the rails enough times so that both you and your horse are navigating them smoothly, and try them at a trot. Then trot, rising at first to establish your rhythm, and then finally ride them in your two seats—half-seat and rising. Both you and your horse should continue to feel balanced and rhythmical through the rails.

WHAT ARE THE ESSENTIALS OF Feel the Alternating Sides of the Horse's Body?

ON THE GROUND

▶ The trampoline simulates the feeling of the motion of the horse's body.

▶ Learn how much joint flexion you need for balance and buoyancy so you can receive upward thrusts from alternate sides of your horse.

▶ Improve turning technique by opening your hip joints.

▶ Come to a halt by using one leg, and then the other.

ON THE HORSE

▶ Obtain stability in the half-seat from leaning forward to touch the horse's ears with your knees dropped, and your lower legs down and against the horse's sides.

▶ In the half-seat, find the two sides of your horse's body, and feel the alternate thrusts.

▶ Learn rebalancing in the half-seat—*ground-center-grow* on a diagonal.

WHAT ARE THE RESULTS?

▶ Your horse's balance and rhythm will stay the same as you change from one seat to another at the trot—half-seat to sitting to rising.

13

Improve Communication through the Quality of Your Aids

With each session, you have been increasing your awareness and strengthening the connection between you and your horse. In this session, you will work on further improving the quality of your aids by becoming more sensitive in the sending and receiving of signals. When a good jumper rider navigates a course in a blazing time, or a top dressage rider performs a fluid test with invisible aids, their bodies are working in cooperation with their horses. Never make the disheartening mistake of assuming this ability is always inborn in these riders, or because you have had trouble being effective with your aids in the past that you are forever doomed to this sort of ineptitude. As you decrease the amount of inadvertent interference from your body, your horse can respond more precisely.

To learn how to improve communication, I'm going to introduce you to a number of new exercises. In *Partners on Chairs*, you will discover how sensitive your horse is to your rein aids, and learn how you can give soft, but clear aids by using your *Four Basics* and *grounding*. The *Buttress* will help you obtain a deep, stable seat, and a refined version of *Fingers under the Armpits* will make you appreciate the potency of aids coming up from your center. In the *ON THE HORSE* session in this chapter, I'll explain how you can use these new communication skills to ride some transitions in all the gaits.

ON THE GROUND

As usual, prepare for your awareness work on the ground by confirming your feeling of inner balance by *centering* and *grounding*. Add another warm-up exercise to release and open your upper body. Remember the feeling of *Feet in the Sand*? Keep this feeling, and with your body free and open, put the tips of your fingers on the edges of your shoulders. Imagine that there are soft rubber bands attached to the tip of each shoulder and grasp one of them in each hand. Then slowly extend your arms holding the bands delicately in your fingers. When you have reached the limit of stretch, open your

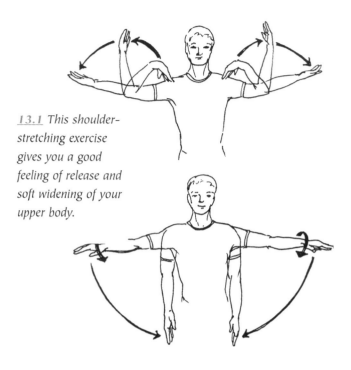

13.1 This shoulder-stretching exercise gives you a good feeling of release and soft widening of your upper body.

fingers outward as you release the rubber bands. Rotate your arms so your palms face downward and let your hands and arms float down to your sides like quiet snowflakes (fig. 13.1). Do this several times remembering that you must stretch the bands slowly so they will not snap. This exercise will give you a tremendous feeling of release and openness through your shoulders and upper body. You can do this sitting down as well, sitting a little forward on your chair. When you are on your horse, use this shoulder-stretching exercise—or do it in your imagination to release and widen your upper body.

Partners on Chairs

I dedicate an entire chapter to "hands" later on, however, I'm also including some information and exercises about hands here because they are so important to the subjects of this chapter: connection and communication.

The *Partners on Chairs* experiment helps you understand just how delicate and precise your hands need to be when in contact with the horse's mouth. For this session, you will need a partner. You will also need two chairs and a set of soft reins from a bridle. Sit facing each other on the front edge of your chair, each holding opposite ends of the reins with two hands, as you would while riding (fig. 13.2). You should hold your hands with your fingers softly closed, thumb side up, and the end of the rein coming out between your thumb and forefinger. The fingers should close around the reins with fingertips not quite touching the palms of the hands. This position gives elasticity to the knuckle of the finger, especially of the ring finger, which has the immediate contact with the rein and can at times give the only rein directive needed (fig. 13.3). Your hold on the reins should have the quality of the *Unbendable Arm*—strength with soft spring. Even if you ride Western using

13.2 "Partners on Chairs." To do these exercises, face each other sitting on the edge of the chair, and hold the reins as you do when riding.

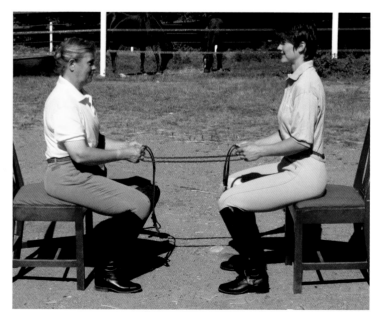

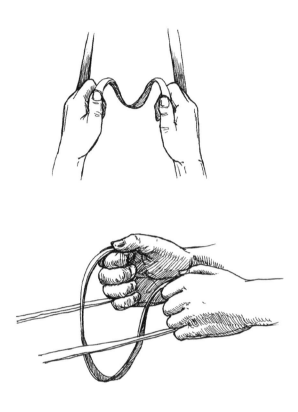

13.3 Two views of the most commonly used English riding hands position—the one I recommend. Note the thumb sides of the hands are on top.

only one hand, you will benefit from this exercise. Good Western riders need to know how to ride with reins in both hands, which they frequently do with a snaffle bit.

Sit with your feet back under you a little, as if you were sitting on a saddle. You will do a number of experiments as the rider, while your partner is the horse. When you have felt the results of these experiments, switch roles with your partner and try being the horse so you can get the benefit of both perspectives. It is important that the horse partner allows herself to react honestly to the aids of the rider partner with no guessing or assumptions as to what the rider wants.

Sit erect and balanced in your chair and become deeply aware of your center. The exercises and experiments you do will be more successful when quiet control comes from there. If you keep your attention on your hands, your horse partner will not like it. If you let your hands be directed as if intimately connected and obedient to your center, you will have a happy partner.

Start this exercise with both you and your partner closing your eyes. It is easier to be sensitive and observant with your eyes closed than with them open. Quietly move your hands back and forth feeling the connection with your center as if you were following the head and neck motion of a young horse at a walk. Position your hands so that there is a straight line from your elbow to the imaginary bit at your partner's hands. The rider may need to open her eyes periodically and momentarily check on this alignment. Find a nice rhythm and enjoy the communication with your "horse" from this ideal connection.

Now try various modifications of this connection to your horse partner and notice her reactions. Continue following your "horse's" movement forward and back as you experiment. In each case, you will try the undesirable way first, and then go back to the centered way.

1. With closed eyes, switch back and forth from hard eyes to *soft eyes* several times.

2. Hold your breath, then *breathe* regularly.

3. As if frightened, let your center rise too high in your body. Then, let it sink to where it belongs.

4. Lose your balance by tipping your torso too far forward and too far back, then establish your balance over your seat bones using your *building blocks.*

5. Turn your hands so the fingernails are down and the knuckles horizontal. Then, carry them correctly with the thumbs on top.

6. Clench your fists on the reins. Then, let the hands and fingers be soft.

7. Carry your hands above the straight line from elbow to bit, and then go back to the straight line.

8. Hollow, and shorten your lower back. Relax, and lengthen your back.

9. Round your back, Then, lengthen, widen, and release it.

How did your horse partner respond to your variations in communication? This whole exercise can be very enlightening on the importance of detail and correctness of form. With each experiment, when you deviated from ideal form, your human horse most likely responded with resistance in some manner. She most likely did not care for it, or found it irritating and unreasonable. The communication became harsh. (A real horse would have responded in some, or all of several undesirable ways, such as holding his breath, setting his jaw, throwing up his head, changing his rhythm, and so on.) My Australian friend, instructor Richard Weis, had an experience with a group of people trying out these experiments but not doing the Centered Riding alternatives (listed above) as well. By the end of the sessions, both horse and rider partners were full of rage.

This exercise makes us realize not only how much our patient horses tolerate and accept from us, but also how

important correct and efficient use of the rider's aids is to the partnership between horse and rider. Careful, sensitive communication with *clear intent* is necessary for your horse to work well for you.

The Buttress

This next exercise is called the *Buttress*. Just as buttresses can hold up a cathedral, a simulated buttress can help you become solid and stable on your horse. Think of how a buttress works. The roof of a Gothic cathedral would likely spread out and fall down if it was not supported and kept in a peak by buttresses, which absorb the energy and the weight through their angles, and being grounded at the bottom. Keep this picture in mind as you do these exercises. All the *Buttress* exercises are, like the *Unbendable Arm*, built on the power and sensitivity of *grounding* and *centering*, with the *Four Basics* and *clear intent* (figs. 13.4 A & B).

Once again, you will need your partner. Stand up facing your partner and have her put her hands on your shoulders. She must now push, not sud-

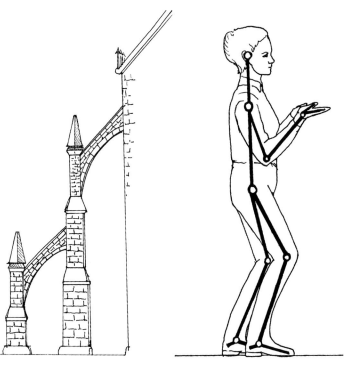

13.4 A & B The "Buttress."

(A) *A flying buttress on a cathedral. Notice how the sideways thrust is directed down into the ground.* (B) *A person in the "Buttress" position.*

denly, but gradually until you find you have to put a foot back in order not to fall over.

Now make yourself into a buttress. Flex your knees and hip joints but let your torso remain upright. Now your center is well established over your feet and your head is over your center. Put your elbows against the front of your sides on, or just above, your hip joints and let your partner again put her hands on your shoulders. Before she starts to push, let the palms of your hands come up under her elbows. You now have a brace between your body and your partner's body from your propped elbows to your hands against her elbows. Maintain the contact between your hands and her elbows with your body rather than lifting with your arm muscles (fig. 13.5).

Now think of your whole body as a huge *bungee cord*. Remember, the end of this bungee cord comes out of the top of your head just above your ears. As you imagine pulling the end of this stretchy cord, you are going to *ground* your feet, and *center and grow*, letting energy go out from your knees and feet. Feel that this is a quick pull, then ease and pull, and ease again. Each time you pull, you are going to have a real feeling of *centering and lengthening*, down and up–out through your knees and grounded feet, and out the top of your head. This lengthening will cause a momentary increase in pressure on the elbows of your partner tending to make her lift her hands off your shoulders. As a result, it is harder for her to push.

Have your partner begin to increase the pressure on your shoulders steadily. You, in turn, will repeatedly pull on your *bungee cord*, and *let your spine lengthen*. These repeated tugs will travel through your body in pulsations. With each pulsation, you will find that your lower back fills and widens. Don't make it happen, just *let* it happen as a result of the lengthening of your body. If at any time you lose the lengthening feeling, your partner will feel the difference. She should pause a mo-

13.5 The "Buttress" stance: Cynthia (on the left) is standing firmly solid on her feet in the "Buttress," and Jineen is unable to push her over. Cynthia's elbows are braced against her body as she sends an upward thrust into Jineen's elbows. Cynthia is using her legs to raise her torso for this upward lift, instead of using her arm muscles.

ment, just as she did in the *Unbendable Arm* exercise, and simply hold where she is until she feels you get your lengthening pulsations going again. She can then go on increasing the pressure. If you keep yourself *grounded*, and *ground-center-grow—* let the energy go up and down through your whole body and out through the top of your head, you will find that your partner cannot move you. You are solid. She can lean her entire weight on you, and you will be as immoveable as a rock.

Again, as in the *Unbendable Arm* exercise, to produce this sort of energy, you need to keep *grounded*, with *soft eyes* and *breathing*. If you are doing this well, your partner could suddenly take her hands off your shoulders, and you would stand there without toppling forward. If you are not doing it well, perhaps leaning toward her, you will fall forward if she takes her hands off. This is a good way to test whether you are balanced and grounded, and really letting your body lengthen.

If at any time in the *Buttress*, you hold your breath, develop hard eyes, tighten your feet or any joints, put tension in your shoulders, neck, and head, or hollow your back, your *Buttress* will disintegrate and have no strength. Experiment while tightening various parts of your body. You will find that your partner can shove you around. Now go back to the correct *centered breathing*, and *grounded stance*, and establish a *clear intent* to stay resiliently solid. Remember your *bungee cord*. Or think of it as an *elastic band*. When you imagine that you are stretching and releasing this band, you are keeping your energy moving both down and up through your body. If you remain inwardly motionless, you will become stiff and stuck, and ultimately vulnerable. Keep your internal energy dynamic and you will find yourself secure, immobile, and grounded as effortlessly as you were in the *Unbendable Arm* exercise.

CROSSED HANDS

Another way to practice the *Buttress* with your partner incorporates the use of reins, and shows you how to use the exercise as a rebalance. In the process of learning this technique on the ground, you will probably use more pounds of rein contact than you will ever use on your horse, whether you ride Western or English. Once you have learned the technique, you will be able to refine your con-

13.6 *"Crossed Hands" stance. In this case, Cynthia is the "horse" and is trying to pull Jineen forward. In the "Buttress" position, Jineen can easily resist.*

nection with your horse through the reins. You will be more able to adjust your rein contact from a positive feel, to a light contact, or to the feather light touch of the Western rider's looped rein.

The exercise is called *Crossed Hands*. You and your partner stand facing each other close enough to hold hands (fig. 13.6). Your partner—the horse—crosses her hands at the wrists, thumbs side up. In this position, you can hold her fingers as if you were holding reins with your thumbs on the top as shown. You are going to combine your *Buttress* with your *Unbendable Arm*. Remember that in the *Unbendable Arm* exercise, your arm is not rigid. It has springy resilience but does not collapse and bend. Now, with the same springy but firm quality, your elbows will stay bent. Flex your knees and hips as if you were on your horse. Let your partner hold your fingers and pull with steady but not excessive pressure on your hands. Do not pull back with your shoulders or elbows, but simply use your *Unbendable Arm* technique. Keep your fingers soft. Repeated small lengthenings with your *bungee cord* will let you do a succession of *Buttresses* that are like pulsations. In each *Buttress* pulsation, you meet your partner's pull with *Unbendable Arm* soft strength and immediately release the pull, ready to redo the *ground-center-grow Buttress*. Feel your repeated *ground-center-grow Buttress* with each one of these pulsations. Your partner will distinctly feel the pulsations and will not be able to effectively pull against them because on each release he has nothing to pull against.

Remember that when you do your *Buttress*, you are *grounding, centering and growing*. When you are on your horse, your body grounds and lengthens, allowing you to sit wider and deeper in the saddle and the horse's back to fill your seat. This depth of seat causes you to flex your knees and bring your lower legs against the horse's side. On your horse, these *centering and growing, breathing* pulsations will be felt as rebalances, and your horse will lighten off your hands and change his balance onto his hindquarters. Remember how important correct *Basics* are to the effectiveness of your *Buttress* and therefore, your rebalances. If you are careful to use *in-out breaths* each time you center and grow, you will not only avoid inadvertently holding your breath and therefore becoming tight, but will be able to apply a clearer aid. *Soft eyes*, a *long, wide back*, and *grounded* foot are essential. Notice how you are learning how to have

powerful aids with a minimum of actual muscle. Your partner will feel that your aids are becoming very efficient and clear.

Combining the Buttress with the Unbendable Arm

Richard Weis found himself on an old codger of a schoolhorse who was stiff, arthritic, totally on the forehand, and hard-mouthed. Richard and I were working on the *Unbendable Arm*, the *Buttress* and rebalancing. He worked quietly and at slow gaits for a long time. Gradually, the old horse's body began to unlock. His neck and jaw softened, he was chewing on the bit, and his glazed eyes began to take on a little sparkle. Richard brought him in to me and said, "Even this old guy responds to the quiet and consistent use of *centering*, the *Unbendable Arm*, and the *Buttress*. It's truly remarkable!"

The *Buttress* is also useful in transitions, and is invaluable in rebalancing yourself and your horse. I have had occasions when students have persisted in riding with their feet out in front of them, and I have taken them off the horse and taught them the *Buttress*. When they remounted, they could understand not only why their feet must stay beneath their centers but also how to keep them there.

Use the Buttress for Control

A good solid, upright *Buttress* seat will be invaluable if your horse bolts or falls onto his forehand and becomes heavy in your hands from imbalance or fear. You can use a series of *Buttresses* to reorganize and control him in just a few strides because your seat is deep but not locked or rigid, and your lower legs and feet are securely *grounded* with the lower legs securely connected to the horse's barrel.

You can demonstrate this use of the *Buttress* with your partner. Sit on the front of the chairs, one with *Crossed Hands*, and have your horse

13.7 A–C

(A) Cynthia, the "horse" (right), is pulling on Jineen who, grounded and solid in her chair, doesn't move. (B) This time, Jineen hollows her back, and the chair tips forward. She has no stability. (C) Now, Jineen rounds her back, and again the chair tips forward.

partner become a puller. Your partner must not jerk but exert a heavy pull on your hands. Use your *Buttress* in the chair, ground yourself and, as you did while standing, use *ground-center-grow* rebalances with arms that are springy but do not unbend. You will discover that you are solid and can keep your horse partner from gaining the upper hand. Your chair remains solidly on its four feet. Try again with your back hollow or rounded, or even leaning back. Suddenly your partner can drag you around and tip your chair forward. If you remain grounded in the correct position, you are firm and efficient with sensitive control. You replace awkward and ineffective pulling and hauling with your *clear intent*, "No," and with your rebalancing, your horse will stop pulling (figs. 13.7 A–C).

The *Buttress* is equally effective when used on a bucking horse. If you let your arms and hands be firm with the *Unbendable Arm*, and use a series of

Buttresses, your bucking horse will find himself putting you only deeper into his back, and he will give up. If, however, you lean your torso forward or back, you will lose your strength and base of support, and your horse will pull the reins away. He will be able to shove you around as your partner did when you resisted her push without a *Buttress*.

One of my longtime students had taken a nasty fall from a horse that was running away. Soon after she was able to ride again, she came for a lesson. All was going well and she was regaining confidence when a pigeon flew off the rafters. Her horse bolted off and she panicked and yelled for help. I repeated, "Buttress," several times, loud and clear. She responded by doing a *Buttress* rebalance, and the horse stopped immediately. She said, over and over, that never again would she be afraid of a horse running away with her because she could always regain control by buttressing.

Refining Fingers under the Armpits

Remember the exercise, *Fingers under the Armpits*? It is explained in Session Three (see p. 71). It is the same subject we are now working, on but with a different approach. So, let's experiment with the exercise a little further. Once again, try this with your partner, bearing in mind that this is an exercise of communication to your horse partner from your center using only your fingertips. It is most effective if the horse partner's eyes are closed. Feel the rhythm. Enjoy the freedom of movement between you and your partner. In that nice swinging walk, begin to take your horse partner in circles, turns, and serpentines, and notice how easily you can direct her, providing that you follow her rhythm using your centered body language for directions (fig. 13.8).

Now asking your partner to keep her eyes closed, deliberately walk out of step with your "horse." You will find that you have to carry your legs further apart or you will step on your horse partner's heels. Now get back in step again. Try taking many more steps than your horse is taking. Notice how disconcerting this is for your partner, who will probably tend to stop and push back. Experiment with how light your fingers can be while still controlling your horse with your body language.

Staying in rhythm, stare intently, with hard eyes, at your horse's mane—the back of your partner's head. Then switch to *soft eyes*, and see your entire surroundings. Go back and forth between hard eyes and *soft eyes* a few times. Alternate between holding your breath for a few strides and then *breathing* normally in rhythm. Don't tell your horse when you are going to do these things so that you can accurately gauge her reactions to your aids. When walking in step again, *center* yourself and let your neck and body lengthen, and then deliberately shorten the back of your neck, which will stiffen your back. Alternate lengthening and shortening two or three times.

13.8 "Fingers under the Armpits." Note Lucy's (in blue and the "rider") excellent "use of self" and "soft eyes" as she communicates forward movement to Cynthia from her center.

Do you remember how you walked while you visualized going down the inside of your legs, and then going down the outside of your legs (see p. 107). As you walk behind your horse partner, alternate between these two images of movement. Try some other experiments to help you discover what a real horse's reactions might be to the ap-

plication of various aids. Get in step with your horse partner in a nice swinging walk and remove one finger from one of her sides. What is your horse's reaction? Many times the first thing she will do is move toward the finger on her ribs before she moves away from it. The one thing she won't do is walk easily, straight forward. So, you can experiment with dropping one finger, then returning it to her ribs, first on one side and then the other.

Remember not to warn your partner what you're going to do. Now with both hands on, try pushing her with your fingers. Don't be surprised if she slows down or stops. These are pushy fingers. If you give a bigger push she will probably go forward, but awkwardly. When you are once again swinging along in step, remove your fingers on both sides. Notice that your horse partner slows down. She doesn't know where you are and feels insecure. She needs your fingers on there to balance and coordinate with you, just as your real horse needs your legs.

Now try some rebalances. Simply *ground-center-grow*, and pull the imaginary *bungee cord* at the top of your head, and notice how your horse partner responds when this is all you've done. She will probably feel more responsive and active with her legs. After a rebalance, try for an extended walk in which you may have to center and grow for every stride. Then do another *ground-center-grow* rebalance, and see if your partner will come down to a collected walk. Go back and forth between the extended walk and collected walk using rebalances each time, and feel the energy grow.

Now go back to a rhythmical walk, and try a little leg-yielding. Before you start, remember that it is important when leg-yielding with your real horse that his rhythm stays the same, and that he goes ahead more than he goes sideways–usually two-thirds ahead to one-third sideways. With your horse partner, you will notice that if you use centered body language in rhythm to her steps to ask her to leg-yield, the movement feels easy. If you use your body out of rhythm, you may really have to punch her over and she won't like that. If you become really good at using your centered body-language signals in rhythm, your horse partner may be surprised to find that she has moved right across your practice area with her eyes closed without ever realizing that she was going side-ways. The partners are working in unison.

Now stop and discuss with your horse partner the sensations she received from your various experiments. What did she feel when you gave your directives *without* your centered body language? Did it confuse her, frustrate her, make her want to resist or give up? When leg-yielding, did she feel your hands as well as your center directing her, even though you were consciously not using your hands? Remember the results of this experiment when you are riding your real horse.

There are an infinite number of experiments you can do with this fun exercise. Try new things, take a turn being the horse, and then being the rider. Try riding all the dressage figures, or Western reining patterns. This is one of the most educational exercises that I know. It brings awareness to the rider of how the horse partner—and her real horse—feel, and how to make connections with them. The use of *grounding* and your *Four Basics*, especially *centering*, is vitally important for you to be a happy, dancing couple. When you can use your *Basics* with sensitive awareness, your work will be characterized by balance, rhythm, and flow—three qualities that are the soul of Centered Riding.

ON THE HORSE

Your work on the ground with your partner has helped you understand the importance of sensitive communication, and given you an introduction into making a connection with your horse. Now take this new consciousness into your riding. It's time to learn how to improve your work with transitions, which we started in Session Four, *Raise Your Horse's Back through Transitions.*

Ride a Square and Add Transitions

You are going to start by doing the *Ride a Square* exercise again, as explained in Session Four (see p. 85). Begin by walking your horse on a long rein with almost no contact. When you have found your inner balance and centeredness, and your horse seems happy with you, start riding a square not more than 20 meters across (approx. 60 feet). Keep your reins long while riding this figure. Before and after each corner, *ground-center-grow*, with *in-out breaths*. Notice again, what each of these *ground-center-grow* rebalances does to your body, and then feel your horse's response. You will again find that your balance is re-established, and that your horse in turn responds by rebalancing himself, stepping more deeply under his body with his hocks and hind feet, and lightening his fore-hand. He may even begin to flex his poll and chew on his bit as he begins to feel balanced and soft.

Still walking, pick up light contact on your reins. Ride your horse in a 20-meter circle and begin to be aware of the quality of your leg aids. Rate the various degrees of leg pressure with values from 0 to 10, with the lightest, 0, being just a thought, and 10 being a good kick. Try some transitions from walk-to-halt and back again, using *ground-center-grow* rebalances. At this point, do not actually use your reins in your rebalance. Make the decision to halt, then *ground-center-grow*, and halt. You may be surprised how promptly and easily your horse halts.

In the transition from the halt to the walk, you may need clear, distinct leg aids at first, using a pressure of 5 or 6, or even more. As you repeat the transitions, gradually reduce the intensity of each directive. In your transitions to the halt, try *breathing in-out* as you *ground-center-grow*—not a big breath, just a gentle exhale. Experiment with both up and down transitions. The down transition will not only begin to feel more prompt but you will also feel that the horse halts in a better balance, from back to front. He steps under more deeply with his hind legs so they carry more of his weight, allow his back to come up, and his front end to halt lightly. This balance will give you a very different feeling from the jarring of a halt on the forehand.

Notice that these *ground-center-grow* rebalances are actually a gentle form of the *Buttress* that you practiced in your groundwork. Notice also that when you *Buttress* on the horse the energy going out your knees and down into your feet opens your seat sideways to allow you to drop deeper into the saddle as his back fills your seat, which in turn allows more depth to your knee and heel. There should be a feeling of balance between the deep knee and heel, giving you a secure and sensitive lower leg on the horse, directly under your center. This effect adds to the directive to the horse to bring his hocks under him for improved balance. Your horse's transitions will increasingly spring from his hind legs and, as a result, his gaits between transitions will become springy as well.

In your down transitions it might help to imagine that you are a pilot bringing a plane in for a landing. If you land nosewheel first you might crash. Instead, you carefully touch down on the main wheels and when they are well connected, you allow the nosewheel to come down. What do you do with your controls to have the plane in this balance so the main wheels touch first? You add a touch of power to bring the front end up just before you land. Your rebalances produce the same result in your horse as that little increase in power just before the plane lands (fig. 13.9 A–C).

When taking off in an airplane, the nosewheel comes off the ground before the main wheels. To do that, you increase the power; you don't just pull the nose up. In the up transition on your horse, a rebalance *before*, and another rebalance *during* your up transition will have the same result and get you off to a balanced start. For all transitions, whether down or up, you will need rebalances to build the important extra energy forward and up from the hindquarters.

To improve your transitions even more, use your *following seat* and *pedal your bicycle backward*. This will let you march into an immediate halt, rather than slowing down until your horse fades to a standstill. So feel the rhythm: one, two, three, four, and then change to feel the rhythm of the hind legs—one and two and one and two. The "ands" are the count for the *front* feet stepping. Remember, you are only interested in the *hind* leg count. Your knees will be dropping left and right with the one and two counts. Your rebalance directives—*ground-center-grow* and *in-out breaths*—are simultaneous. You are marching one and two. You make the decision to stop. So, with your rebalancing, you drop a knee and leave it down, then drop the other knee and leave it down, and hold those hind feet on the ground by gently embracing your horse with your lower legs. This makes a vigorous, tidy, square halt with the horse attentive to your further instructions. At the halt, breathe normally.

After you have done two or three more walk-to-halt transitions, pick up a trot, still on the 20-meter circle. Trot two strides, walk four strides, trot two strides, walk three strides, and so on, noticing how your horse becomes increasingly balanced, light and attentive. Now change the exercise while still riding the 20-meter circle. Walk a quarter of the circle, and trot half the circle. Keep carefully using your *ground-center-grow, breathe-in-out* rebalances to prepare for, and initiate each transition, and then afterward to keep the new gait balanced.

If at any time your rebalance seems ineffective and does not come through, either you are not using your body correctly or your horse is not listening. Check your own *use of self* and ride one or more transitions to a full halt to regain your horse's attention and balance.

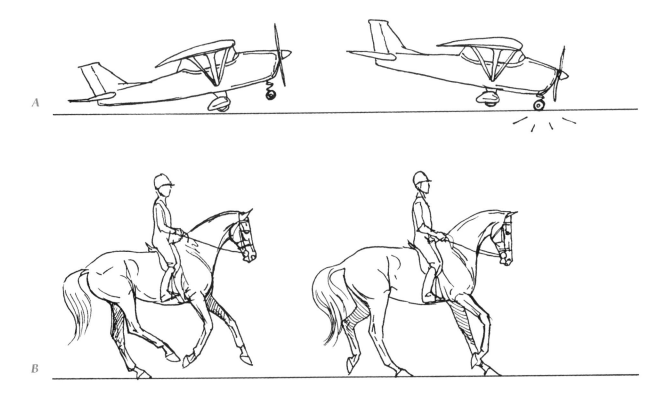

<u>13.9 A–C</u> Down transitions.

(A) A good landing in an airplane requires the pilot to "rebalance" the plane just before landing so that the main landing gear lands first. In a bad landing the pilot allows the front wheel to touch down first.

(B) Similarly, in a good down transition, you ask your horse to bring his hind legs under him to rebalance so that he is carrying more of his weight toward the back, lightening his forehand, and making it easier for him to stop or slow down.

(C) This horse is landing on the forehand, abusing his body—an example of a bad down transition.

Now begin using the whole ring to try some trot-walk transitions, keeping the *Buttress* in mind as you do your rebalances. The amount of energy you need to use in your *Buttress* will depend on how balanced and forward your horse is at that moment. By this time your horse will be doing the transitions so completely from back to front, that it is as if he were stepping with his hind feet up into your receiving seat and hands. Your hands need not move. Your horse fills them and your effortless *Unbendable Arm* intent says, "No further!" Your horse is "in front of your leg."

The Power Triangle

As you ride, feel the full width of your center, hips, and elbows, which hang softly at your sides, not pinched in nor flared out. Let your forearm, hand, and rein form a straight line to your horse's mouth on each side. These straight lines form the two sides of a triangle, the base of which is formed by a line running from side to side through your center. The apex of the triangle is your horse's mouth. From your center, allow the triangle to fill up with power. I call this the *Power Triangle*. Wherever the *Power Triangle* points you can go. Just build the energy in your center and let it release forward into the power triangle (fig. 13.10).

Ride a bit with your *Power Triangle* in straight lines, circles, and serpentines. Notice that when you add the image of the *Power Triangle* to your rebalances, the horse's balance remains positive and steady through corners, transitions, or changes

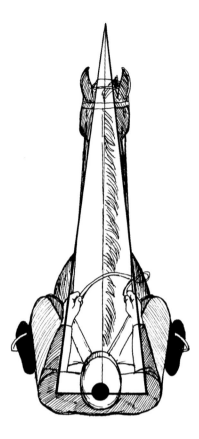

13.10 Release your energy from your center into the "Power Triangle," which consists of your center, pelvis, and elbows at the base of the triangle, through your hands connected to the apex at the bit.

of stride. The more energy you invest in the triangle, the more vigor and power you give to your horse who is in front of your leg.

Point your *Power Triangle* out ahead of you and ride some transitions, big flowing circles, serpentines, and changes of direction. You will probably discover that you are only using quite light leg aids. Don't be surprised if your horse is beginning to come onto the bit and reach softly into your hands as he works.

At this point, the balance of your horse should be totally ready for the canter depart. From either the walk or trot, whichever you prefer, *ground-center-grow,* fill your *Power Triangle,* and allow him to step into the canter. Remember to maintain your upright balance through the transition. If you find yourself tipping or lunging forward, you will throw your horse off balance and actually prevent him from cantering. Like the plane taking off from the runway, your horse must step into the canter with his forehand light and his hind legs coming up under his body.

Ride your horse around the ring adding canter transitions to your halt, walk, and trot transitions. What have you done in this session? In your work on the ground, you found sensitive ways of communication with your horse as you worked with reins as *Partners on Chairs.* Then, you found the soft power of the *Buttress,* which you will find very useful in many aspects of riding. You have discovered how subtle directives to your horse can be done with only the touch of your fingers, and on the horse, you used these skills for smooth transitions that balanced your horse as he developed lots of forward motion and energy. He is more attentive and obedient to your lighter and more accurate aids. You feel that his hind legs are directly connected to your hands, and that he is beginning to come into these soft and receiving hands—not from them being fussy—but through correct and sensitive use of your body. ≫

WHAT ARE THE ESSENTIALS OF
Improve Communication through the Quality of Your Aids?

ON THE GROUND

▶ The *Partners in Chairs* holding-reins exercise demonstrates how using a centered body increases your ability to be sensitive with the reins.

▶ The *Buttress* with the *Unbendable Arm* technique teaches you how to obtain a more stable seat, and shows how you can create a soft barrier to your horse's (sometimes undesired) forward movement.

▶ Practicing *Crossed Hands* with *Buttress* pulsations will add sensitivity to rebalances on your horse.

▶ *Buttress* into a chair so your partner cannot pull you out. This is the feeling you need when on your horse's back so he cannot pull you forward.

▶ Doing the refined *Fingers under the Armpits* exercise with *centered* control will give you the ability to have a more sensitive connection to your horse.

ON THE HORSE

▶ *Ride a Square* doing *ground-center-grow* rebalances as small, gentle forms of the *Buttress*.

▶ Add transitions to *Ride a Square*. Do small *Buttresses* to become softer and more accurate.

▶ To further refine the transitions, use the image of an airplane taking off and landing, *pedal backward*, and point the *Power Triangle* in the direction you want to go.

WHAT ARE THE RESULTS?

▶ Your horse will be balanced and ready with forward energy for transitions.

▶ He will be attentive and obedient to light, accurate aids.

▶ You will become a dancing couple.

14

Learn Straightness before Lateral Work

Very few people walk truly straight and balanced. Very few animals do, either. Think of how a dog travels happily at the trot and "canter" with his hind feet on one side or the other of the track of his front feet. Horses will travel in this crooked fashion as well, particularly at the canter. However, for maximum athletic efficiency while carrying a rider, a horse must travel straight. His hind feet must travel in the same track as his front feet whether he is moving in a straight line, or on a curve.

ON THE GROUND

Walking in a Straight Line

In order to begin lateral work and really utilize the supporting and strengthening benefits this work provides, your horse must first be able to move in a straight line. It is, of course, unreasonable to expect him to be able to walk in a straight line until you can walk in a straight line yourself. So, let's do some groundwork to prepare for lateral work on your horse.

Stand quietly and allow your body to organize itself as you have been doing in your previous groundwork sessions. With special awareness of *centering* and *soft eyes*, walk quietly in straight lines, noticing if your pelvis and shoulders are re-

ally traveling in a position perpendicular to the line you are walking on. Does each foot travel the same distance in a stride, or does one cover more ground? Does each foot land with equal weight, or is one heavier on the ground? How does the movement of your legs and feet relate to the positioning of your pelvis and shoulders?

It will be helpful to have someone watch you to report if you are straight and, if not, where the unevenness originates. Watching yourself in a mirror can also be revealing and helpful. Remember to be aware that an incorrect habit may feel correct, and the correct movement may feel wrong. So, take time to become aware of how you move, and how it should feel when you are actually moving straight and evenly. Practice until you can move this way confidently and comfortably.

14.1 *Claudia demonstrates a lateral step to the left.*

Lateral Moves

Now that you are able to move straight, stand quietly for a moment and prepare for a lateral move to the left with the control coming from your center. Think about the *ball*—your center—just touching the top of your sacrum as it floats with a slight backward rotation in your pelvis. Visualizing your center will allow your hips and knees to soften. Now let your center, in whatever form you like to imagine it—a *ball* or a mass of energy—rotate on its vertical axis a few degrees to the left while continuing its slightly backward rotation. It should not roll sideways, or change position within your

pelvis. Notice how this small rotation changes the feeling of the positioning of your body. Your pelvis will want to rotate left. Allow your torso, shoulders, and head to follow this slight rotation. Keep your left leg and foot *grounded*, and you will feel this leg stretch a little back as you rotate. Your right leg will soften as it crosses over.

Now, let's try the leg-yield exercise while walking. Walk forward in a straight line. The energy and directions for a leg-yield will come from your center. Rotate your center a little left, flex your right knee and allow yourself to move diagonally forward and left with your right leg crossing over in front of the left (fig. 14.1). After a few steps, go straight again, reorganize, and move left again. Repeat this sequence several times. Become aware that if you let the rotation of your center pulsate in rhythm with your strides, the movement is easier and more stable.

When moving left feels easy, try the same routine to the right. Keep your body upright and pretend you are the horse; your legs are his hind legs, your hands can move in the air to represent his front legs. Finally, try a few steps left, straighten, then a few steps right. Be sure that the straight steps have a good forward impetus because when you are on your real horse, this forward energy is especially important to keep him straight and responsive to, and in front of your legs.

At this point, it will be interesting to experiment on your own feet with a variety of lateral movements. Pick a sizeable area—lawn, yard, or an arena. Begin walking in patterns. Within these patterns, keep switching from walking straight to walking diagonally. Be aware of your flexibility, balance, and forward motion. Imagine your feet leaving footprints like your horse's hoofprints. Now begin playing with placing his haunches first to the right, and then to the left while moving in a straight line, or a pirouette where your feet keep stepping around in a tiny circle. Try a Western

14.2 A & B Lateral work.

(A) Cynthia is straddling Jineen showing intent to move to the left, but nothing is happening because Cynthia has not released her left leg, which discourages the "horse" from moving.
(B) Now, Cynthia has opened her left knee, inviting Jineen to move left. The initiative to move sideways comes from Cynthia's right leg.

spin. Experiment and have fun. Remember to reestablish your forward impetus by periodically walking straight forward.

How much effort should you put into the control from your center? When working from your center, keep in mind the phrase, "less is more." Try using a lot of effort, and notice how ineffective you become and the contortions into which you put your body. So stand again, reassemble your *soft eyes, centering,* and *breathing.* Be careful that your center points in the same direction as your nose. Be careful not to twist your head beyond the line of your desired direction. Notice how over-rotating your head and neck reduces your stable balance. Discover what a small amount of effort you can expend and still make your directive work. The equivalent of a clear whisper will be more effective than a shout.

Work on All Fours

Try some movements on all fours, on a soft carpet, or wearing kneepads. Though you will not be able to move with the lightness you had when walking, this is a good way to understand the sequence and use of your horse's legs. As the horse, remember to imagine that your eyes are on the top of your head so you can lengthen your neck, especially at the *slippery spot* at the poll. To start each movement, allow your back to fill and lengthen and don't lose that slightly backward rotation of the *ball* in your center. Let the movement of your limbs be automatic as they follow your *clear intent.*

Now try having a partner straddle you, like a rider, without putting weight on your back (figs. 14.2 A & B). Have your partner ask you to move laterally by putting pressure on your sides with her legs. You will discover that it is almost impossible to move laterally toward your rider's leg if she puts pressure on your body on that side. In order to move to the left, for example, the rider's left knee and thigh need to be soft, almost open, and inviting. The initiative to move left must come from the rider's right leg in unison with your motion. The rider's right leg will ask you to move to the left as your right leg comes off the ground and crosses in front of the left.

By now you will probably feel that you are both horse and rider. You can move gracefully in balance, straight forward, or sideways. With *grounding* and your *Four Basics*, you can float over the ground. And, with the soft but precise directives from your center, the movement becomes effortless. You are now ready to try these exercises on your horse.

ON THE HORSE

First, Be Straight Yourself

As you warm up your horse, remember that he must be able to travel straight before you can ask him to move laterally. Before you can ask him to be straight, however, you must be sure that you are in balance and straight yourself. As you begin your ride, become aware of your own body as you check on your own straightness. Are your seat bones carrying equal weight in the saddle? Are they both in the deepest part of the saddle, or is one a little bit ahead of the other? Check to see that your forward and back balance is correct (do the *Teeter-Totter* exercise, p. 36). Do your legs lie comfortably on the same spot on your horse's sides, or does one tend to be ahead or behind the other? Is the weight in your stirrups equal? Do your shoulders hang squarely with your horse's shoulders, or does one want to pull ahead or behind the other?

Try a few exercises as you warm up to help you take care of any of these potential problems. Be aware of the changes in your body as you do them.

1. Put one arm up, fingers reaching softly toward the sky, with your thumb pointing to your horse's tail. Use whichever arm you prefer.

2. Allow your feet to be equally grounded.

3. At the rising trot, change diagonals every few strides until your feet feel alike in the stirrups.

4. Siphon weight out of one foot, up through the leg and the pelvis and back down into the other foot until your feet feel equally weighted. Sometimes it helps to siphon the weight back and forth until it becomes even.

5. Gently pull the bungee cord on the top of your head above your ears.

6. Imagine your shoulders are a coat hanger. Let the rest of your body hang freely and evenly below the coat hanger and over your horse.

If your horse is crooked, you may have some difficulty completely straightening yourself, as his crookedness will affect your position. However, if you start your work by focusing primarily on your own straightness, you will ultimately be able to correct your horse. Remember the *Comparable Parts* of you and your horse.

Straighten Your Horse

As your own straightness improves, start to become more aware of your horse's body. On a straight line and in large, easy circles, do his front and hind feet track in the same line (fig. 14.3)? Most horses need muscular development to carry themselves perfectly straight, so you will probably have to help him. First, put your horse's hind feet on the track you wish to travel. Now you are going to put his forehand directly in front of his hind feet. In order to do this, be sure that your seat bones are even on the saddle and that your horse is nicely balanced between your legs and hands. Use your legs to stabilize his hindquarters on the track. If your horse's shoulders are displaced a little to the right of this track, center yourself, keep equal contact in both reins, and rotate your center a little to the left. You can use a small opening left rein and a careful right, indirect rein against his neck to shift his forehand to the left. In short, take both your hands a little to the left. Be careful not to simply move his head and neck in the desired direction, but remember that your objective is to move his entire forehand, his shoulders and front feet, to track directly in front of his hindquarters.

Starting Lateral Moves

When your horse is moving obediently and promptly from your aids and he is straight and balanced, he is ready to do some lateral work. You, in turn, must be aware of your *building blocks*, be *centered*, and *grounded.* Establish a nice breathing connection from your center with your horse. This will mean that from your center, you feel as if the skin of your seat was the skin of his back, your legs draped around his sides are free to give exact aids as needed, and your center through your hands connects to his mouth, which in turn connects through his body to his hind legs.

The energy and directives to move laterally will still come from your center. Use your *ground-center-grow* rebalances before, during, and after each directive. As your center rotates slightly in the direction you and your horse are moving, you may feel that the rotation has slight pulsations in rhythm with your horse's strides. Keep your nose lined up with your navel. If you turn your head more than your body (a great temptation), you will unbalance your horse.

Initially, keep your weight evenly on your two seat bones. Only when you are secure in your ability to use them equally, can you begin to weight them separately and precisely.

At first, move his whole body sideways at a very shallow angle and only for a few steps before

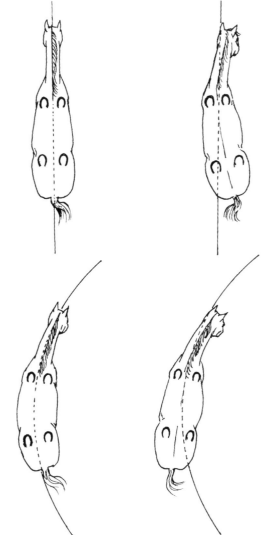

14.3 A straight versus crooked horse, on a straight line, and on a curve. When the horse is crooked his hind feet do not track up in the same line as the front feet.

moving forward in a straight line again. This is a little leg-yield—a movement where the horse goes forward and sideways with his body almost straight (see fig. 14.5 A). Keep your body balanced and perpendicular over your horse's spine and your seat bones on either side of it. Allow your torso, pelvis, and shoulders to rotate a little with

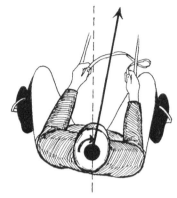

14.4 Rotation of the body doing a shallow-angled lateral move. Let your center be the primary directive.

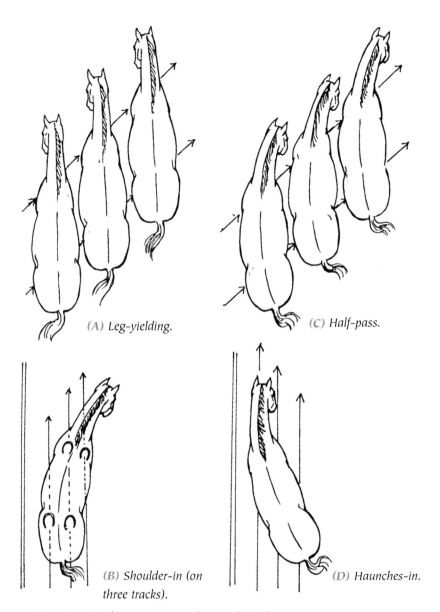

(A) Leg-yielding.

(C) Half-pass.

(B) Shoulder-in (on three tracks).

(D) Haunches-in.

14.5 A–D Lateral movements used primarily in dressage.

the directives from your center. Be careful not to over rotate. Let your center provide the primary directive (fig. 14.4).

Spend some time experimenting with different parts of your horse's body. You have moved his whole body as a unit in your simple leg-yields. You can also move his different parts independently, remembering that your center and hands control

the horse's forehand, and your center and legs control his quarters. So, move his shoulders off the track a little and back again, a movement, which with refinements becomes a shoulder-in (a lateral movement where the horse's shoulders are brought in off the track while his hind legs remain on it) in dressage. Move his haunches in a little to the inside of the track and back again, a haunches-

_14.6 A–C_ Quality of lateral work.

(A) _Correct and "up." Good balance, with the legs crossing over freely._ (B) _Incorrect, falling sideways._ (C) _Incorrect, obedient but stiff._

in. Try a bit of half-pass where the horse goes sideways and forward, bent toward the direction he is going (figs. 14.5 A–D).

If you want lateral work to be valuable in improving the quality of your horse's movement, you must maintain good _use of self_, your _building blocks, centering, soft eyes, breathing_ and _spine lengthening._ You can then reasonably ask your horse to stay balanced and engaged without tension. He too must be soft-eyed, and breathing easily. Good lateral work can and will help him free up so he can move correctly and in balance, crossing over freely with minimum of effort. He can avoid falling sideways, or even when obedient, being stiff. He will be a pleasure to watch and to ride (figs. 14.6 A–C).

Take a moment to picture a working cutting horse (fig. 14.7). Remember when you were doing your groundwork and directing your movement easily to the right or left through the power of your center? The movement of the cutting horse is an extreme demonstration of this effect. The horse initiates every move from his center, just below his lumbosacral joint (see fig. 6.10). His forward energy flows through his body and out his poll. In a quick turn, a cutting horse will frequently move his forehand as a unit, both feet and shoulders at once, right or left. In a smaller turn, when he moves his front or hind legs separately, one always crosses over in front of the other, never behind. His energy is always forward and directed from his center. Though the moves of the cutting horse are more extreme than most lateral work, the image of his lightness and mobility can give you a good guideline for the

_14.7_ A cutting horse: this is a wonderful example of a horse and a rider moving and following from their centers.

smaller motions you will be practicing in all movements of lateral work.

You are now ready to take these basics of lateral work into more advanced movements in any discipline. Whether you are doing competitive dressage, Western reining, or simply trail riding, the basic concept remains the same.

WHAT ARE THE ESSENTIALS OF **Learn Straightness before Lateral Work?**

ON THE GROUND

- ▶ You must be straight yourself before you ask your horse to travel straight.
- ▶ Practice straightness in front of a mirror.
- ▶ Walk the lateral movements yourself.
- ▶ Try some work on all fours, with or without a partner playing the rider or the "horse."

ON THE HORSE

- ▶ Any lateral directive must come from your balanced center. Be sure to keep your nose directly above your navel with every rotation of your torso.
- ▶ Horse must become obedient to your aids to independently move his forehand, or his haunches.

WHAT ARE THE RESULTS?

- ▶ Good, basic lateral work will take you into more advanced movements in all different disciplines of riding.

15

The Joyful Canter

The canter can be the most beautiful of gaits with soft lift, rhythm, and swing—a joy to ride in harmony with your horse. Horses like to canter. In fact, foals canter in their first hours of life, often before they trot. Yet, many people are worried about riding the canter, possibly in fear that it might become an out-of-control gallop. A rider stiffens, locking her hips and her back. In turn, the horse stiffens, and the softness of the canter degenerates into a rigid, uncomfortable bounce. Fortunately, the Centered Riding techniques that you have been developing in your walk and trot work can take you directly into the canter. Whether you are a beginner or an experienced rider, working on improving your canter work will help you remain in balance with your horse and apply your aids (seat, legs, hands, and even breathing) with more ease and clarity.

ON THE GROUND

Let's analyze the motion of the horse's feet as he canters. The canter has a three-beat rhythm with a moment of suspension. Stand and let your feet represent the horse's hind feet, and your hands become his front feet. You need not actually put your hands on the ground. You are going to pick up the right lead. Put your left foot forward and put weight on it as shown in figure 15.1 A. This represents the left hind leg of the horse and this is beat number one. Now bring your right foot and left hand forward at the same time. This step with diagonal legs is beat number two as shown in figure 15.1 B. On this step, the horse shifts his weight forward over the diagonal legs as the left hind foot

comes off the ground. Now put out your right hand—beat number three as shown in figure 15.1 C. On this step, your horse's weight rolls forward over his right front leg. As his weight continues to swing forward, he moves into a moment of suspension (fig. 15.1 D) until the left hind leg reaches forward and catches his weight again to begin the sequence once more (fig. 15.1 A). The rhythm is *one*-two-three, *one*-two-three, and the suspension is of such short duration that you cannot count it out loud.

Some groundwork can help you ride the canter in balance without stiffness. Follow the drawings in figures 15.2 A–F for a right lead canter. Imagine a square with the sides the same length as the width of your shoulders. Place one foot on the back

(A) The first beat: simulating the horse's movement, Jineen's left foot is taking her weight.

(B) The second beat: her right foot and left hand are on the ground at the same time.

(C) The third beat: her left foot comes off the ground as her right hand starts to take the weight.

(D) Her right hand on the ground is the rollover into suspension.

<u>15.1 A–D</u> The three beats of the canter. In right lead canter, Jineen's feet are representing a horse's hind feet, while her hands become his front feet.

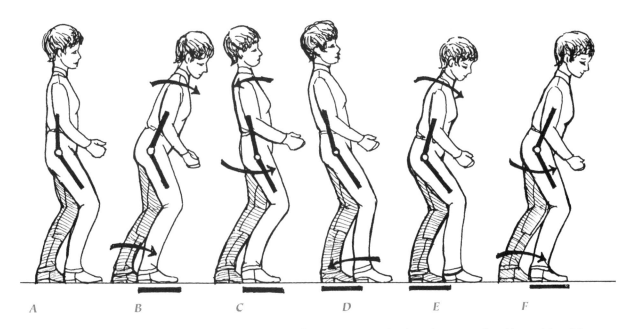

_15.2 A–F_ Feeling the canter motion (right lead) with "Monkey/Reverse Monkey/Monkey," or "closed/open/closed."

(**A**) Balance position: right foot slightly forward. (**B**) "Monkey" (closed): weight on right front foot. (**C**) "Reverse Monkey" (open): weight on right front foot. (**D**) "Reverse Monkey" (open): weight on left back foot. (**E**) "Monkey" (closed): weight on left back foot. (**F**) "Monkey" (closed): weight shifts to right front foot.

corner of one side, and the other foot on the front corner of the other side. Flex your hips, knees, and ankles. Your knees should be flexed forward, and slightly out, and your hips a little closed and back. With your shoulders, head, and arms somewhat forward, balance with your center over your feet in the _Monkey_—the hips-closed position (see p. 109). Now slowly move into _Reverse Monkey_ or hips-open position. Keeping your back straight, open your hip joints until your hips are ahead of your feet and your hip joints are fully opened. Your shoulders will be behind your feet and you will feel that your belt buckle, and the lower half of your body, is leading. Move back and forth between the closed, open, and closed positions several times to review the coordination of ankles, knees, and hips and how they change position relative to each other as you move.

Feeling the Horse's Canter Motion

This _Monkey/Reverse Monkey_ exercise will help you begin to feel how your hip joints can follow the oscillations of the horse's canter.

Another way to "feel" the canter is to think of a _seesaw_. Imagine you are straddling it in its middle over the supporting point. As the end of the seesaw in front of you goes _up_ and you keep your back upright, your hip joints close into _Monkey_ position. When this front end goes _down_, your hip joints open into _Reverse Monkey_ position. This closely resembles the back of the cantering horse—as you can see in the drawings (fig. 15.3). Keeping your back upright leaves all the responsibility of receiving the canter oscillations up to your hip joints, and results in your having a very quiet seat on your horse.

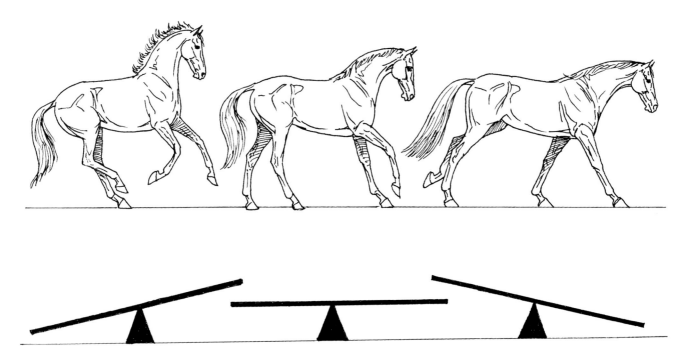

<u>15.3</u> *Phases of the canter showing the "seesaw" effect.*

You can also add to the canter "feelings" discussed above, the image of a surfboard or a ship sliding up, over, and down a wave. Your three joints—ankles, knees, and hips—must coordinate smoothly as the board slides up the wave, close as the board rolls softly over the top, and open as you slide down to start all over again (fig. 15.4).

Feeling the Canter Rhythm

This understanding of motion of the horse's body will help you follow the rhythm. You will be able to improve the timing of your canter aids and influence the balance and quality of the gait. To find out how the horse feels during canter work try slapping out the canter rhythm. While sitting down, clap your hands together once, slap the top of one thigh with one hand, and then slap the other thigh with the other hand. This is your *one-two-three* canter beat. It is similar to the feeling of dancing to a waltz in three-four time. Now back on your feet, and as you may have done as a child, experiment with a nice easy canter and then see what happens when you include some common rider faults, and how much they can influence the horse.

Canter on the wrong lead by turning in a circle to the right leading with your left leg. It is unbalanced (fig. 15.5).

Canter with inconsistent tempo—fast, slow, fast. It is disorganized.

Hold your breath. This makes you stiff (fig. 15.6).

Canter on the forehand leaning too far forward, and looking down. Heavy on your feet, the canter becomes unstable (fig. 15.7).

Canter around a circle, leaning inward. This feels even worse if you go fast.

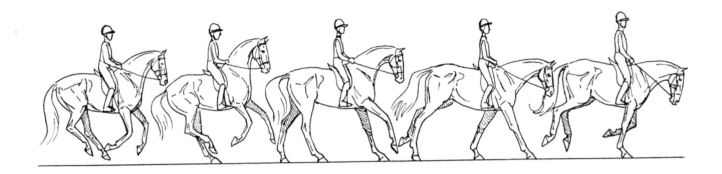

_15.4_ *"Riding the Wave" follows the motion of the canter. Note the slight closing and opening of the hip joints, so the torso remains vertical.*

Canter as if your "rider" is forcing you to go too slowly. This makes you tight, stiff, and restricted.

Canter with a hollow back. This shortens the back of your neck and stiffens you (fig. 15.8).

Canter "flat," without suspension. You land harder on the ground with a dead feeling (fig. 15.9).

Think about becoming upright and in balance and do a round, springy canter. It is actually easier than doing all those canter aberrations, and more athletic and fun. Notice how the quality of your canter improves when you *drop your sacrum* and add the now familiar directives—*ground-center-grow*.

Try some counter-canter. Then skip, and do some flying changes of lead. You will need more spring and suspension, but if you achieve them and stay tall, you will be able to take the weight off each upcoming, new inside leg.

The canter is a joyous gait!

ON THE HORSE

What Makes a Good Canter?

1. Rhythm is essential. Three clean beats without shuffling, or breaking up into a four-beat canter. The canter must also have a steady, constant tempo. A canter does not need to have a lot of speed. A really balanced horse can canter as slowly as he can walk.

2. Correct balance. A horse's balance in the canter is dynamic, not static. The more balanced a horse and the more he is not on his forehand, the easier he will be to ride.

3. Engagement. There are two kinds of engagement, and both have their purposes. "Swinging" engagement where the horse's hind legs swing far forward underneath his body. "Sitting" engagement where the horse

15.5 *The girls are "cantering" to the right on the wrong, left lead. This is awkward, as you can clearly see.*

15.6 *Holding your breath stiffens you and your horse.*

15.7 *"Cantering" on the correct lead, but with their heads down and leaning too far forward the girls are heavy on their feet and unstable.*

15.8 *Notice how the girls' hollow backs cause shortening of their necks and overall stiffening of their bodies.*

<u>15.9</u> *This photo shows a cantering comparison. The girl on the right is "cantering" heavily, without spring, and the girl on the left is "cantering" lightly, with suspension.*

<u>15.10</u> *Claudia is in a deep seat (three-point), with her seat bones over her feet.*

tucks his hindquarters underneath him and "sits," causing him to bend the joints of his hind legs more than usual. I like to think of these joints as *"mattress springs."* In a good canter the horse shifts his weight backward to some degree, and moves with "carrying power."

The more a horse engages his hind legs, the greater his power, spring, balance, and security. Good engagement makes it easy for him to carry his rider. None, or poor engagement can lead to such problems as a weak, flat canter, breaking into a trot, going with a hollow back, and slipping dangerously on a turn.

Learning the Canter

Earlier, at the trot, you learned the exercise of *Three Seats at the Trot*: half-seat, sitting trot, and rising trot, in repeated and prolonged sequences. To help you stay in balance, you can now practice *Two Seats at the Canter*—sitting in an upright, deep (three-point) seat, and the half-seat (two-point). See figures 15.10 and 15.11. When sitting to the canter you will need to allow your pelvis and knees to move forward on the saddle, one at a time, as you keep your seat bones over your stirrups or your feet depending on the type of saddle. When in the half-seat at the canter or gallop, your feet will be more under your knees, with your toes slightly in

_15.11_ *Here, Claudia is cantering in a half-seat (two-point), with her seat bones off the saddle.*

front of an imaginary *plumb line* hanging from your kneecap as your pelvis and knees move back in the saddle (fig. 15.11). Your center will be over your stirrups, and your feet on the stirrups are your base. If you keep your feet squarely under you, you will discover that you can stay quietly in the middle of your horse in either seat. Practice shifting smoothly from the half-seat to sitting, and back again. The transition from half-seat to sitting is easier to establish if you raise the arm on the leading-leg side of the canter over your head, with your fingers softly pointed toward the sky. You will also find that your knee on the leading-leg side will slide slightly more forward

than the other following the horse's leading shoulder as it reaches forward (fig. 15.12). Now canter for a while until you can swing along and fully enjoy the movement.

The movement of your body at the canter should not be overdone. While following the motion of your horse, your center should stay quiet, whether sitting or in the half-seat. Your well-oiled joints can absorb the motion and keep your feet under you. To anyone watching, your body should appear to be still—not moving.

Tension in the knees and thighs is the worst enemy of a good seat in the canter. Too often, the rolling motion of the canter makes the rider feel a

<u>15.12</u> Val is doing "Hand Over the Head." This valuable exercise while cantering helps you soften the inside knee in order to free the horse's shoulder.

bit insecure, so her knees and thighs unconsciously grip the horse. This gripping locks the joints of the knees and hips and causes the rider to bounce on his back. Gripping also upsets the horse by pinching his back, often causing him to tense, speed-up, and hollow his back. To counteract this, you must first be in balance. With each rolling stride release your knees and soften them (even exaggerate and let them go off the saddle a few times) allowing them to drop and your weight to sink down past them into your *grounded* feet. It may help to imagine a thin cushion of air between your knee and the saddle flap. Don't squash it! Let your knees "roll" in a circular motion as if polishing the saddle flap with the fleshy pad at the inside of your knee. (When practicing this, it often helps to concentrate on one knee for a while. As you release one knee, the other will get better too.)

You can practice releasing the knees when sitting deep or in the half-seat. Try riding a steady canter and alternating between deep seat and half-seat for four to five strides of each. Notice that as your knees release, your leg drops softly down and around your horse's barrel, *grounding* your feet and making a soft, rhythmic leg aid at every stride.

The Suspension in the Canter

The rider's sense of suspension, that lovely floating feeling—the place in the canter stride that you want to save—comes from the thrust of the horse's body. This thrust begins on beat two and carries you through beat three into the moment of suspension. Suspension is the point in the stride where you change from *Monkey* to *Reverse Monkey* and the start again of *Monkey* (see p. 175). It is easy to overdo the thrust motion of *Reverse Monkey*. To avoid this, try to float through your *Reverse Monkey*, letting the horse's motion guide you. The longer you can maintain the moment of floating through *Reverse Monkey*, the longer will be your period of suspension. Suspension or "airtime" is essential to a good canter, and it is a necessity for clean flying changes. With suspension, the canter is light, buoyant, and springy. Without it, the canter becomes flat, labored, and hollow, and brilliance and athleticism are lost.

The suspension in the canter comes from the horse engaging his hindquarters–think of it as loading the *mattress springs* (the joints of the hind legs)–which send his body upward. To load the *mattress springs* the horse must shift his balance back a little and "sit" on his hindquarters. The rider must let the horse's back and withers lift up in order to allow this thrust of the horse's body upward. Sitting stiffly, heavily, or out of balance, inhibits this upward thrust.

The gallop has suspension, but it's a different kind. The horse is propelled forward and up, not by him "sitting" and bending his joints, but by the long powerful strides of the gallop and immense swinging engagement of the hind legs.

One simple way to encourage balance and suspension is to "ride the up" in the canter. You have already considered the *seesaw* effect in the canter groundwork section of this chapter, so now try riding the canter to see if you can identify the moment of "up" on the first beat of the canter as the hindquarters come under, and the withers, neck, and forehand rise. At first, just identify the moment of "up." Say "now," or "up," as you feel the front end rise in each stride. For contrast, see if you can also identify the "down" beat (the third beat of the canter), in which the hindquarters come up and the neck and head go down.

Once you can find the "up" moments for six or seven strides in a row, you can begin to rebalance in the "ups." It is easier if you are *breathing*, *centered*, and *grounded*. Let your spine briefly lengthen upward and downward (stretch the *bungee cord* in both directions) on the "up," then release. Don't freeze, and hold it. At first, you may only be able to rebalance on an occasional "up," then per-

haps you will be able to do it on every fourth "up," then every other one, and eventually on every "up" for six, seven, or more strides. Remember, this won't work unless your rebalance is a split-second *ground-center-grow spine lengthening* and release. If your rebalance takes too long, or you freeze and hold it, it locks you up and prevents your horse from responding.

What is the result of rebalancing on the "up"? Your rebalance is timed during the first beat of the canter as the horse's hind legs are coming under him. He increases his engagement, rebalances, and "sits" more on his hocks. Your instant release allows him to send his energy upward in the next stride. Your rebalance asks him to fix his balance momentarily, while it puts your legs on him briefly for more energy. During clinics, when riders practice "riding the up," we often hear comments like, "That's the best balance he's ever had in the canter," "Now he's so easy to ride," and "Hooray, he's actually in balance!"

Straightness and Vertical Balance

Straightness of horse and rider (I discussed straightness in detail in the last session) is essential for good movement in the canter. Moving crookedly, even a little bit, dissipates the horse's energy and stops this energy from coming through the whole horse. It's as though some energy leaks out when the horse is crooked–one hip carried to the inside, or a shoulder bulging out of line. Riders are often amazed at the power and spring they feel when the horse becomes truly straight.

This isn't easy, however, because horses (and riders) are not naturally symmetrical. They have stronger and weaker sides, as well as other body issues such as stiffness and odd habit patterns, which make it easier for them to canter slightly sideways. Horses often do this to spare a weaker hind leg the stress of bending its joints and carrying its share of the load. Riders frequently have one hip joint or side that is tighter, which inhibits the horse's movement on the same side. Consequently, the canter with its diagonal, rolling motion from outside hind to inside foreleg, is often more difficult to straighten than the walk or trot.

Ride on the Train Tracks

Helping the horse to stay really upright, helps his straightness immensely. Imagine that your horse is a train going through turns. Ride a simple corner or circle in the canter, then ask yourself, "Did my 'train' stay upright around the curve, or did he lean dangerously inward threatening to come off the tracks? Did his hind feet stay on the tracks, or skid outward–'losing his caboose?' How about his shoulders? Did they pop out and jump the outside track, or fall in and leave the inside track?"

Once you've identified the part of your horse that tends to leave the rails you can ride through the same turn or circle again prepared to help him. In all cases, keep your own body vertical and turn your center as if shining a headlight from your belt buckle down the track ahead. If the horse starts to "lose his caboose," use your outside leg to say, "No, stay on the tracks." If his shoulders fall in, don't lean with him, stay upright and use your inside leg to remind him to stand up instead of leaning over. If he's popping the outside shoulder and letting it run off the track, sit deep and tall, turn your center a little toward the inside, and use your outside rein to "catch" his shoulder and say, "No, stay on the tracks."

If you are comfortable doing it, you can ride the canter with a small degree of shoulder-in. Sometimes it works best to just "think shoulder-in" as you canter. Remember to stay upright, swivel your center a little to the inside, and use your outside aids to regulate the bend and inside leg to ask for more bend and power.

The Lope

The lope–a Western gait–is a slow, relaxed canter with minimal suspension. It is performed in self-carriage on a light or loose rein. Because it has little suspension or bounce, it is very smooth to ride. The horse should be well balanced, with his hind legs engaged, but a Western horse's balance and frame are usually more horizontal than the more upward-looking and upward-feeling canter of a dressage horse. The lope should always have three clean beats (figs. 15.13 and 15.14). It must never degenerate into a four-beat shuffle, which is a sign of poor balance and engagement (a Western horse should be capable of stopping on his hindquarters at any time). A good lope looks and feels almost effortless to ride, but in reality, it is quite hard work for a horse to lope slowly in good balance. It requires good engagement and use of the hindquarters, back, and shoulders to do well.

Riding the lope feels easy, but it's important to get the details right or the gait will quickly deteriorate. A Western rider is centered, grounded through her feet and seat bones and allows the motion to flow softly through her joints and her whole body. Since she cannot use strong continuous rein pressure on Western bits, she must be especially good at using her body to subtly ask for, and regulate stride, direction, and balance. The *Pianissimo-Crescendo* exercise (see p. 64) is particularly useful in adjusting the horse's stride in the lope. An accomplished Western rider has wonderful "feel," and a soft, subtle, and well timed touch with her reins. She does most of her communicating with her horse through her seat and balance, only using her hands as a finishing touch. As before, it is important to stay vertical to keep the lope straight and balanced laterally, and to turn from deep in your center.

How the Rider Affects the Quality of the Canter

Your position is vital in all canter work. If you plunge your upper body forward in the transition to canter, you will throw your horse onto his forehand, making the transition difficult for him. Again, if you plunge forward over the leading leg

_15.13_ Val, sitting softly, deep, and well-balanced is being rewarded with a lovely three-beat lope.

_15.14_ In order to get Show Lightly to produce this four-beat "shuffle," Val had to significantly alter, and spoil the nice seat that she showed in the previous photo.

as it lands, you will tip him off balance sideways.

How does the rider positively affect the horse's engagement in the canter? First, you do it by riding in balance, with a smooth, non-interfering *following seat*. If you're out of balance backward, the horse will hollow his back, which prevents him from engaging his hind legs. If you're pitched too far forward, he will lean on his forehand instead of "sitting" on his hindquarters.

You also encourage engagement by using your leg and seat aids in rhythm with the canter, and by doing *ground-center-grow* rebalances. These must be modulated to suit the sensitivity of your horse. Even doing the *right* thing too hard or long, is as bad as doing too little, being stiff, holding your breath, or being out of rhythm, which inhibits the horse's rhythm, balance, and engagement.

Be sure to keep *breathing* and let the motion of the horse help your breathing rhythm. A cantering horse will breathe in and out with each stride. The folding and unfolding of his body controls the action of his diaphragm. You should find yourself breathing with *his* stride, whether you breathe with his every stride, or every two or three of his strides. If you get tense and hold your breath, you will find that he does too, and his strides will become choppy and uncomfortable.

Now, using the suggestions I've given you above, you'll find that with some practice you will be able to ride the lope, canter, or gallop anywhere you want. You will be *grounded*, in balance, and have full use of your *Four Basics*. You will have softness, power, and resilience and be able to use any aids you need in the most efficient way.

WHAT ARE THE ESSENTIALS OF The Joyful Canter?

ON THE GROUND

▸ Understand the sequence of the horse's legs when cantering.

▸ Doing *Monkey/Reverse Monkey/Monkey* you'll get the feeling of the canter through your hip, knee, and ankle joints. Think of the *seesaw* effect.

▸ On your own feet, canter correctly and incorrectly. Try right and wrong leads, different breaths, balance, and tempo.

▸ Skip, and try some flying changes.

ON THE HORSE

▸ A good canter has a three-clean-beat rhythm, dynamic balance, steady constant tempo, and engagement with the horse swinging his legs under him and sitting down bending the joints of his hind legs.

▸ Practice *Two Seats at the Canter* in the deep seat, and the half-seat.

▸ At the moment of suspension, float through *Reverse Monkey,* letting the horse's motion guide you.

▸ Ride the *train tracks* to keep your horse straight.

▸ To encourage balance learn to "ride the up." Then, do rebalances on the "up" with split-second *ground-center-grow spine lengthenings*, and release.

WHAT ARE THE RESULTS?

▸ The ability to ride the canter, lope, and gallop with softness, power, and resilience.

16

Hands That Help, Not Hinder

"If you want a horse to 'come to your hand,' you should have a giving hand. Then feed him in your giving hand the food of your well-understood legs, and feel him melt underneath you." Michel Vermeulen (see p. 43), describes good hands to his students in this most delightful way.

How can you achieve an ideal connection with your horse through your hands? First and foremost, to have good hands, your seat must be sensitive, well established, and grounded. Let's assume that by now you have achieved this, and are ready to fine-tune your hands.

ON THE GROUND

Let's begin with some work on the ground. Give yourself a *Shake Out* (see p. 30). As you shake out your wrists, elbows, and shoulders, notice how soft they all become and how your shoulder release affects the ability of your wrists and fingers to release.

Next, you will need to *ground* yourself. Grounding is as essential to having sensitive, skillful hands as it is to all your other work. Begin with a look at how *grounding* affects the use of your hands. Stand comfortably with your arms in a position as if they were holding reins. Now, thoroughly connect yourself with the ground. It might help to use the image of your *Feet in the Sand*. You

do not feel heavier, but only more warmly connected to the ground. You will also notice that you feel taller, and that the *grounding* has softened your shoulders, arms, and hands.

Now experiment a little. Move around and "unground" yourself. Put some stiffness in your hips, knees, and neck. You will discover that you have lost the softness in your hands. Ground yourself once more, and remember the importance of keeping yourself grounded for all your exercises.

As part of *grounding* yourself, *center and grow* as you keep the energy in your center gently rolling backward. Good *use of self* is essential. Remember that *use of self*, and therefore of your hands, must come from your center. Imagine that your shoulders, arms, elbows, and wrists are empty

A

B

C

16.1 A–C Check your shoulders.

(A) Correct: shoulder blades hang naturally behind the rib cage.
(B) Incorrect: shoulders pulled forward and hunched.
(C) Incorrect: shoulder blades pinched and pulled back together.

Check your shoulders. Are your shoulder blades hanging down naturally behind your ribs, not rounded, or tied back close together (fig. 16.1 A–C)? Check the front of your chest, your collarbones, and the points of your shoulders. Are they caved in? Your shoulders should be hanging outward and open, not wrapped around or pointed forward. Check your front and your back. Many people tend to tense themselves forward which over-muscles the front of their bodies. Feel your back drop down, as your front opens up. This takes you to your center. With your arms in the position of holding one rein in each hand, thumbs on top as if following your horse's mouth, find the sensation of connection from your hand along the bottom of your lower arm to your elbow, up the back of your upper arm to your shoulder, and then down your back to your center. Elbows must drop down, not backward. You will find your hands connected to your center, and later to your horse's mouth.

Let's review the position of your arms for holding the reins. Your elbows should hang softly at your sides, not pinched or tight. Your fingers curve softly around the reins with your thumbs on top, and your thumbnails facing up or slightly

conduits through which directives from your center can travel through the reins and to your horse's mouth, and from there, back through his body to his hind feet.

Hands cannot be any better than the arms they are attached to. Arms are no better than the shoulders. Hands, arms, and the shoulder girdle must hang from a centered, balanced, and grounded body. Many problems that appear in the hands originate in the connection of the arms to the body, or in the body itself.

<u>16.2</u> *This is an exercise to help you learn to pick up the reins correctly. Your arm and hand rotate as you swim the backstroke, and you rotate your hand at the top of each stroke so that it always pushes water away. This "scooping" motion is what you are looking for when you pick up your reins.*

inward. This position is necessary whether you hold your reins with one hand or two, whether you ride English or Western. This position allows the two bones in your forearm to lie parallel to each other and the muscles on the insides of your forearms to be soft and supple. If you hold your hands so that your knuckles are on top, your arm bones will cross each other and your forearm muscles will become tight and unyielding.

Many riders share the common bad habit of riding with their elbows out like chicken wings. If you put your arms in this position, you will no-

tice that it encourages your knuckles rather than your thumbs to be on top and tends to pull your shoulders down and round. This round-shouldered posture will induce your horse to drop onto his forehand. The most effective position for holding your reins is, therefore, thumbs up, shoulders hanging open, and elbows at your sides.

Try an exercise that will help you learn automatically to pick up the reins correctly. Make big, backward circles with your arms as if you are swimming the backstroke, pushing the water with open hands. As each hand comes in front of you, the thumb will be on top. This scooping motion is what you should feel when picking up your reins (fig. 16.2).

Now make yourself comfortable, sitting or standing, and consider the flexibility of all the joints in each hand. Notice that each finger actually begins at the end of each wrist. If you have a pair of t'ai chi balls, bring them out for play exercise. With the two balls in one hand, move them all around, using all your fingers. Roll them over each other. You will find that rolling them over one way is fairly easy, but rolling them the other way may feel quite difficult. Keep working at it. It will probably be easier to roll them both ways with one hand more than the other. This exercise frees your fingers to move independently, and will help them be soft when holding the reins.

Feeling the Reins

To improve your understanding and feel of your horse's mouth through the reins, you can do an exercise with a partner. You will need reins for this activity. If real reins are not immediately available, lengths of clothesline, or even soft dog leashes, work well instead. Sit facing each other on hard chairs, sitting upright and forward on the seats so that you don't use the backs of the chairs. Once again, one of you will be the "horse," receiving directives, while the other one is the rider,

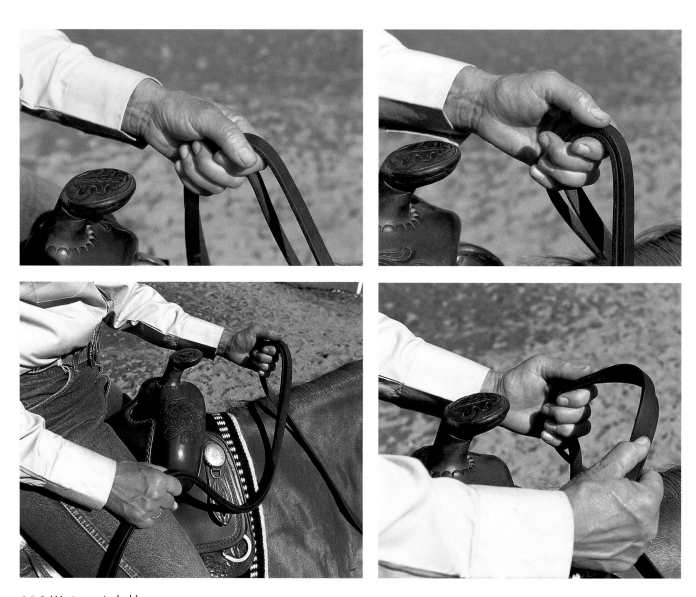

_16.3_ Western rein holds.

providing them. It is most effective if the horse closes her eyes. You will be experimenting with how sensitive these directives can become. If you ride Western, you will still benefit from the following exercises, which are explained as if you were riding English. The drawings (figs. 16.3 and 16.4) illustrate common, acceptable Western and English rein holds.

Pick up your reins, one in each hand, thumbs on top. The rein comes from the bit to between your ring and little finger, and goes up and over your first finger with your thumb on top. In this way, your thumb and first finger keep the rein from slipping, while your ring finger, with its direct connection to the bit, is the one most responsible for the conversation between you and the horse.

16.4 *English rein holds.*

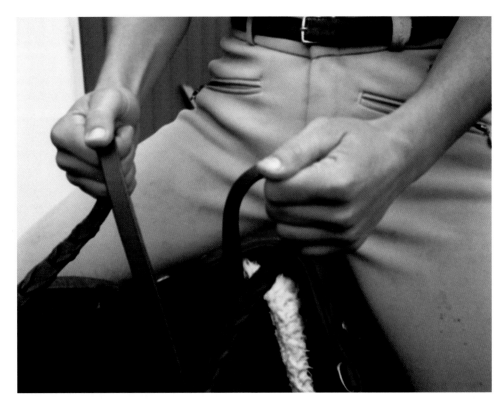

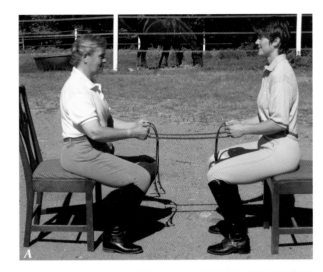

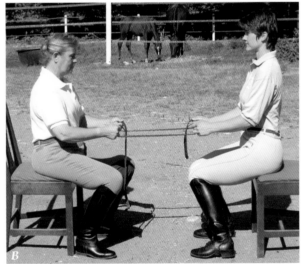

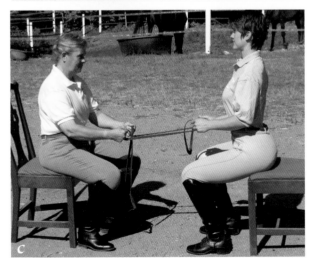

Have your partner–playing the horse–pick up the reins in her soft fists and hold them as if her hands were the horse's mouth. Now make a comfortable connection with this "horse's" mouth through the reins. The horse partner can move her hands gently back and forth to imitate the horse's head motion at the walk. You, the rider partner, will need to follow this motion. In order to do this sensitively, you must check your *use of self*, become *grounded* in your feet and seat, have both your seat bones headed straight down, and your torso, head, and neck tall and balanced above them. Remember to *center* yourself, *breathe*, and use *soft eyes*. From your center, allow your hands to follow your horse's mouth with contact–without resistance or a slack rein (fig. 16.5 A). The horse partner may find that a slight backward circular motion with her hands will approximate the motion of a horse.

Begin to think in terms of "feel"–the feel of the reins in your hands, the feel of the connection with your horse's mouth, and the quality of the feel. Thinking about feel softens the hands. A sensitive feel cannot be found through tight fists, so if you find yourself making tight fists, stop and begin again.

After savoring how pleasant this feel is for both horse and rider, you can try a few alternatives. Re-

16.5 A–C "Feeling the Reins." Claudia, the girl on the right, is the "rider."

(A) A comfortable connection: note Claudia's soft and grounded body—you can sense the depth and resilient "heaviness" in her seat. Lucy (the horse) is relaxed.
(B) Claudia pinches her knees together and her back tightens. Her arms and shoulders become tense and the reins "hard." Lucy hangs on. (C) This time, Claudia really hollows her back and tenses her entire body, which makes her feel like a piece of wood to Lucy, who you can see is getting irritated at the lack of sensitivity.

strict or hold your breath. Clench your fingers around the reins, or pinch your knees together (fig. 16.5 B). Use hard eyes, or tighten your buttocks and hollow your lower back (fig. 16.5 C). Lean too far back or slump. Sit crookedly in your chair. You will discover that all of these activities will cause your horse partner to become resistant and even annoyed. She may try to evade you by pulling the reins out of your hands. You, in turn, may find yourself becoming angry with her! So *center*, *ground*, and quiet yourself and remember the gentle power of the *Unbendable Arm*. You will find your horse partner cooperating with you once more.

You are beginning to discover the feel of a sensitive hand. Now let's explore how you will have to use your hands in your directives to the real horse. Your objective is to have your horse become sensitive and easily responsive to your aids. In order to do this, your horse will have to maintain his balance so that his forehand is light. You will have to help him with this balance, because a horse is built with more of his weight carried on his front legs than his hind legs. However, if at any time, you take a steady, strong hold on the reins, you will find your horse saying, "If you want to hold up my front end, I'm happy to let you," and he will become heavy on his forehand, losing his engagement.

So now with your horse partner, try some directives for these all-important transitions and turns, which help your horse become light and agile. Most people tend to start communication with a horse through the reins. After all, we can see the reins and the front end of the horse when we are riding. However, it is the back end of the horse that we need for all our starts and changes of movement. So now, begin by *centering* yourself so that your directives will come from your body first and then through your hands.

Try a down transition. *Ground* your seat as you quiet your hands. Your horse partner should understand without any need for you to pull on the reins. If you find that your directive needs to be stronger, use the quality of the *Unbendable Arm*, as well as *clear intent*, along with your *grounding*. This will give you a gentle and irresistible power, which your horse partner will not oppose if you ask and then give several times.

Sensitivity Exercises

Try experimenting with turns. Remember to initiate the turn by rotating the *ball* in your center (p. 40). Point your belt buckle in the direction you want to go. You will find that this small motion will take your hands along as well as your torso and shoulders. Your hands actually play a secondary role in initiating the turn; the directive for the turn comes from your center. Now switch roles with your partner to experience how it feels to receive these directives through the reins.

To help improve the sensitive and effective use of your hands, try some further exercises before you get on your horse. Once again, hold your arm in a position as if you were holding reins. Have your partner place one hand on your arm just above the wrist and her other hand on your hand just below the wrist. With good *use of self*, your partner should let her hands separate almost imperceptibly, suggesting that you allow there to be an extra inch of length and space in your wrist (fig. 16.6). It will feel as if you are emptying your wrist. Notice how your fingers on that hand become very soft and sensitive, and attentive to your center.

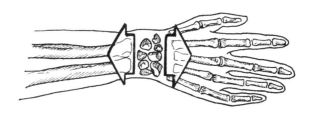

16.6 This is what it feels like when you allow your wrist to lengthen.

<u>16.7</u> *Have your partner encompass your wrist in her hand so it cannot bend. You get the feeling of how soft your straight wrist can be.*

Many riders have difficulty maintaining their connection to the horse because they allow their wrists to break inward, thus interrupting the feel to the horse's mouth. Here is another exercise with your horse partner that can help you avoid this common problem. Allow a straight line along the outside of your forearm to continue along the back of your hand to your knuckles. Have your partner gently enclose your wrist with her hand, as if it were a plaster cast, so you cannot bend your wrist (fig. 16.7). Notice how soft the muscles on the inside of your forearm become, and how easily you can manipulate your fingers from this position.

This will help you learn to use your fingers without bending your wrists.

Now stand up and try some experiments while walking. With your fingers around the stems, take full champagne or wine glasses in both hands and walk around the room. Notice how much easier it is to not spill the "champagne" when you are grounded, centered, and soft with your fingers, than when you tighten and hold the glass stems with tense hands.

Try walking around the room while carrying a large bowl with a ball in it (fig. 16.8). A t'ai chi ball works well, but any small ball will do. Hold the bowl loosely with your arms relaxed, your thumbs just under the outside of the rim, and two or three fingers underneath. Experiment with what you need to do to keep the ball quiet in the bowl, not rolling around, as you walk. You will quickly discover that you must not try too hard, hold your breath, or keep a tight hold on the bowl with your hands. If you try to keep the bowl still by tightening your hands, the ball will roll around rapidly. Instead, balance your pelvis by softening your hip joints, and *dropping your sacrum*. Use your *Basics*: *ground* yourself, keep *soft eyes*, *breathe* easily, *center* yourself, and maintain *your spine lengthening* both up and down. Remember to use your *Unbendable Arm* quality as well, and you will discover that your hands become very sensitive in the way they carry the bowl, and the ball will be surprisingly quiet inside it. You would like to have this quality of hands when you communicate with your horse through the reins and bit.

ON THE HORSE

After you are comfortable and at ease on your horse, and before we get into specifics, do these shoulder exercises. Lift the tips of your shoulders straight up and let them drop limp three times. Lift them up and then back and let them drop limp

16.8 Lucy is carrying a large bowl with a tennis ball (it can be any small ball) in it. She is experimenting how to move while keeping the ball as still as possible.

down, and vice versa. Last, give your shoulders a *Shaggy Dog Shake* and see how great you feel.

Now you can apply some of the groundwork exercises on your horse. As you pick up your reins, remember the swimming-the-backstroke motion (see p. 191). Using this as you begin will help to not only bring your hands into the correct, thumbs-up position when you pick up your reins, but will also open your shoulders and the front of your body.

As you walk on your horse, review your *Four Basics* and *grounding.* Find that pleasant connection from your center through your hands to your horse's mouth. From your center, you can allow your hands to follow the motion of his head and neck through your well-oiled shoulders and elbows. As you felt with your partner on the ground, you may find your horse moving your hands in a slightly backward, circular motion.

Keep your reins short enough so that your hands are not back near your belly but are slightly reaching and have a forward feel through them. The energy flow must always feel forward, even during a down transition. Try imagining champagne bubbles floating forward through your arms, wrists, fingers, and reins to your horse's mouth.

After you achieve your pleasant connection with your horse's mouth, try some of the incorrect alternatives that you experimented with on the ground. Your horse may become annoyed with you, so apologize to him after each unsatisfactory experiment by softening your hands. You can try holding your breath, using hard eyes, putting your center high up rather than low in your body, pinching with your knees, tightening your buttocks, sitting off balance, or stiffening any part of your arms or hands. It will become obvious how your *Basics* and *use of self* are integral to the connection of your hands to your horse's mouth.

Combing the Reins

There is an effective way of asking the horse to reach softly down into the bit with an exercise

three times. Take them forward, up, back, and down three times. Then the other way around: back, up, forward, and down. Do a different type of circle where, instead of moving your shoulders identically, allow one to lift while the other goes

16.9 A & B "Combing the Reins."

(A) *Starting with her hands high, Beth reaches with one hand on both rein as far forward as she comfortably can. Her index finger pointing down divides the reins.*

called "combing the reins." With your first finger pointing down between the reins, take the reins softly in one hand as far forward as you can comfortably reach (figs. 16.9 A & B). Now draw your hand back toward your center, softly letting the reins slide through your fingers as you extend your other hand to repeat the motion. This repetitive motion will encourage your horse to relax his back and jaw and he will want to reach down toward the ground as your hands gradually lower. The unfamiliar position of your hands as you comb the reins is also an excellent tool for developing the "feel" of soft hands connected to your center, as well as helping to loosen your shoulders, whether you ride English or Western.

Switching Hands

Another interesting exercise for discovering feel and softness involves shifting your reins from one hand to the other as you put the other hand behind your back (fig. 16.10). Try this leisurely at the walk and then more rapidly at the walk, trot, and

(B) *She then draws this hand softly back to her center. She constantly repeats the exercise alternating hands until the horse's head gradually lowers.*

"Switching Hands." Beth is shifting the reins from one hand to the other, alternately placing her free hand behind her back. This is a good exercise for discovering feel and softness.

canter. Not only will this help you become adept at changing reins in your hands without disturbing your horse, but you will also discover that it cannot be done if you keep your shoulders and arms tense, are unbalanced, or hold your breath. Try doing this exercise for a number of times around the ring, and you will find yourself centered, laughing, relaxed, and feeling carefree with a happy horse under you. Notice how grounded you have become in your seat and legs, and how relaxed your arms and shoulders are. You are on

your way to developing those all important "feeling hands."

It is important in the rising trot that your hands do not move up and down with you as you rise up and down. They must stay still and level in relation to the horse's withers. Therefore, as you rise up, your elbow joint must open, and then close again as you come down. I help my students appreciate how much motion is needed in that elbow joint by standing beside the horse, stabilizing my arm against the horse's shoulder and offering my finger for the student to hold as if it were the rein. When the rider (with the horse standing still) goes up and down as if rising to the trot, she must not pull my finger up and down. If she does, I protest loudly! Once you realize the amount of elasticity needed in the elbow, it will become easier for you to trot with quiet hands.

Now, using your *Basics, ground-center-grow* and ride your horse at all three gaits. Incorporate some turns into your work making sure that your body carries your hands along with it. It is easy to make the mistake of rotating the torso but leaving the hands behind in an awkward and ineffective position. Visualize a flashlight beam that shines from your center out through your belt buckle in the direction you want to go. The flashlight beam should always shine out between your two hands.

With correct understanding and *use of self,* you will be able to maintain the connection to your horse, and discover that you are using your hands to feed your horse the "food of your well-understood legs." ⌇

WHAT ARE THE ESSENTIALS OF Hands That Help, Not Hinder?

ON THE GROUND

- ▶ Good hands require a good seat.
- ▶ Soft hands require being well grounded.
- ▶ Imagine your shoulders, arms, elbows, and wrists are empty conduits through which directives from your center can travel through the reins.
- ▶ Review the position of your shoulders, collarbones, chest, and arms.
- ▶ Just thinking about "feel"–the feel of the reins in your hands and their connection to your horse's mouth–will soften your hands.
- ▶ *Feeling the Reins* exercises: turns with little rein. Initiate by *centering, grounding,* rotating the *ball,* and pointing your belt buckle in the direction you want to go.

ON THE HORSE

- ▶ Think about "swimming the backstroke" to pick up reins correctly.
- ▶ *Combing Reins* to develop feel.
- ▶ *Switching Hands* exercise for sensitivity and softness when shifting reins from one hand to another.
- ▶ Elasticity in elbows to keep arms and hands steady in the rising trot.

WHAT ARE THE RESULTS?

- ▶ You will be able to feed your horse "the food of your well understood legs, and feel him melt underneath you."

17

SESSION THIRTEEN

Centered Jumping

BY SUSAN E. HARRIS

It is a long time since I have taught jumping, and even longer since I, myself, have been over a fence. Therefore, I did not feel comfortable about writing a chapter on Centered Jumping. Susan Harris, a Level IV Senior Centered Riding Instructor, was one of my early apprentices, and is currently teaching jumping using the full complement of Centered Riding techniques. I feel she is uniquely qualified to do the job. I am grateful to her for putting together the following chapter.

Along with Susan, I feel that jumping is an integral and important part of all riding. Jumping is a large subject so this chapter has become quite long in comparison with other subjects covered in this book, but Susan has given such clear, comprehensive, and sensible instructions that I do not want to sacrifice any piece of her work for the sake of brevity. By following her advice, both the beginner as well as the more experienced rider will gain knowledge that will make her more capable, and therefore more safe, to enjoy whatever her level of jumping might be.

Jumping is an integral part of riding. It should not be seen as something difficult, dangerous, or completely different from good basic horsemanship. While you do need good basics in flatwork and a correct and safe approach to jumping, it isn't necessary to wait until you're perfect on the flat before you can think of learning to jump. Such an approach tends to intimidate people by making jumping too much of a "big deal." On the other hand, you must be balanced, secure, and in control enough to handle the extra thrust caused by riding over cavaletti poles or jumps. Encouraging a beginner to jump before she can even canter safely is asking for trouble!

A low jump is much like a canter stride but bigger and rounder. Basic jumping exercises, such as those using cavaletti poles and low gymnastics, can help you learn to stay in balance and use your joints to absorb bigger movements in rhythm, while your horse learns to use his back, legs, and body better. Even if you are not interested in the jumping sports, or don't ever want to jump higher than a few inches, basic jumping exercises can help your balance, flexibility, and security, giving you extra confidence when your horse shys or bucks.

No jump takes place in a vacuum. The line you choose, and the pace, balance, rhythm, timing, and impulsion throughout the approach, all combine to produce the kind of jump you get. Each jump is part of a line, a course, a performance, or just getting from one field into another. Most difficulties in jumping are actually problems that occur when riding between the fences, and it is there that most jumping problems will be solved.

Jumping bigger fences means dealing with more power, thrust, and speed, and the elements of approach, takeoff, and timing become more critical. A jump is a brief moment in time and a good jumping rider's reactions are automatic, almost reflexive. Often in competition, schooling over larger fences, or other demanding jumping, you have little or no time to think about how you should use your body; instead, you must rely on your habits and reflexes. When learning to jump, it's important to take time to put the right things into your pattern of balance and movement, as this is what your body will revert to whenever you jump. It is much more difficult to fix incorrectly learned habits than it is to develop the right habits in the first place.

ON THE GROUND

The groundwork for jumping uses many of the Centered Riding concepts you have learned earlier in this book. In this chapter, you will learn how they apply to jumping, along with some exercises and ideas specifically designed for jumping and work in a half-seat.

How the Four Basics and Grounding Apply to Jumping

The *Four Basics* and *grounding* are as essential in good jumping, as they are in everything else you do in riding. I'm reviewing them briefly below emphasizing how they pertain specifically to jumping. It's important to learn and practice these *Four Basics*, first on the flat, then in simple exercises and low gymnastics over ground poles, cavaletti, and crossrails. Once you have established use of the *Basics* as a habit, it will be much easier to apply them over the size and type of fences you school, or compete over. If you complicate the process by trying to learn the *Basics* while jumping demanding fences, you will be distracted and the results may be disappointing. As you have discovered in your work in this book so far, the *Basics* are interrelated. If you use one, it enables you to use the others.

Soft Eyes

How you use your eyes in jumping can make a tremendous difference since eye control is essential for control, balance, and safety. A jumping rider can have three kinds of eyes: *"no eyes," hard eyes*, and *soft eyes*.

Having "*no eyes*" means that you don't know how to use your eyes, or you lack eye control; you may shift your eyes from point to point, or worse, look down over a jump. This causes your head and balance to shift unexpectedly; the horse feels it and may falter, change his balance, jump awkwardly, or refuse.

Hard eyes, which are fixed tightly on a point, are better than "no eyes" because they at least keep your head and upper body in balance, and enable you to see and ride your chosen line over a jump. However, the price you pay for over-focused eyes is mental and physical tension. This tension tightens your body and locks your joints, and is transmitted to your horse. It also blocks "feel," and can interfere with seeing a takeoff distance. The narrow focus, or tunnel vision, associated with hard eyes makes it difficult to be aware of what is going on around you, such as another rider approaching your path in a crowded schooling area.

As you know by now, *soft eyes*, when focused on a specific target at eye-level in line with the center of the jump, but relaxed and able to view the area around the target with wide-angle vision, are the best way to use your eyes when jumping. They allow you to see your line, the jump, the area around it, and enable you to feel your horse's pace, rhythm, balance, and stride better in order to see a distance. They also increase your physical awareness of your body and your horse, improving your feel.

Breathing

Jumping is more physically demanding than flat-work so good *breathing* is essential. Breathing well frees your body to move in a supple, athletic way. It also oxygenates your body, which helps stave off fatigue and lets your muscles function more efficiently without cramping—very important in jumping cross-country, or over a demanding stadium course. Breathing deeply with the diaphragm lowers your center of gravity, making you deeper and more stable, and helps you stay relaxed and supple. Taking time to breathe can help you wait for a jump instead of anticipating, and you will find that you seem to have more time to think when you remember to breathe.

Many riders hold their breath, or breathe high and tight in the chest when jumping. It's some-times from fear or nervousness, but often just from excitement or effort. Holding your breath, or breathing tightly, raises your center up higher, which makes you feel unstable and top heavy, so you may tend to either get left behind the motion of the horse or overcompensate by standing up and jumping ahead of it. It also stiffens your body and locks up your joints, especially the hip joints, which makes it hard to absorb the thrust of the jump, the shock of landing, or let your weight sink down into your feet for security. When you breathe in, you must not hold it, but let yourself exhale as your horse jumps. Breathing allows you to feel and to be one with your horse.

Centering

In jumping, *centering* enables "feel," rhythm, and timing. It is especially important when riding with *clear intent*, which is essential for control without conflict. Centering also helps you stay calm and confident, shut out extraneous influences, and re-member your course and how you plan to ride it.

Building Blocks

In jumping, as in other riding, balance is dynamic, not static. Your *building blocks*—your balance—must be united with the balance of your horse, with your center remaining over your feet and over the horse's center of balance through the approach, takeoff, flight, landing, and as your horse resumes his gait after landing. Jumping in good balance feels secure and is exhilarating, but even a small loss of balance can make you involuntarily stiffen, grip, or overcompensate. Nothing is more demoralizing to a horse than feeling his balance threatened by an unstable rider when he is trying to get to the other side of a jump. When balance is lost, both you and your horse can lose your confidence.

When jumping, the rider is in the *half-seat*, and her *building blocks* are a balance of angles, instead of the vertical "stacking" of the body in the *deep seat*. The angles of your upper body, thigh, lower leg and foot, as well as the angles of your upper arm and lower arm, change to follow the movement and absorb shock as the horse's body rises, rounds, hollows, and dips during the jump. If your center is misplaced, or any of your angles are not functioning correctly, your balance suffers and your body will have to clutch, grip, or try to save you in some way.

Grounding

Grounding can make you feel safe and secure over a jump, as if you are standing on the ground. In jumping, *grounding* means feeling where your feet are, underneath your body, and the ability to allow your weight to settle deep into your feet and legs. It also helps you keep your center low, over the center of the saddle and your horse's balance point, instead of being thrust precariously forward, up, or backward, away from your horse. True *grounding* is accomplished by letting your weight sink past the knees into your feet and ankles, which also keeps your center lower and in a better place for balance and security. Only when you feel securely grounded can you release your joints to absorb the thrust of the jump and the shock of landing, or allow your hands and arms to follow the horse's balancing gestures freely and sensitively.

"Heels down" is essential in jumping, but overdoing it or getting your heels down incorrectly can create problems almost as serious as riding with your heels up or with insecure, swinging legs. In an effort to get their heels down, many riders jam their heels down as far down as they can, locking their ankle joints and driving their feet forward. This stiffens all your leg joints, making you stiff, ungrounded, and pushing your center of gravity (and your center) up where it makes you less stable.

Grounding of the Feet

Grounding the feet is essential in jumping; it gives you a wonderful sense of balance and security. Especially in landing from a jump, *grounding* gives you the sensation of landing on your feet, instead of being pitched forward onto your knees, or backward on your seat. Review the *Bubbling Spring* (see p. 38); *Feet in the Sand* (see p. 37); jumping up and down in the *Horse Stance* position, (see p. 111); and the *Chair Exercise* (see p. 126).

Try this *grounding* exercise: stand with your feet about shoulder-width apart, toes at a comfortable angle (not forced in or out), and knees slightly bent. "Think" your way around the edge of one foot, feeling its contact with the ground. Consider a suction cup. In order to stick to a flat surface, all the edges of the suction cup must be in contact with the surface. Does one part of your foot touch the ground less than another? Now, explore the inner surface of your foot and the way it contacts the ground. Experiment with shifting your weight very slowly, in tiny increments—toward the front, toward the rear, and into the center of the foot. Can you locate the *Bubbling Spring* point? Finally, compare the foot you have been exploring with your other foot. Which one feels wide, solid, and deep in the ground. Which can receive your weight better? Which foot would be a better base on which to balance yourself?

Balance in a Half-Seat
Jumping Position: the Teeter-Totter

A good jumping position gives you a basis from which your body adapts to the horse's thrust, balance, and movement. This position is never fixed or rigid, but it must be functional.

The *Teeter-Totter* (see p. 36) helped you discover the freedom and security that comes from being in true balance. Repeating this exercise in a jumping position will help you find a balance that is very secure, at the same time freeing your joints to absorb thrust and shock. It is also the least fatiguing balance position—a real advantage for not only cross-country jumpers, but foxhunters, trail and distance riders, and anyone else who must ride for long periods in the half-seat or galloping positions.

To find a central balance in a jumping seat (whether half-seat, or galloping position), place your feet about shoulder-width apart and let your knees and hips bend equally as you fold into the jumping position. Keep your neck and back long and flat, and look ahead but not excessively high. Shift your weight slightly forward and backward until your weight is distributed evenly over your feet and you do not feel extra tension in your calf muscles or the muscles of the front of your thigh.

Now shift your weight backward, over your heels. Which parts of your body tighten up to keep you from falling over backward? Do you stiffen up and lose your flexibility? Shift your weight back to a central position and check your balance again. Try shifting your weight forward so that most of your weight is over your toes. Where do you feel tension, and what happens to your joints? Finding this central balance will give you an efficient, comfortable, and secure jumping position that you can maintain while trotting, cantering, galloping, or jumping.

Your Joints as Springs and Shock Absorbers

Joints are where movement takes place; in jumping, they are your *springs* and *shock absorbers*. Good use of your joints helps you go smoothly with your horse's movement, absorb the shock and thrust of jumping, and keeps you safe, secure, and comfortable; it also makes you much easier for your horse to carry. Your ankle, knee, and hip joints are the major shock absorbers; they protect your back and enable your other joints to work smoothly. Joints are vulnerable to injury if overstressed or misused. The shorter stirrups used in jumping bring the joints into greater play, and consequently put more stress on them if they are not used correctly.

In order to use your joints well, your body must be in balance—the long bones need to be in their natural alignment. In addition, the muscle

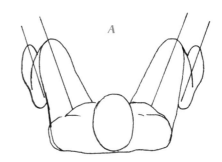

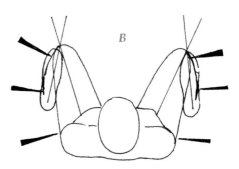

_**17.1 A & B**_ _The angles of the feet._

(A) *The angle of the foot should be the same as the angle of the knee.* (B) *Forcing the toes in more than the angle of the knee stresses the ankle, knee, and hip joints.*

tone should be balanced. If the muscles on one side of a joint are tighter than on the other, not only does the joint lose its flexibility, there will be extra stress on the joint, bones, muscles, tendons, and ligaments.

When you are in natural alignment, the long axis of your foot (or the direction in which your toes are pointed) should be parallel to the direction of your femur (thighbone) (fig. 17.1 A). Forcing the toes and foot inward parallel to the horse's side, rolls the foot sideways on the stirrup tread, locks the ankle joint, and prevents the foot and ankle from *grounding* properly and sinking under the rider's weight (fig. 17.1 B). (The opposite position—

excessive toeing out—pulls the knee, thigh, and inside of the leg away from the horse, and causes the rider to grip with the back of the calf.) With jumping-length stirrups, most riders' knees and feet will point out a bit more than they do with longer stirrups. It may help to remember to let your knees go out over your toes (review the *Deep Knee Bend* exercise, p. 124). It's also important to allow the whole width of the foot to lie evenly across the stirrup, instead of rolling the foot sideways and riding on the inside or outside edge of the foot.

To experience this on the ground again, place your feet about shoulder-width apart and point your toes straight ahead, or even a little bit inward. Begin to sink down, bending your knees. Stop when you begin to feel discomfort. Do your feet begin to roll sideways, onto the outside edges? Notice where your joints are complaining, the outside of the knee, ankle, or elsewhere?

Stand back up and readjust the angles of your feet; let your toes point outward a little—about 15 degrees outward from straight ahead. This time let your knees go out over your big toes as you sink down. Can you sink lower with less stress and better balance? Try turning your toes outward too far, and notice where the strain occurs as you sink down. Also, notice which position allows your feet to stay *grounded* and helps you keep your balance better. Don't overdo this exercise—it should help you find the most efficient way to use yourself, not stress your joints.

Toes and knees that stick out excessively often go along with a hollow back and a tight band of muscles across the back of your sacrum and lower back. If you can *center* yourself, *breathe,* and allow your *spine to lengthen and widen,* you may feel more freedom in your hips and thighs, and your entire leg may become more correctly aligned.

Now that you have found a balanced alignment for your legs and feet, test your *springs* by bouncing softly in place in a rhythm similar to a slow jog trot. (It may help to do this on a jogging trampoline.) Notice that there are two parts to each springing motion: one, sinking down, and two, releasing your joints to handle the upward rebound. You may find that one or the other is more difficult for you. Check your balance, including the balance of your head and neck, center, spine, and the distribution of your weight over your feet, and remember to *breathe*—people often forget to breathe when they are thinking. The better your balance and *springs*, the easier it will be to stay deep, safe, and secure when jumping.

Opening, Closing, and Freeing the Hip Joint

The rider folds, or "closes down," into a balanced crouch as the horse takes off; the angles of the hips, knees, and ankles close and open to follow the changing thrust and movement of the horse's body as he jumps. You can't guess which angle will be needed and try to assume that position beforehand. Instead, you must stay in balance and just allow the thrust and motion of the horse to open and close your angles as needed. This is a key component in jumping without getting ahead of, or behind the motion, and being safe and secure over fences.

Your hip joint plays a major role in the angle. Ideally, your legs and feet remain under your body and quiet on the horse's side, and the flexing and opening of the hip, knee, and ankle joints allow your body to go with the jump. However, excessive tension can lock up your hip joints and interfere with the free, smooth, and balanced opening and closing of this essential angle. When this happens, the hip joint doesn't completely freeze up, but it becomes less mobile than it should be and closes superficially, instead of deep in the joint. Stiffness in the hip joints will cause the legs to pivot forward or backward out of position. Some riders bend at the waist instead of flexing enough in the hip joints, causing a round, or "roached," back. Hips

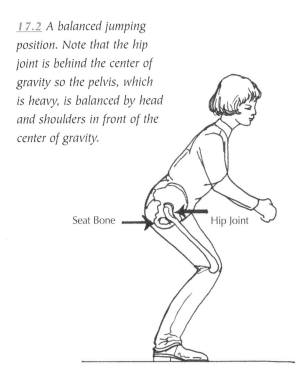

**17.2** A balanced jumping position. Note that the hip joint is behind the center of gravity so the pelvis, which is heavy, is balanced by head and shoulders in front of the center of gravity.

Seat Bone — Hip Joint

that are tight may fail to fold enough so the rider falls behind the motion, or they may fold too little and then tip the rider forward, making her precarious and ahead of the motion.

In Chapter 5, you explored the location and structure of the hip joint while standing upright. Now I want you to review this in a jumping-seat position. Locate the front of the hip joints with your fingers, but realize that the ball of the femur and the actual hip joint are deep inside. The ball of the femur is about 2 inches in diameter–about the size of the ball on a trailer hitch. As you sink into a half-seat jumping position (with your hands as if you were holding reins), breathe out and feel your hip joints closing deep and far back inside the socket. Notice also that as the hip joint folds deep in the socket, your pelvis tips and your seat bones slide backward, pointing _back_ and _down_ (fig. 17.2). This is quite a different feeling from the one you get when doing this exercise in an upright, deep-seat position.

Stand up and try it again, but this time hold your breath, and tighten your seat and hips. Notice that if you fold only at the front of the hip joint, you tend to lose your balance more easily. Your seat bones do not slide as far back, and they may point back and even _up_, like a bird with a turned-up tail.

Practice again, by breathing out and allowing your hips to close smoothly and farther back up in the joint; you will find that you can sink deeper and more quickly, as if jumping a big fence, but with less strain. Allowing your knees and toes to line up naturally will also help; you can't have free hips with tight knees!

Control and Lengthen the Spine and Torso

Your head, neck, and spine are the essentials in the balance of your upper body when jumping and riding the approach to a fence. They should work together as a coordinated unit, keeping your balance together in a manageable "package" instead of breaking up into many uncoordinated separate parts. This unit needs some muscle tone to keep it from becoming loose, floppy, and uncontrollable, but it also needs spring, resilience, and grace. Smooth, balanced control of the upper body is crucial for independent hands and control of your horse. The ideal back appears flat (although it still has the natural curves of the spine), not tensely arched, or round and slumped.

The best way to achieve a good functional back and upper body for jumping work is to keep _letting your spine lengthen,_ as you have practiced all through this book. Even though the back is angled forward more than in the upright, deep seat, it is equally important to lengthen the spine. A hollow back is a shortened back, and a round (or roached) back shortens the front of the spine. Both positions stress the back and make it harder to keep your balance and use your joints as _springs_.

When learning to jump, it is common to hear instructors say, "Hollow the loins," or "Arch your

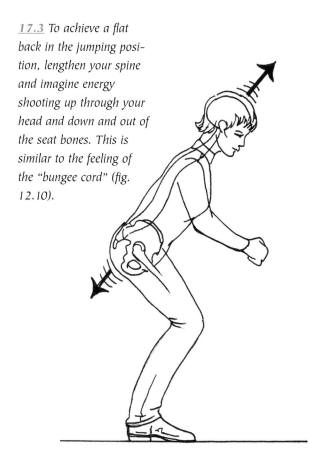

17.3 To achieve a flat back in the jumping position, lengthen your spine and imagine energy shooting up through your head and down and out of the seat bones. This is similar to the feeling of the "bungee cord" (fig. 12.10).

back." These commands go back to the very beginning of the forward seat as taught by Federico Caprilli, and they are still a common way of getting a slouching rider to straighten up. However, hollowing the loins, or arching the back is often overdone, causing a stiff, tipped-forward pose that causes stress, stiffness, and lower back pain. *Lengthening the spine* is a better way to achieve a flat, functional back, along with a more athletic way of using the body.

Try folding into a jumping position over your feet, allowing your spine to lengthen briefly. For this exercise, allow the top of your head to follow the same angle as your spine (fig. 17.3). As you take a breath, notice the lengthening of your head, neck and rib cage along the angle of your upper body. During your next breath, notice the slight stretch in your lower back, loins, and abdomen, and the space

between your last ribs and the top of your hipbones. Notice how your sacrum and seat bones seem to stretch backward and downward for a split second, lengthening the lower part of your back and seat.

Another way to achieve this lengthening is to imagine a rubber band running through your spine being briefly stretched in both directions, out the top of your head, and out of your seat bones. Notice that when your spine briefly lengthens, your hip joints, knees, and shoulders, also become free and elastic.

Head and Neck: Looking Ahead Without Tightening Up

Your head and neck are the top of your balance, and the head is one of the key components in balance, direction, and control. The human head weighs 10 to 13 lbs—about the same weight as a bowling ball—so the balance of your head (a heavy weight at the top of your body), has a strong effect on your overall balance. Your horse feels and reacts to quite small movements of your head, especially when you look down or to the side. Countless riders have found out that a quick peek down at the base of a fence can trigger a mistake on takeoff, a refusal, or even cause them to jump the fence without the horse!

Your eyes control the position and direction of your head, and therefore lead your balance, especially in the split-second timing of jumping, so it is important to look up and ahead when jumping. Just keeping your eyes up is not enough—you need to aim your eyes at a focal point on the center of the jump at your eye-level. If you have to squint, stare, or glare to do this, you'll wind up with hard eyes, which make you tense and lessen your ability to feel. (Even so, hard eyes are better than looking down!) Select a focal point, or "target," in the middle distance at your eye-level and allow your eyes to relax and see a big circle around this target—your *soft eyes* are staying directed while allowing freedom and feel.

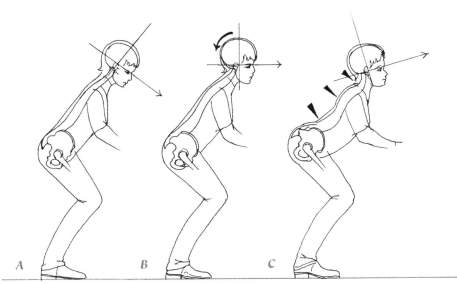

17.4 A–C Rotating the skull back to look ahead without shortening the neck.

(A & B) Correct: first, lengthen your back and neck, which will cause you to look down. Keeping that position, rotate your skull back to raise your eyes and look level and straight.
(C) Incorrect: a shortened, "crunched" neck and back.

It is possible to look up too high. Setting your focal point up in the clouds cramps your neck and back, and makes it harder for you to see where you're going.

In addition to looking at a focal point, it's important to keep your neck long and free—looking forward without shortening. Sticking your chin out shortens and cramps the back of your neck as if crunching it. If the head and neck crunch, your lower back becomes stiff and hollow, because your neck and lumbar spine have the same type of curve. This can lock up your hips, also cause your shoulders to stiffen.

To keep the neck free while looking up and ahead in jumping position, you need to go back to the work you did on the atlanto-occipital joint (see p. 54). Now, close into a jumping position, but keep your head aligned with your upper body—your nose and eyes should be pointing toward the ground a few feet in front of you. Place your hands on the sides of your head and gently rotate your skull until you can look ahead with your gaze level (your "looking-level" position), keeping your neck long and the atlanto-occipital joint free. Your back can also stay long and free, and your neck and body are unconstrained and free from crunches (fig. 17.4 A–C).

Next, keeping your neck long, practice sinking slowly into a jumping position, at the same time as you allow your head to rotate to a looking-level position. This takes practice, and at first, you'll have to do it slowly enough to be aware of *how* you are doing it. As you learn the technique, you can fold into the jumping position with just a quick thought of "long neck," or "long back."

Shoulders, Arms, and Hands

The shoulders, arms, and hands have a different role in jumping; they act with control on the approach, but over the fence, they must release and follow the motion of the horse's head and neck. The joints of the shoulder, elbow, wrist, hand, and fingers all absorb shock, and prevent the *springs* and *shock absorbers* in your body from being transmitted through the reins to the horse's mouth. This is especially important when jumping on contact or using an "automatic release." (I'll describe "releases" in detail ahead on p. 223.) The hands cannot be any

17.5 A–C
Heavy elbows.

(A) When the elbows hang heavy with the shoulder blades dropped down behind the rib cage, your arms can swing freely forward.
(B) Shoulder blades pulled up produce a round upper back and restrict the free move-ment of upper arms.
(C) Shoulder blades pinched together in back result in a tense back and neck, and rigid hands and arms.

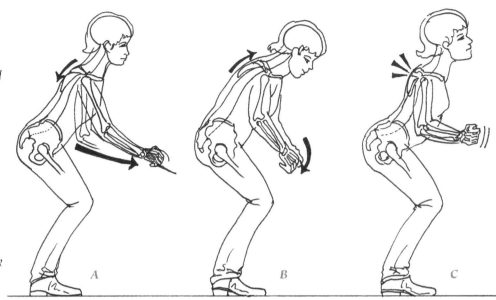

better than the arms they are attached to, and the arms are no better than the shoulders; hence, good hands start in the shoulder girdle.

In jumping, it is often necessary to control a horse that is strong, excited, or moving fast. At the same time, hard or over-controlling hands will quickly spoil a jumping performance and ruin a tal-ented jumper. Dropping the shoulder blades down behind the ribs allows you to use the muscles that run down your back and the back of your arms, in-stead of tugging with the biceps and the muscles at the front of the arms. Dropping the shoulder blades also opens your chest and keeps the shoulder joints free, allowing your arms to follow the reach of the horse's head and neck. The mus-cles between the shoulder blades also help, but if overused, which they frequently are due to in-structions to "pull your shoulders back," can cause tension in the upper back, and locked, stiffened shoulders. This tension, in turn, leads to loss of

your *centering*. It is much more effective to drop the shoulder blades and elbows down than to try to pinch the shoulder blades together in back (figs. 17.5 A–C). If your shoulder blades are pulled for-ward and up, your upper back becomes rounded and it restricts the free movement of your upper arm. As is so often the case, what seems to be the long way to get there is really the shortest way to the balance, softness, and *centering* essential in any activity.

In a jumping position, standing on the ground, check your balance, feet, and long back, then breathe as you shrug your shoulders upward and drop them down. Shrug your shoulders again with your elbows bent, feeling the weight drop down the back of your arms and into your "heavy el-bows." Now ask a friend to gently support your forearm and wrist, and slide your arm backward and forward. Allow your arm to hang heavily into your helper's hands, and let her move your arm.

17.6 A & B

(A) Claudia (right) is demonstrating a nice neutral position with heavy elbows, and shoulder blades dropped down correctly. (B) Here, she is able to move her arms forward freely with no change in the position of her torso when Lucy asks for more rein.

This is harder than you might think; most people discover that they hold their arm themselves, or that their arm tries to "help" and take over the movement. When your arm hangs with a heavy elbow, your partner should be able to move it freely without encountering stiffness, or bumping into an unyielding hand. When you ride on contact, your horse will appreciate this (figs. 17.6 A & B)!

Keeping your hands close to vertical (with thumbs upward on top) will help to keep your wrists straight and your hands light yet effective. Hands, which go "flat" on top (with knuckles on top, palms down) are stiffer, because the two bones of the forearm twist and cross in this position. The hands are also "heavier," dropping the entire weight of the arms onto the bit and reins. People who ride with flat hands are forced to use the biceps and muscles on the front of their arms, which leads to "elbows out," and "gorilla arms." These positions go along with the front of the shoulders pointing in, which cave the chest in, and hunch the shoulder blades up in the back. All this makes it difficult to control the horse through contact and balance. Instead, the rider finds herself reduced to pulling, curling the wrists, and "nipping" backward with the hands.

Applying the Basics on Foot

When training the horse and rider for jumping, we often make use of cavaletti poles and gymnastic-jumping exercises to help the horse with his stride and balance, teach him to use himself, and be aware of his takeoff point. The rider is also concerned with the takeoff point and getting the horse to adjust his stride to arrive at it perfectly. We ask our horses to do this all the time, but how many riders who jump horses have tried to do it themselves—on foot?

For this exercise, set a jump pole (about 4 inches in diameter) on the ground. Walk in a large enough circle to pick up a normal walking stride and rhythm, the way you walk when you're not thinking about how you are walking. Finish your circle and walk straight on over the pole. Stop a few steps afterward, and consider: did your last stride end at the right spot to step easily over the pole, or did you have to shorten or stretch your stride to step over? Try walking over the pole in various ways, noticing how the following suggestions affect your stride, balance, and "takeoff":

- Walk with a steady rhythm, *breathing,* and counting or humming as you approach and step over the pole (fig. 17.7). Then try it with an uneven rhythm, or many small steps.

- Approach the pole looking at your focal point—a target at eye-level out ahead—with *soft eyes.* Then try it with hard eyes, looking down, and shifting your eyes around.

- Choose a line that will take you over the center of the pole. You can also experiment with a curving approach on an angle. Then, try an inconsistent approach, starting from nowhere in particular: weave, zig-zag, and change your direction. How does this affect your "takeoff" step?

- *Center* yourself, dropping your center deep into your pelvis, and allow the movement of your walk to come from your center. For contrast, try walking over the pole with your center too high, too far forward (at your belt buckle), or off to one side.

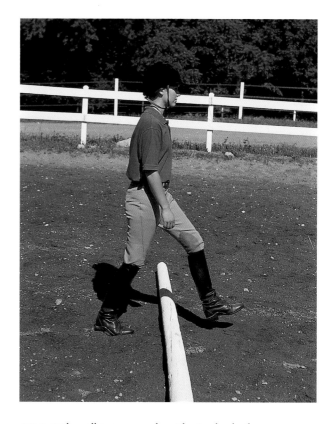

17.7 Beth walks over a pole with steady rhythm— breathing and humming as she goes. Her gaze with soft eyes is straight ahead looking at her focal point.

- Breathe out as you step over the pole. Does this affect your step? What happens if you breathe tightly with shallow breaths, or hold your breath?

- Allow your shoulders to hang down and your arms to swing freely as you walk in toward, and step over the pole. What happens if you hold your shoulders stiffly? Imagine someone tying your arms down with a strap around your middle. How does this relate to your horse's head and neck freedom?

- Walk in and over the pole while allowing your back to *release and lengthen,* keeping your back and neck long and your *slippery spot* free. Try it with your back arched, neck

17.8 A & B *Beth (in dark blue) is influencing Amanda with her hands and energy.*

tight, back rounded. Especially notice the effect on your ability to take a long stride and lift your legs over the pole.

- Have a helper "ride" with you by walking in step beside or behind you, holding her hands lightly on your sides, or holding hands with you. How does the presence of another person affect your balance, breathing, concentration, and use of your body? What happens if your partner tries to make you adjust your stride right before you step over the pole, and urges you on or holds you back? How does her breathing, centering, balance, and type of eyes (or lack of any of these things), affect your performance (figs. 17.8 A & B)?

Next, set up a series of 3 to 5 cavaletti for people to use. Use poles about 4 inches in diameter, set approximately 2 feet 6 inches to 3 feet apart. You will have to experiment to find the right distance for you so that your feet land in the center of the spaces when you walk or jog through this grid. Try this and notice how your balance, rhythm, breathing, length of stride, and *springs* and *shock absorbers* are affected by the grid. You can also set up combinations and lines of fences scaled for humans, and experiment by negotiating them at a walk, jog, or "canter" (skipping with one leg ahead will even let you simulate canter leads and changes of lead). The way you use your body on the ground will reflect your body's habitual patterns that you unconsciously use when jumping. This allows you to develop more body awareness and learn how to make changes where they might help. This kind of exercise is also helpful in understanding what you are asking your horse to do when negotiating turns, jumps, grids, and combinations, and how the way you ride the approach to a fence affects the way your horse will jump it.

ON THE HORSE

Now that you have explored the use of your body in jumping-related groundwork, it's time to put this knowledge into practice. But, before you start jumping, here are several essentials that you need for safe, confident, and effective riding over fences.

Confidence, Fear, and Clear Intent

Jumping with confidence can be one of the greatest thrills in riding, but jumping with fear can be a terrifying ordeal. Confidence comes from successful experience, based on sound fundamentals. False confidence, or overconfidence, often based on ignorance (as in, "Well, I've never had a lesson and he's never done it, but I *know* I can get my horse over a 3-foot jump!") is foolish, dangerous, and abusive to the horse. Lack of confidence is often only caused by inexperience, and is easily helped with good, systematic instruction, but it can come from gaps of knowledge in the basics of security, control, balance, and understanding the process of learning to jump. And it is to be expected, because jumping does involve more speed, thrust, and athletic movement than flatwork or slow trail riding, and riders who are not yet comfortable with the idea of cantering or going a little bit faster are often apprehensive.

Probably the two most important factors in developing confidence in jumping are safe, system-atic instruction at the student's own learning pace, and a suitable horse to learn on. Jumping requires control, communication, and cooperation between horse and rider. A horse that is too green, too quick, or too difficult can overface a student, and you'll be constantly distracted by control issues rather than concentrating on what you are doing and feeling. Obviously, this situation is unsafe and can cause loss of confidence, as well as ruin your horse. If this is your case, have your horse schooled over fences by a more experienced jumping rider while you take jumping lessons on a reliable jumping horse.

You can stretch your confidence gradually, but overfacing yourself or allowing someone else to push you beyond your confidence limits can give you a bad experience and increase the fear factor. Fear breeds tension, locks up your body, and interferes with your ability to ride, feel, and use your body well. Some degree of tension is inevitable in certain situations even enhancing your performance if channeled into a positive mode, such as being excited or "up" for a competition. However, if you are hampered by fear and tension, it's a signal to go back to basics and recheck your fundamentals. Work on simple jumping or pre-jumping exercises within your range of confidence. When you find yourself beginning to become a bit bored with them, it's a good indication that you're ready to move up to the next step.

Clear intent is a fundamental part of control. It gives you confidence, because you know what you plan to do and what to focus on. It is also essential for your horse's confidence and obedience, especially in jumping. When you lack *clear intent*, a horse is left confused and rudderless, and he may fill the vacuum by taking charge and ignoring you, or may lose his confidence and become erratic, nervous, and upset. Clear intent comes from making a clear decision, particularly about where you plan to go—straight over that jump, down that line of jumps, around that turn on a particular track—and how you plan to get there. Some riders are diffident about making decisions; they are afraid they may be wrong or that they will mess up the horse. If you wait until you are a perfect expert to make a decision, you'll never get there. It's more important to be clear than to be perfect! Having *clear intent* is another way of expressing the old saying, "Throw your heart over the fence, and your horse will follow it!"

Jumping Basics Check

In order to jump safely and with feel, your jumping basics must be in order and must be developed enough for the demands of the level at which you are working. Here are some basic points to review.

Jumping Seats

The jumping seat gives the rider security, control, balance, and unity with the horse over fences. I'd like to briefly review the variations of the seats used when jumping.

Two-point contact is a position in which the rider is balanced with her seat suspended over the saddle to free the horse's back. The two points of contact with the horse are the rider's two legs (inner knee and calf), and her seat (the third point) is out of the saddle. The stirrup length determines how high her seat is above the saddle (fig. 17.9 A).

Three-point contact means that the rider is seated in the saddle, with all three points (both legs and seat) in contact with the horse. In both two-point and three-point contact, the rider's body angle may vary from vertical to quite forward, and the rider should always be balanced with feet under her center. Three-point contact is often used in riding approaches to, and between jumps, but is not normally used over jumps, except for a special

purpose such as jumping a drop fence. A three-point contact seat is also the *deep* seat talked about so much earlier in this book and used in a great deal of Centered Riding on the flat.

A *light seat* refers to a position with *three-point* contact where your seat bones *lightly* touch the saddle, but your body is angled forward rather than upright. This position is light and easy on the horse's back and it allows you to easily close, open, and adjust to the horse's changing back and

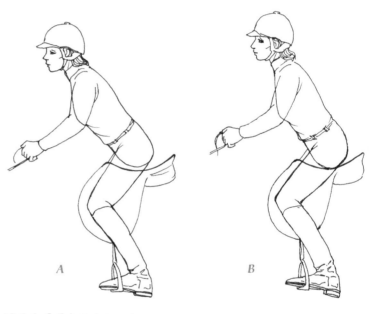

17.9 A & B *Jumping seats.*

(A) Two-point contact: half-seat. (B) Three-point contact: light seat.

jumping movements. As in *two-point* contact, you must be balanced with your feet under your center. The light seat is versatile and useful for schooling over fences and for riding approaches and courses that require turns and adjustments of stride and balance (fig. 17.9 B).

STIRRUP LENGTH

Correct stirrup length is critical to jumping well, as the length of stirrup helps determine the angles of the ankles, knees, and hip joints. While too short

_17.10_ The four lines represent different stirrup lengths and their relationship to your anklebone. The top line is for jumping medium height fences. The second line is a good length for basic jumping. The third line is for flatwork in an all-purpose saddle, and the fourth line indicates the length for doing dressage.

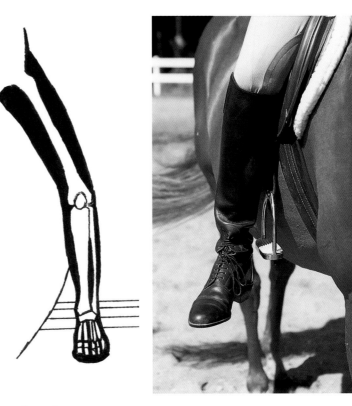

_17.11_ The correct stirrup length for jumping medium height fences—the equivalent of the top line in figure 17.10.

stirrups cause exaggerated angles and can be uncomfortable, stirrups too long for jumping ruin your _springs_ and _shock-absorbing qualities_—throwing you out of balance, and dropping your seat down onto the horse's back over fences. Because you are insecure and unable to _ground_ your feet, you grip with your knees, which cause the knees to pivot. This action, in turn, swings the lower legs and heels up. Often a rider who rides with stirrups that are too long sits back on the approach, then has to stand up, or lunge forward as the horse jumps, putting her ahead of the motion. While the correct stirrup length is always best, it is usually better to ride a bit too short over fences than to have the stirrups too long.

The correct jumping-stirrup length depends on the kind of jumping being done, the height of the fences, and to some extent, on the rider's length of leg, the size of the horse's barrel, and the design of the saddle. For a good, basic jumping length, the bottom of the stirrup iron should reach to the center of the rider's anklebone. For jumping medium fences (3 feet and higher), the iron should reach to a spot just above the point of the ankle. The stirrups should be raised one hole for every foot increase in the height of the fences; for show jumping over big fences or galloping over steeplechase fences, the stirrups should be well above the top of the anklebone (figs. 17.10 and 17.11).

FOOT AND STIRRUP POSITION

In jumping, correct positioning of the foot in the stirrup can make a tremendous difference in how well you are _grounded_, and how well you use the three major _springs_ of your hip, knee, and ankle joints. Placing the foot in the stirrup so that some part of the stirrup tread supports the _Bubbling Spring_ helps you feel where your feet are and allows your weight to sink past your knees and be received by your stirrups, ankles, and feet. It is more useful to think of allowing your weight to _sink_ into your feet than to _drive_ your heels down. Forcibly driving your heels down locks your ankle joints, robbing you of these important _springs_ and _shock absorbers._ The forcing also often causes a rider to jam her heels forward, which puts her leg

17.12 A & B Jumping position.

(A) A correct jumping position. The leg and foot are well grounded acting as a "spring" and a "shock absorber."

(B) This forced-down heel is jamming the foot forward and locking the ankle joints.

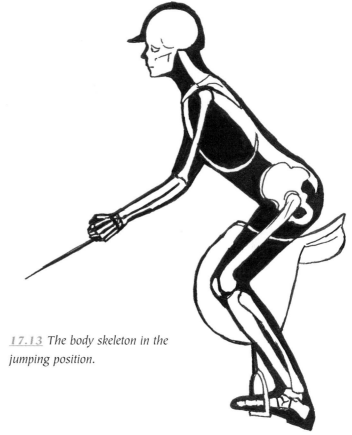

17.13 The body skeleton in the jumping position.

too far forward with resulting loss of balance (figs. 17.12 A & B).

BODY POSITION

Your position in jumping should be functional, never a faddish, meaningless mannerism. Good position really means an athletic and efficient use of the body. While a few riders may be successful with a highly individual style that's anything but classical, this is not a sensible trend for others to copy. There is a practical reason for every position detail. You will have to work out exactly how to use your body in a good jumping position, and make minor adaptations to suit your individual conformation and the size and shape of the horse you are riding.

Here is a brief jumping-position checklist (fig. 17.13):

SEAT: half-seat or light seat. The upper body is angled more or less forward, in balance with horse.

CENTER: dropped down deep in your body, in front of the sacrum, and balanced close to the saddle.

LEGS: in contact with the horse's sides. The angles of the hip, knee, and ankle joints should be similar. The *Bubbling Springs* under your feet should be directly under your center.

THIGHS: rolled inward, with the flat parts against the saddle. They should not grip, but just have frictional contact.

KNEES: the inner parts of the knees are in contact with saddle, but not pinching. The knees act as springs and shock absorbers.

LOWER LEGS: slightly stretched through the back of legs; the inner sides of the calf are in contact with horse's side.

ANKLES: flexible, sinking under weight of rider, and not locked or twisted.

FEET: stirrups are placed under natural balance

17.14 A–C The rider's back in the two-point jumping position.

(A) Correct: a good, functional, flat back for jumping work.

(B) Incorrect: hollow, excessively arched back.

point of the foot–the *Bubbling Spring*–and the heels sink down and backward under the rider's weight but not "jammed." The weight should spread out across the width of the stirrups, which should not be *rolled* in or out, and the toes and feet should lie at the same angles as the knees and femurs.

BACK: long, flat, lightly stretched, not roached or excessively arched (figs. 17.14 A–C).

SHOULDERS: shoulder blades are dropped down be-

hind the rib cage in back, with the shoulders wide–not hunched, or pinched together in back.

CHEST AND COLLARBONES: chest is open, *breathing* into the *lengthened* body. The upper chest and collarbones need to be wide and free, not caved in.

NECK: long and free, an extension of the spine. It needs to be mobile at the atlanto-occipital point, not "crunched."

HEAD: balanced freely, with *soft eyes* looking ahead at focal point. Your jaw should be relaxed.

(C) Incorrect: round, or roached back. Notice the locked hip, pinched knee, and foot pushed forward.

UPPER ARMS: hang naturally from the shoulder joints, free to swing forward to follow the horse's head and neck movement.

ELBOWS: hang as if heavy, with a natural bend to act as a cushion effect on the bit.

FOREARMS: in a straight line from elbows to wrists to bit.

HANDS: hands should hold reins in soft fists with the fingers closed. They are part of the straight lines of the forearms from elbows to bit.

OVERALL POSITION: the rider is in balance, with equal weight on both seat bones, or both stirrups depending on the seat used. A vertical line of balance runs through the center to the feet. The head and shoulders are in front of this line balanced by the seat behind it.

Pre-Jumping Exercises

Pre-jumping exercises are a way to explore and apply the *Four Basics* and *grounding* as they apply to jumping. Most importantly, pre-jumping exercises allow you to feel your use of your body in slow motion. If you take time to practice the pre-jumping exercises with awareness, the right feel, habits, and reflexes will all be there—faster than you can think—when you need them to operate over a jump. As you become more familiar with how they work, you can build them into actual jumping exercises progressing from ground poles, cavaletti grids, single fences and lines, to gymnastic jumping exercises.

BALANCE FIRST

Every time you ride to a jump, you need balance working for you. This means that first you need to check your horse's balance. Does he have a nice, balanced trot or canter from which to jump, or is he stiff, crooked, or on the forehand? Check his balance by riding a large (20-meter or larger) circle at the end of the ring. If you like his balance, continue down the long side, maintaining balance and rhythm. If his balance is not right, stay on the circle to improve his balance.

The next consideration is the state of your own balance. Are you in balance *with* your horse, or are you *ahead* of, or *behind* his balance? If your own balance isn't quite right, take time on a circle before the jump to get yourself in balance with your horse.

SOFT EYES EXERCISE

This exercise begins by riding each side of the ring at walk or trot with your eyes on a specific target

17.15 A–C Centering with the seat belt.

(A) *Center yourself in a deep seat, then fold at the hip joint to a jumping position.*
(B) *Imagine a seat belt low across the hips for security and balance.*
(C) *Contrast the feeling by standing up and leaning forward. Your center falls forward onto to the horse's neck and your balance feels insecure.*

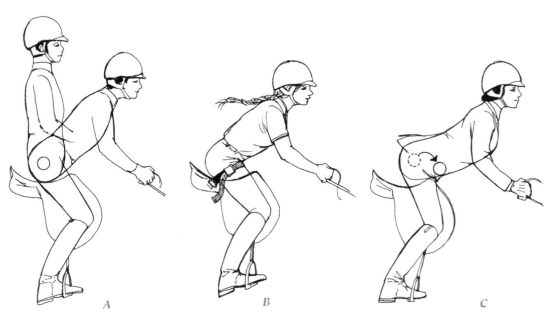

A   B   C

or focal point as you practiced on the ground in the first section of this chapter. Select a target that is at your eye-level, in the middle distance, and lined up straight where you want your horse to go. Practice keeping your eyes on your target as you ride to the end of the ring, then shift your eyes and turn your center to a new target for the next line. Can you keep your eyes on your chosen target without looking down? Are your eyes soft or hard? If you find yourself with hard eyes, what happened to make them hard? Check your horse's response by halting at the end of a straight line with your *soft eyes* on your target, then check to make sure he is straight, with front legs, hind legs, head, and spine all lined up on the target.

Next, practice the same exercise over a ground pole flanked by standards. Note your *soft eyes* and choose the line over the pole to your target as you turn the corner beforehand. Maintain *soft eyes* all the way to the end, and halt. By the way, this is a good exercise to teach an impetuous horse to relax and associate jumping with straightness, calmness, and control.

ADD BREATHING

Now, as you ride over the pole, concentrate on your breathing. Breathe out as your horse steps over the pole, as if you were blowing out a match or candle. This helps you keep your balance, drops your center down, and softens your joints as your horse steps or jumps over. It also helps to relax a "quick" or tense horse, and teaches your body to associate jumping with breathing. As you practice, keep breathing normally—before the pole, after the pole, on the approach, and during the halt afterward—but remember you must breathe as your horse goes over the pole.

CENTERING AND THE SEAT BELT

To discover how to center in a jumping seat, you'll first have to center yourself sitting in an upright, deep seat. Breathe your center back and down so that you feel yourself sink down into the saddle. Your center should feel as if it drops down in front of your sacrum.

Now, find your hip joints and imagine a *seat belt* low across your hips (figs. 17.15 A–C). Leave your center deep in your body as you breathe and fold forward deep in the hips. As you fold, let your hips slide back a little. Now, with your center deep and back, you will feel secure and balanced, and your joints sink easily under your weight ready for jumping.

For contrast, try standing up and leaning forward, imagining your center is up toward your belt buckle, as if it might fall out onto the horse's neck. Does your back feel tight and arched, and does your balance feel "tippy"? Are you now folding superficially, instead of deep in the hip joints? Would you feel secure in this position if you were jumping?

"Feel" the *seat belt* and practice breathing out as you fold forward deep in the hip joints, while leaving your back long and your center deep—first at a halt, then at the walk, trot, and canter, and then over ground poles, cavaletti, and low fences.

SINKING, NOT STANDING

As I mentioned earlier, good jumping uses your joints in balance. Because jumping is done in a forward balance, many people tend to stand up forward in an effort to get with the horse's jump. However, this can put you ahead of the motion. It often goes with open knees, jammed heels, and rigid, locked joints, and throws your body out ahead of the saddle over the horse's neck.

Learning to sink into your joints helps your security and enables your *springs* to do their job better (figs. 17.16 A & B). Practice by taking a normal balanced jumping position with two-point contact (your seat should be out of the saddle). Breathe and release your knees (soften the pressure so the connection against the saddle is soft), and sink an inch or two down and backward, into your knees and ankles. You will feel your heels and ankles sink back and down, your knees flex, and your hips sink back a little. Your lower legs and calves will sink closer into your horse's sides. Your seat bones sink backward, a little closer to the seat of the saddle, but they don't hit the saddle, nor

should you fall backward as if you were being "left behind" over a jump. Sinking is not sitting down. If you find yourself bumping the saddle you are doing it too vigorously, or your stirrups may be too long. Sinking correctly is using your three joints well, making you feel deeper and more secure. Practice sinking at the halt, walk, trot, and canter, and then over ground poles.

Which forward position would leave you secure if your horse should make a mistake on takeoff, stumble, or stop suddenly? Which one would make you feel as if you might sail on over the jump without your horse?

TOUCHING TOES

Here is an exercise that can help you become limber. You learn to sink into your joints, keeping

17.16 A & B Sinking down versus standing up.

(A) Correct: the two-point position where the upper body closes forward but is ready to sink into the joints, while the hips and legs sink back and down.

(B) Incorrect: the two-point position where the upper body tips forward but with the pelvis much too high. The knee angle opens instead of closes to absorb the thrust of the jump.

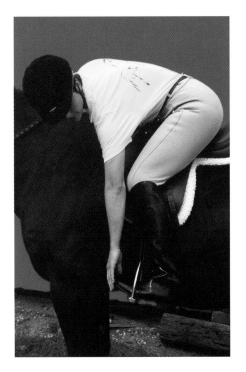

17.17 A–D Touching Toes.

(A) *"Touching Toes" on the left side. Correct: a view of Claudia's left leg, which is in a normal position with her body balanced over the "Bubbling Spring." She should, however, be looking ahead while doing these exercises.*

(B) *Touching Toes on the left side. Incorrect: a view of Claudia's left leg where her knee has stiffened, pushing her seat too far back in the saddle, and her leg forward. Her toe is ahead of her knee.*

(C) *"Touching Toes" on the right side. Correct: Claudia's soft left knee is directly over the tips of her toes.*

your balance and improving your leg position (figs. 17.17 A–D). Take the reins in your right hand. Reach down and briefly touch your toes on the left side with your left hand, and then come back to a normal jumping position. Switch hands and repeat on the other side. Keep your eyes ahead, and don't stiffen your knees or let your lower legs come forward. As you practice this exercise, alternating sides at walk, trot, and canter and eventually over low fences, you'll discover that your *springs* and *shock absorbers* work better, and your seat and balance become more independent and secure.

Releases—the Following Hands

"Releasing" means using one of several methods that allow the horse to stretch his neck as he jumps without restricting the use of his head and neck, or catching him in the mouth. If you fail to release properly and interfere with his jumping effort, his mouth gets pulled, and he may lose his confidence. (Every time you jump a horse, you are in effect promising him that if he does as you ask, you won't hurt his mouth, so you owe him a good release.)

There are several types of releases, and it's important to use the right one for the horse you are

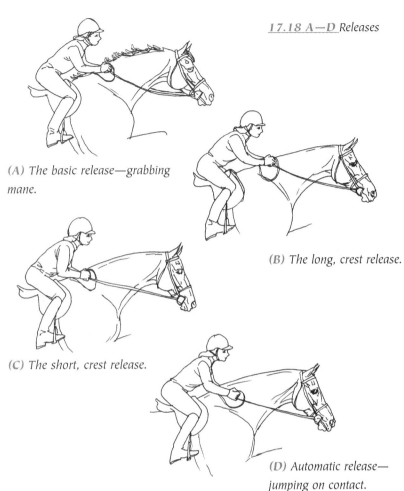

17.18 A—D Releases

(A) *The basic release—grabbing mane.*

(B) *The long, crest release.*

(C) *The short, crest release.*

(D) *Automatic release—jumping on contact.*

(D) *"Touching Toes" on the right side. Incorrect: Claudia's stiff left knee is pushing her seat way back in the saddle and her toes are way ahead of her knee.*

riding, the job you are doing, and your skill level. You should learn to use and practice all of the various releases listed below in order, and then use the best one for the circumstances (figs. 17.18 A–D).

BASIC RELEASE

The *basic release* (grabbing mane) allows the horse complete freedom to use his head and neck and protects him from a jerk in the mouth. This can happen not only from a beginning rider becoming unbalanced or a young or green horse making an erratic takeoff, but also in an "emergency" situation when you just need to stay aboard and avoid interfering with the horse. If you learn how to correctly grab the mane like this, you'll be on your

way to the next release—the *crest release* where your hands and arms follow the motion of the horse's head and neck. However, when you grab the mane you also give up a certain amount of control, so this release is not the best choice when you need extra control—on a headstrong horse, for instance, or when you plan to turn or rebalance immediately after the jump.

To execute this basic grab-the-mane release, hold the reins normally in both hands, open your thumbs and forefingers and reach forward approximately 12 inches to one-third of the way up the horse's neck. Place the knuckles of both hands side by side, on top of the crest, pinch the roots of the mane firmly (close your fingers!), and press your knuckles firmly forward into the crest. Don't let your hands just touch the neck and then fly up. Keep your hands pressed into the mane until your horse has landed, then pick up your hands and regain the contact gently and smoothly.

CREST RELEASES—LONG AND SHORT

A *crest release* is an intermediate step up from the basic release and the more advanced releases, allowing you to take some support from the crest while protecting the horse's mouth against accidental mistakes, but also giving you more control options than just holding the mane does. However, it does not offer as much control, precision, or communication as the *automatic release*. A crest release breaks the line from elbow to bit upward, but it still allows the horse considerable freedom to use his head and neck. A *long crest release* (approximately one-third of the way up the horse's crest) allows a horse maximum freedom of head and neck over a spread fence, through gymnastics, and when encouraging him to make the maximum use of his neck. A *short crest release* (your hands move only a few inches forward up the crest) allows more control for collecting, or turning immediately after the fence.

To execute a long crest release, extend your hands and arms forward and press your knuckles, side by side, into the top of the crest about one-third of the way up the neck. Press forward firmly in the direction of the bit with your forearms, as if you wanted to push the horse's neck forward and down. Keep your knuckles pressed firmly into the crest until your horse has landed, then pick your hands up and return to normal contact gently. For a short crest release, extend your hands forward a shorter distance to the crest (usually about 4-to-6 inches), closer to the withers. This release allows the horse less room to stretch his neck so it is better suited for vertical jumps rather than spread fences, but it offers more control and is quicker to

pick up after the jump. When using either crest release, keep your knuckles, wrists, and forearms in a straight line, and press forward in the direction of the neck—don't drop your hands alongside the neck or rotate them up and back.

AUTOMATIC RELEASE

The *automatic release* also known as *jumping on contact* or *following through the air*, affords the greatest degree of communication and control. It is the ideal that all jumping riders should aim to master after learning the basic and crest releases. To follow the movement of the horse's head and neck while maintaining contact without interfering with his balancing gestures, or committing the cardinal sin of catching your balance with the reins, you need an extremely secure seat, joints that are fluid *springs* and *shock absorbers,* and good timing. You also need to be in good physical shape and in practice. Any mistakes you make will be paid for by your horse—in his mouth! Expert riders may jump on contact most of the time, but when things go wrong, they will quickly use a crest release, slip their reins, or even grab the mane rather than grab the mouth.

This release is called an "automatic" release, because it happens automatically. If you ride a good approach with normal contact with your hands and arms clear of the horse's neck as he jumps and extends his head and neck, he will draw your hands and arms forward through the air. If you are balanced and secure, and your shoulders, arms, and hands are free and independent, the contact stays exactly the same throughout the approach, takeoff, flight, landing, and recovery. This gives you the potential to turn in the air, to collect on landing, and even to make subtle adjustments to your horse's jumping effort. It's important to keep a straight line from the elbow to bit, as this is the least likely to make the bit interfere with the horse's bascule (the position of the horse as he moves through his jumping effort).

Using Cavaletti to Find Your Springs and Shock Absorbers

As explained in the groundwork section, three joints—the hip, knee, and ankle—act as *springs* and *shock absorbers.* They flex and sink under the weight of the rider, absorb the thrust of takeoff and shock of landing, and allow the body to adapt to the horse's movements during approach, takeoff, flight, landing, and recovery. They only work well when the body is in balance. If you are even slightly out of balance, your body and legs will instinctively grip or tighten, and your joints cannot adjust smoothly and freely to your horse's movement.

Riding over some grid-work exercises (a series of poles set on the ground at fixed distances to regulate the horse's stride) is a way to develop good use of your joints in motion. They should be set for your horse's average stride, so that his feet fall in the center of the spaces between the poles. (A good basic distance is 4 feet 3 inches to 4 feet 6 inches for trotting grids; 3 feet to 3 feet 6 inches for walk work; and 10 feet to 11 feet for canter grids. But remember, these must be adjusted to suit the horse. (figs. 17.19 A & B).

Before you begin, check your stirrup length for jumping and make sure that your stirrup is under your foot at the *Bubbling Spring,* and that your feet feel grounded. Practice riding in a two-point position at walk and trot, and allow your knees to release. Resting your knuckles of both hands on the horse's crest, and taking a little support from his neck, can help to free your knees. In the trot, feel the alternating thrust that lifts one knee and then the other; in canter, (which I'll discuss below), feel how the horse rolls your knees in circles. You can also practice breathing (do not hold your breath), and "sinking" into the jumping position. Remember, in order to free your joints and find your *springs* and *shock absorbers,* you will have to be in balance over your feet and in balance with your horse. Carry this feeling into work over cavaletti or grid work, allowing your weight to sink down past your knees into your grounded feet, and your joints to spring and sink with the bigger, springier strides your horse takes over the poles. This is excellent work for your horse as it frees his back, encourages him to swing his hind legs forward, round his back in a bascule, and bend the joints of his legs. It's strenuous so don't overdo it, especially with a horse that is not very fit.

Cantering over a cavaletti grid can be ridden in a two-point seat, but it is often more useful to ride a canter grid in a light seat, allowing the horse to rock your body forward and back a little at each stride while your center stays balanced over your feet and your joints absorb the rolling motion (figs. 17.20 A & B). Horses canter with more roundness and suspension over ground poles, and some horses feel to the rider as if they are taking a series of connected jumps. In addition to preparation for gymnastic jumping, this can be a good exercise to motivate a lazy horse, or restore the suspension to a canter that has gone "flat," but it is essential that the distances set are a comfortable stride for the individual horse (figs. 17.21 A & B).

Gymnastic Jumping and the Seesaw Effect

Gymnastic jumping exercises are made up of a set of closely related fences, or fences and poles, which regulate the horse's stride and takeoff and affect the way he uses his body. They are used to train horses to balance themselves, to adjust their strides for takeoff, and to use themselves correctly while in the air. They can also help riders learn balance, rhythm, timing, and other techniques. Because good gymnastic exercises set up horse and rider for a good rhythm, they can help both develop confidence as well as good style, and the repetition helps both "get into the groove."

It's important to set up the gymnastics line safely and correctly for each individual horse, and to keep the level of difficulty appropriate for both

17.19 A & B Trotting poles.

(A) *Beth trotting over poles in a light seat with a lovely connection to the horse's mouth, but her horse is stepping a little short. More impulsion would help.*

(B) *This girl in a half-seat is having a bad ride because she is not balanced over her feet. Her torso and pelvis have come too far forward so she has tightened her shoulders, hollowed her back, pinched with her knees, and pressed her heels too far down. She has succeeded in keeping her hands soft.*

<u>*17.20 A & B*</u> *Cantering cavaletti.*

(A) *In a light seat, Beth shows good balance and folding, with a nice crest release.* (B) *Here, Beth has lost her balance a little, is tipping forward with her heels up, has a round back and tight shoulders.*

17.21 A & B

(A) Claudia is cantering through a grid in a light seat. Her eyes, leg angle, and balance are good, but her short release and broken, backward wrists restrict her horse's use of his head and neck.

horse and rider. Most gymnastics should be approached in a lively, rhythmic, but not too fast trot. It is often useful to begin a gymnastic line with a short series of trotting cavaletti. Cantering into gymnastics should be reserved for experts on experienced horses. Because they are a successive series of efforts, a mistake at the beginning of a gymnastic tends to get worse with each successive fence, so badly conceived or constructed gymnastics can cause scares, falls, and refusals, and ruin a horse's or rider's confidence.

Gymnastic jumping exercises are an excellent way to learn to keep your balance and wait for the horse to jump up to you, instead of you lunging forward and trying to second guess his takeoff. A series of "bounces," or short, one-stride jumping efforts, can help you discover the "*seesaw* effect" (see p. 175) and the balance that lets you ride the *seesaw* fluently. This effect will serve you well in jumping combinations, also in riding a balanced approach and "waiting" for the takeoff (fig. 17.22).

A gymnastics exercise can be ridden at various levels of difficulty, so be conservative and start out with one that is easily within your horse's, and your own ability. If you're worrying about the height of the fences or the difficulty of the exercise, you'll tense up and your joints will tighten, and you won't be able to get the feeling this exercise offers. (If you're not experienced at setting and riding gymnastics, you should do this in a jumping lesson with a knowledgeable jumping instructor.)

As you know, the *seesaw* effect is the rocking motion of your horse's body, and you can feel it in a rhythmic canter as well as when your horse jumps down through a gymnastic jumping line. His body rocks up toward you, then rocks down away, then up

(B) She lands with good legs, angles, and balance, but her shoulders are tight, her back is round, and she is looking down a little.

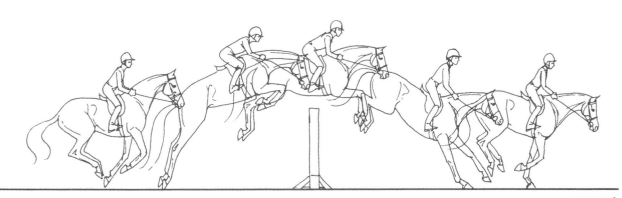

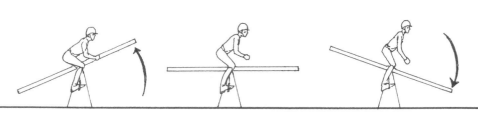

17.22 The "seesaw" effect. A jumping rider stays over the fulcrum, or balance point, of the horse or seesaw.

17.23 A—D Jumping a gymnastic with the "seesaw" effect.

(A) The horse "jumps up to meet the rider," who is nicely balanced with her angles closing in the "up" phase of the seesaw.

(B) The down phase: the rider is balanced over her feet as her angles open to accommodate the horse's downward tilt.

again, over and over, like a rocking horse. The same motion happens in a single jump, but many riders are too stiff or distracted to be aware of it. If you can find your central balance and allow your joints to absorb the up-and-down rocking motion, you can stay in balance and allow your body to follow your horse's jump smoothly. This also enables you to wait easily for the takeoff. *Grounded* feet, *breathing, leaving your center back*, folding deep in the hip with a long back,

and *finding your springs* will set you up for discovering this feeling (figs. 17.23 A–D).

When you ride through a gymnastic, use your balance, aids, and contact to set your horse up during the approach. Keep your *soft eyes* on the target at the end of the line, and breathe over every fence. Once the horse begins the exercise, just go with the flow—don't try to hold him back, adjust his strides, or even maintain contact with his

(C) Incorrect: Beth tips forward, pivoting on her knees instead of staying balanced over the fulcrum. Note the strain in her hollow back, her stiff shoulders, neck and elbows, and her heels coming up.

(D) Oops! Beth shows what happens when you get behind the fulcrum. She rounds her back, slips her reins, and braces her legs forward in a "survival seat." The horse isn't very happy about it, either!

mouth. It often works best to release as he steps over the first ground pole or rises to the first fence, then press your knuckles firmly forward into his crest and keep them there until you have landed after the last fence. (One exception to this is if your horse tries to swerve. In that case, take one hand off his neck, and steer him by using a leading rein sideways in the direction you need to keep him straight.) If you press your knuckles firmly into the crest and press forward with your forearms in the direction of the bit, you will be training your hands and arms to follow the reach of his head and neck as he jumps. Pressing firmly forward into the neck also helps to flex your hips, knees, and ankles, and discourages standing up and getting ahead of your horse in the jump.

Riding a series of properly spaced ground poles in a canter is a good way to begin to feel the *seesaw* effect. And then, as you learn to stay grounded and balanced, and let your joints adjust to the motion, you can ride over different types of grids, bounces, and gymnastic lines. These gymnastic exercises that follow are set with fairly short distances to encourage the horse to stay in balance and rock his forehand up more sharply. This teaches the horse to jump off his hocks, and be tighter with his forelegs. The heights and distances are set for an average, 16-hand horse, but please make sure your distances are adjusted to suit your horse's size, stride, and capabilities.

GYMNASTIC NUMBER ONE. A progressive gymnastic, suitable for a green horse (fig. 17.24).

- Trotting grid of three cavaletti each spaced apart at 4 feet 6 inches;
- 9 feet to crossrail (18 inches high);
- 17 to 18 feet (one short stride) to small vertical (18 inches to 2 feet high);
- 18 to 22 feet to small oxer (crossrail oxer or step oxer, 2 feet to 3 feet 3 inches high, 2 feet wide).

GYMNASTIC NUMBER TWO. Series of bounces (fig. 17.25).

- Ground pole; 9 feet to the first of a series of four small verticals or crossrails (18 inches to 2 feet high), spaced 10 feet 6 inches to 11 feet apart.

GYMNASTIC NUMBER THREE. Progressive gymnastic with placing poles (fig. 17.26).

- Trotting grid of three cavaletti spaced apart at 4 feet 6 inches;

- 9 feet to small vertical or crossrail (18 inches to 2 feet high);
- 10 to 11 feet to small vertical or crossrail bounce (18 inches to 2 feet high);
- 9 feet to ground pole;
- 9 feet to small vertical or crossrail (2 feet to 2 feet 3 inches high);
- 9 feet to ground pole;
- 9 feet to small vertical or crossrail (2' to 2'6");
- 9 feet to ground pole.

Rhythm and Timing

Rhythm and timing make it easy to go with your horse's movement, and allow you to begin to "see a distance," tell where your horse will take off, and to jump single fences "in stride" at the canter or gallop. They also help you to string a series of fences and lines together for a seamless performance over a course, and make jumping much more pleasurable.

Rhythm must be developed on the flat first, but eventually, you'll need to make the connection between rhythm and jumping, especially at the canter. This depends on having developed a balanced canter that you can maintain, control, and adjust.

One thing that can help is connecting your breathing to the rhythm of all the gaits, especially the canter. Start out in the walk. Breathe and count to a one–two, or a 1-2-3-4 beat, until your breathing is deep and effortless and your horse has steadied his tempo to follow your lead. In the trot, look for a breathing pattern that allows you to breathe deeply, steadily, and easily, and allows your horse to relax into his best working tempo. Some people prefer to hum, sing, or chant a phrase in time with the gait; others like to count.

When timing the canter, you'll probably find that you can't count (or sing or hum), "1-2-3," as fast as your horse puts his feet down. Instead, it works better to count one beat every stride (as in

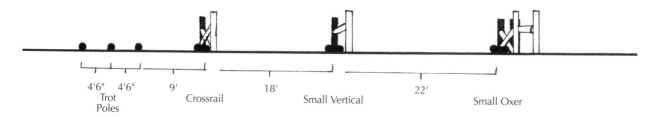

4'6" 4'6"   9'   18'   22'
Trot   Crossrail   Small Vertical   Small Oxer
Poles

17.24 *Gymnastic Number One.*

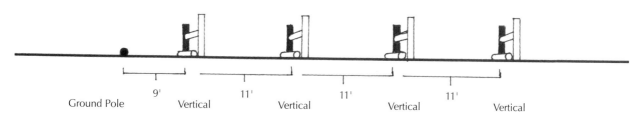

Ground Pole   9'   11'   11'   11'
              Vertical   Vertical   Vertical   Vertical

17.25 *Gymnastic Number Two.*

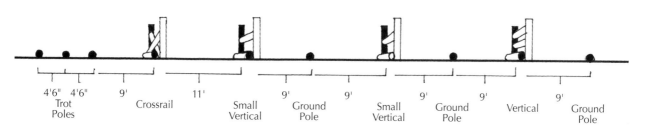

4'6" 4'6"   9'   11'   9'   9'   9'   9'   9'
Trot   Crossrail   Small   Ground   Small   Ground   Vertical   Ground
Poles   Vertical Pole   Vertical Pole   Pole

17.26 *Gymnastic Number Three.*

saying, "Stride, stride, stride," or singing "row, row, row your boat," or to sing, or say something like, "da-DUM, da-DUM, da-DUM," in time with the canter. Whatever you choose, practice cantering and becoming aware of indicators of rhythm—your horse's hoof beats, the creak of the saddle, your horse's rhythmic snorts, and especially, places in your body where you can feel rhythmic movement. Canter circles and straight lines in both directions and on both leads, and become familiar with your horse's best working tempo and balance in canter. This is the canter you'll want to jump from.

Seeing a Distance

Seeing a distance–also called "seeing a spot"–means knowing, at some distance from the fence, where your horse will take off. This makes it easier to jump in stride and to avoid unpleasant surprises and last-minute attempts to "fix" a bungled takeoff. If you see a distance far enough back, you may be able to "rate," or adjust your horse's stride to make the takeoff distance shorter, longer, or however you want it to come out. Some people are gifted with the ability to see distances easily and naturally; others find this difficult.

Seeing a distance could just as well be called "feeling a distance," because "feeling" is equally important. When you see a spot, your body feels the pace, the stride, the balance and impulsion, and the rhythm, while your eyes get an instantaneous "flash picture" of how much distance is left between you and the jump. You get a flash of awareness, "If we keep going like this, we'll take off long (or maybe short, or just right)." The components that allow you to do this are your feel for balance, pace (speed), length of stride, and rhythm. You also need to be able to ride straight along your line and keep your *soft eyes* on your target. If any of these components are not working well, or if your horse changes something before you get to the jump, you cannot get that moment of awareness, or what you see may not be what you get.

Seeing distances depends on having all the components in place, which gives you a chance to see a spot, and having the relaxation to feel, and the confidence to believe in what you feel. It cannot be forced. In fact, the quickest way to mess up this capacity is to "push your eye," or try to force yourself to see a distance when you don't.

Experience and practice help, but it's important that it be good experience. What you can do is practice the components that let you see distances over fences that are small and simple enough so that a mistake will not be a disaster. At first, you would like to learn to simply recognize a short, long, and perfect distance. When you're able to do this fairly consistently from three or more strides away, you can begin to ask your horse to adjust his stride and make the distance better.

A simple exercise that helps you begin to see (and adjust for) distances is riding over a single ground pole at a steady rising trot (fig. 17.27). As your horse goes over the pole, notice and say out loud whether his step was perfectly "in stride" (just the same as the rest), or if it was long (he had to "stretch" his step to make it over), or short (he had

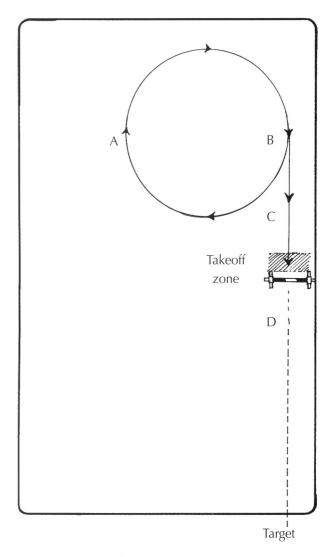

17.27 An exercise for learning how to "see a distance."

A: Circle for balance, rhythm, and preparation.

B: Your "soft eyes" look toward the target and have the opportunity to "see the distance."

C: Maintain the same rhythm and balance through the approach.

D: Ask yourself, "Was it short, long, or just right?"

to shorten, or almost tripped). Keep your *soft eyes* up and on target, and *feel*–don't look down to see what happens! Eventually you may find yourself automatically adjusting your horse's trot stride to come out right, but be careful to maintain the rhythm as you do. When you are getting pretty accurate at the trot, try the same exercise in canter, first on a straight line and then on a large circle. It is often easier to adjust the distance on a circle, because you can cut the circle a little, or widen it to make the takeoff come out right.

For the next exercise, set up a simple crossrail (18 inches to 2 feet 3 inches high), in the middle of a line in your ring. Make an opening circle to establish a nice balance, rhythm, and pace in the canter, and as you ride through the corner, use your *soft eyes* to pick out your target and establish your line. As you ride down the line, breathe and maintain rhythm, balance, and *soft eyes*, on over the fence. After the jump, ask yourself, was that a perfect takeoff? A bit long? A bit short? An instructor, or helper on the ground can give you feedback.

As you become more accurate at judging whether the takeoff was short, long, or just right, ask yourself if you knew beforehand that the takeoff would be short (or long, or just right), or was it a surprise? When you realize that you "knew" how a jump would come out, ask yourself, *where* did I know that? One stride out? Two, three, or four strides away? At whatever point you knew what the takeoff would be, you *saw a distance.* Congratulations!

At first you probably won't see a distance every time, and often you won't see a distance until you are pretty close to the fence. Just relax, keep your rhythm and balance, and let your horse take care of it. If your horse needs some help with distances, you can set a placing pole approximately 9 feet from the base of the fence. You can also practice appropriate gymnastic jumping exercises to help him learn to take off at the right place. When

you do see a distance, relax, keep your rhythm and balance, and enjoy the fact that you saw it. This begins to build confidence in your "eye" and gives you the habit of keeping your rhythm and balance, and allowing your horse to do the jumping. As you begin to see distances more consistently from three or more strides away, you can begin to ask your horse to adjust his stride occasionally. It is usually wiser to learn to "add strides" by shortening his strides and taking more, shorter strides before the takeoff spot; if you try to leave out a stride by pushing your horse to lengthen, he may fall onto his forehand and arrive at the takeoff spot in poor balance.

Centered Jumping in Various Disciplines

Centered Jumping has applications in all of the jumping sports and disciplines. This chapter has focused on the fundamentals of jumping, which are the tools you need in any jumping specialty. These same fundamentals are important whether you are just beginning to develop your jumping skills, solving jumping problems, or using them to get the best performance in demanding jumping competition at advanced levels. You can use *clear intent, soft eyes, breathing,* and *centering* to gain a new level of feel and connection to your horse for a smooth, sophisticated round in the show jumping ring, hunter seat equitation, or to improve the use of your body and joints so you can enjoy a long hunt or cross-country ride with more security and less fatigue, pain, and stress. Getting your feet *grounded,* your *springs* and *shock absorbers* working smoothly, and finding a central balance in the *seesaw* effect, can help you ride a jumper cleanly through a tricky combination, or help an eventer negotiate a multi-part obstacle without losing the rhythm of his gallop.

One of the most important applications for Centered Riding is in helping jumping riders solve problems of technique, or use of their bodies by coping

17.28 Claudia having fun jumping a natural fence in the woods.

with the body they have since it's the only one they get in this lifetime! It's especially useful for teachers and students to help figure out how they get their bodies to do what they are made to do, and how to teach jumping in a way that is safe and attainable.

Centered Jumping isn't just for style or to look pretty. Using your body well helps horses jump better. Many jumping problems—refusals, poor jumping style, and control difficulties— are related to the trouble a horse experiences with his rider's balance, control techniques, and use of her body. A sensitive horse is quick to react to the feelings he gets from his rider's body, balance, aids, and mental attitude—he is disturbed and irritated by heavy hands, loose legs, or a tight, tense, or unbalanced rider. And a horse gets frightened and defensive when he gets unclear signals from a rider's body language, or the rider's balance or timing is wrong. He may fumble his takeoff, hesitate, or even refuse, especially if the rider gets ahead of the motion. Centered Jumping and better use of the body can help a rider become more secure, better balanced, softer, and better at getting with his horses, enabling him to jump with confidence and freedom, and to use himself better over fences.

WHAT ARE THE ESSENTIALS OF Centered Jumping?

ON THE GROUND

- ▶ Good balance in the half-seat is essential—the *Teeter-Totter*.
- ▶ *Grounding* of the feet.
- ▶ Your joints act like *springs* and *shock absorbers.*
- ▶ Align your feet parallel to your thighbones.
- ▶ Keep your spine *lengthened.*
- ▶ Your *soft eyes* look ahead at a focal point; your head and neck are long and free.
- ▶ Apply the basics of jumping on foot yourself; walk over poles and discover how easily you can spoil your take-off stride.

ON THE HORSE

- ▶ *Clear Intent* at all times when jumping.
- ▶ Jumping basics include: an educated use of the half-seat and the light seat; correct stirrup length and position with feet *grounded* on the *Bubbling Springs.*
- ▶ Pre-jumping exercises: *soft eyes* on focal point; *breathing, centering* and *the seat belt.*
- ▶ Sink into your joints in forward balance, don't stand. *Touching Toes.*
- ▶ Allow the thrust and motion of the horse to open and close the angles of your hips, knees, and ankles.
- ▶ Hands with correct jumping releases to keep your horse comfortable.
- ▶ The *seesaw* effect as learned in gymnastic jumping.
- ▶ Rhythm and timing: breathe in rhythm with your horse.
- ▶ "See" a distance. Is it long or short? Adjust stride.
- ▶ *Allow* the horse to do the jumping.

WHAT ARE THE RESULTS?

- ▶ Centered jumping with good use of your body results in a horse with more confidence, freedom, and better use of his body over fences.
- ▶ Safer jumping, with fun.

PART THREE

18

Reducing Pain through Centered Riding

A student once told me, "Before I rode with you, my lower back always hurt, but since participating in your clinic, the pain has disappeared." I was delighted and from then on, I began correlating the use of Centered Riding techniques with the relief of pain.

Your body can produce various common sorts of pain as it works. Pain can be caused by the build-up of lactic acid in your muscles during exercise that is aerobic. Even a body well in balance will feel this sort of pain during periods of extreme stress or fatigue such as speed skating, riding in races with short stirrups, and endurance riding.

Other sorts of pain are the result of your body being out of balance. When this happens, not only is movement less efficient, but also the joints involved are put under stress even with ordinary daily activity. The pain produced by this kind of stress is the body's way of telling you that all is not well–that it needs help. One of my students told me of a quote, "Pain is God's megaphone." You should listen to any message of pain from your body because when you are using your body within reasonable limits, you should be able to work free of pain.

General Pain Felt When Riding

Let's consider pain in various parts of your body when you ride. First, you should realize that, in most cases, you should be comfortable on your horse. You need not assume that riding will produce discomfort. Keeping this premise in mind, let's examine how the mechanics of your body can affect your level of comfort.

Our bones are meant to support us. When you are standing, for instance, the knee is most efficient when you balance the femur directly above the fibula and tibia bones and do not flex the knee forward, or lock it back. Keeping in mind that balance is dynamic, not static, you will realize that the delicate balance of your knee is maintained by constant little adjustments of the muscles around the joint. The muscles on the front and back of the leg alternately take the responsibility of not allowing the leg to over flex either way. For instance, a knee flexed constantly a little forward overuses the muscles of the front of the legs while other muscles suffer from inactivity. The result of this imbalance will be some level of pain.

Another factor in efficient and pain-free body use is the function of the different layers of muscle. The muscles that lie closest to the bones are the involuntary muscles (work automatically) that respond to the autonomic nervous system. These are the muscles that a baby first uses—as he kicks and waves his hand aimlessly—with little coordination. His coordination improves with practice. As he begins to do things on purpose, the outer, voluntary muscles come into play. As we learn skills, we begin to direct these muscles. But, sometimes as a result of our being influenced by fashion or the people around us, we learn to move with these muscles in inefficient ways—slouching is a good example.

Our bodies work most efficiently when the involuntary muscles are allowed to work without unnecessary interference—like tension—from the voluntary muscles. The effectiveness of the involuntary muscles also depends on the correct articulation of the skeletal structure. When you "ride with your bones," you are more balanced and efficient. Rather than pushing your way into position, with your voluntary muscles, you are allowing the involuntary muscles to work properly.

The strength in the *Unbendable Arm* is an example of this.

Examine some of the places that riders tend to feel pain. The most common trouble spot is the lower back. This pain comes from hollowing the lower back excessively and sitting on the front of the seat bones. When you sit on your horse and you allow your lower back to hollow, you tip your pelvis down in front and up in back. This position causes stress to the lumbosacral joint (see figs. 6.2 A–C and 6.3, p. 51), because you place it in a much steeper angle than normal. It also puts the joint directly over the seat bones instead of slightly behind them, and this produces jarring. The result is pain in the lower back, as well as tension in the hip joints. This sway-backed position will also produce a rounded upper back, a shortened back of the neck, and protruding chin. In turn, this position of the upper body can cause pain in the shoulders—the shoulder blades and collarbones (see figs. 6.7 A–C, p. 53).

The best remedy for this awkward and painful position is simply to *center and grow*. This may seem like an over simplification, but in fact, *centering and growing* allows your back to *lengthen and widen*, releases your sacrum down, and lets you balance further back on the *rocker* of your seat bones which is the middle of them, thus relieving the stress and associated pain at the lumbosacral joint. Your upper body will realign and your shoulders will relax as they are carried over this more stable position. A normal, well-muscled lower back with the correct degree of curve actually looks flat as the muscles fill in the curve.

Sitting with your pelvis properly balanced will help alleviate much pain in your head, neck, and shoulders. Sometimes, however, not only will a hollow back shorten your neck, but a short, tight neck can hollow your back. Releasing one of these tight spots will loosen the other. In addition, a tense neck will also tighten the shoulders, ultimately causing pain between the shoulder blades.

To release this tightness in your upper back,

try becoming distinctly aware of this area in your mind. It can be helpful to have someone put her hand with slightly open fingers on your back to help you increase your consciousness of the area. She can let her fingers be moved a little apart and together by your breathing. Now softly move your shoulder blades over your ribs, up-and-down and in a circle. Allow your ribs to move when you breathe. Some riders have been told so many times to "keep your shoulders back" that they become rigid, and the ribs and spine are actually hollow between the shoulder blades when they should be full and moving.

The ribs, as you know, hang from your spine, a pair of ribs on each thoracic vertebra. With each breath, your ribs should spread slightly sideways, back and up between your shoulder blades, and sideways forward-and-up in your chest. Breathe so that your front and back expand equally, remembering that your upper arm should hang in the middle of your side. Usually, it is the rib movement in the back that becomes stuck. Once you are able to allow this motion from breathing across the back, the front will usually begin to move as well. Most people breathe too much (are too full) in this part of the upper back, so it helps to imagine that this area can "melt" forward and up through the neck and out the head.

Be careful not to try too hard with this breathing and so over-do it thereby creating another form of tension. Over a period of time, with a clear knowledge of the anatomical ideal, and a frequent intent to let those ribs fill and breathe, your upper back should become more relaxed and comfortable.

There are many other ways we misuse our bodies and cause pain when we ride. Many of us have been taught to jam our heels down, a practice that can produce pain in the ankles and calf, and often drives the foot too far forward. This position disrupts your *building blocks* and creates more tension as you struggle for balance. Putting

the stirrup under the *Bubbling Spring*–the balance point of the foot–will produce a springy ankle and good overall body balance. The foot will be essentially level but the heel will go softly deeper when needed as in approaching and landing over a jump.

We are often instructed to keep our feet parallel to the horse's body. This position may cause difficulty depending on the rider and horse body types. To understand the problem, stand on the ground as if you are sitting on your horse. Note that your knees will be surprisingly far apart. Allow your knees to bend, pointing them forward and out as they do when you are in your saddle. Remember that knees are delicate joints with no rotary motion. Most of the rotary motion of the leg is in the hip joint and some in the ankle joint. Knees only flex forward and back, and for greatest comfort and efficiency, your feet will need to point in the same direction as your knees and thighs. If you are correctly positioned, you will see that your feet are following the same angle out as your knees and thighs, and that just your big toes, not more, are visible inside your knees. Notice how comfortable you feel in this alignment.

Now adjust your feet so that they are *parallel* to each other while you once again keep your knees wide apart, as your horse would shape you. Ouch! There is rotary stress on each knee, which will cause pain. Furthermore, this position tends to roll your foot onto its outside edge. In fact, it is almost impossible to keep your foot flat on the floor. This means there is stress in the foot and ankle and your connection with the ground in your riding will be diminished. People who ride with their feet parallel mostly ride only on the outside edge of the foot in the stirrup. This is a very unnatural and stressful position for the knee and body, which interferes with the freedom of motion of both your knees and hips.

I once had a student who told me in her first lesson that her knees hurt when she rode and that she could hardly stand or walk when she got off after a vigorous lesson. She rode with her feet strictly parallel and was amazed when I suggested she experiment with letting them turn out a little. But, she agreed to do it, rode the whole lesson without pain, and to her added delight when she dismounted, she walked off normally—still with no pain. In talking it over she said her instructor was absolutely insistent that she ride with her feet parallel. Then after a moment she said, "But come to think of it he walks with a cane and he is only 40!"

Reducing Pain
Caused by Physical Damage

Centered Riding can also help alleviate pain associated with physical damage such as an injury, or arthritis. Muscles around a joint are tense so they pull the bones of the joint together producing pressure and reducing freedom. And, if there are any roughened bones, or bony spurs, in that joint, as can occur in arthritis, trauma and pain result. Releasing the tension of the muscles, and aligning the bones in more correct balance, can reduce or relieve the pain. When not exacerbated, the roughened bony spurs frequently reduce.

A few years ago, I taught a clinic where the students worked on the ground the first day with an Alexander Technique instructor, Peter Payne. On the second day, they rode with me. On the first day, I had noticed a woman named Dorothy arrive at the clinic. Her body was distorted with arthritis and her face showed a life lived in pain. I watched with interest during the Alexander Technique session as her body become more normal and her face more serene. She said later that she had arrived thinking she would have to leave early because of the pain. To her surprise, when she finally left at four o'clock, she had less pain. Though much of this relief lasted into the next day when she rode with me, there was still some tension in her neck and face as well as in her tight hip joints and drawn-up legs.

She told me of her arthritis, so when I worked

with her body, I handled her with great care. As we worked, the lines of tension in her neck disappeared, her lower back softened and filled, her hip joints and thigh muscles let go and her legs dropped down around her horse. Both she and her horse loved the change and she rode the rest of her lesson free from pain. When she went home, her doctor was amazed at the changes in her body.

A year later, Dorothy rode with me again on a new and fancier horse, working on dressage and doing some eventing. Like most arthritic people, she still has days when she is in pain, but most of the time, she lives and rides largely pain-free.

Another problem is the pain cause by old injuries. When you are recovering from an injury, like a broken coccyx for instance, there is pain. It hurts to sit down, especially on a saddle, so you tighten to keep that coccyx off the saddle, and you probably also pull one side of your pelvis up more than the other. By the time the healing is complete, and the actual pain has disappeared, you have developed a faulty posture habit.

A number of years ago, Kim Walnes, the double Bronze medal winner in the Three-Day Event at the 1982 World Championships, and a US National Champion, came to a clinic with me in just that situation (fig. 18.1). She had broken her coccyx and though it no longer hurt, she was hollow-backed and crooked. She was delighted to find that with knowledge of Centered Riding techniques and some practice, she could have a deep, balanced, pain-free seat again. In this case, her problems were cured mostly by freeing her head and neck to allow her back to be long and wide, and putting one arm up over her head to correct the crookedness. Accident prone, Kim came back to me each year for several years with some new post-accident crookedness, which, each time, required a new combination of releases. She was fortunate to have a Centered Riding instructor on the ground to help analyze and address each of the new problems as they came up.

_18.1_ _Kim Walnes on The Gray Goose wearing her two bronze medals won at the 1982 World Three-Day Event Championships in Dublin, Ireland. The upper-left corner of this photo contains the handwritten message, "Sally, we couldn't have done it without you!"_

Ignoring Your Pain

If your horse is uncomfortable or in pain, you stop working him and take care of the problem or call the vet. You don't simply say, "Well the horse will get over it," and keep going. Many a rider, however, seems to feel that her body is invincible and she only has to simply persevere to get over any problems that arise. Think about it. You take a bad spill from your horse. You really shake yourself up and

one shoulder hurts. You may very well say, "I don't have time to stop. It'll get better, let's keep going!"

So you keep on going and eventually a lot of the pain does go away, but there is a residue that lingers there until you finally decide to address it. By this time, months later, it may be very difficult to help. So, when you get hurt, treat your body exactly as you would treat your horse's body. Take care of it.

Closely related to this concept of treating yourself as you would your horse is the adage, "If you have no pain, you have no gain." This is not a universal truth. Remember that you would not put your horse in pain to teach him something, or to develop his muscles. You teach him what is within his capacity to learn at that moment, and you give him exercises to develop the necessary muscles. If he starts working in pain, he will get discouraged. On the other hand, if you are working in pain, you may grit your teeth and say, "I can bear it," but your body isn't being as efficient as it should. Remember that pain is nature's way of saying, "Wait. Give me a chance. I need a break. I need air." Ease off, as you would with your horse, and start again another time at a slightly lower level and gradually you will be able to work up to more and more vigorous work. Learning does not require pain. It requires work. It requires judgment. It requires a lot of *intent*. But it does not require pain.

Pain produces tension. We often tense up in anticipation of, or in avoidance of pain. In either case, tension is built up as a protection from the pain, and this tension interferes with your breathing, causes hard eyes, and makes your center start to climb in your body (see p. 82). To your horse, all of these consequences of tension immediately frighten him. This is the last thing that you want to do. Go back, quickly and often, to *grounding* and the *Four Basics*.

Sometimes people will just shut down areas of their bodies a result of pain. I had a very dramatic case of this in a young woman who had injured her lower back seriously so that she had some disc problems as well as other damage in the lower back and sacral area. She suffered intense pain for over a year until finally she had surgery on her lower back. The doctors fused some of the discs and put some pins in her pelvis and sacrum, and the intense pain went. The relief was fantastic, but she was left with lesser pain both from the pins and when she moved incorrectly as her body made adjustments after the surgery. This pain was so much less than the original excruciating pain, that she discounted it. She didn't call it pain, and didn't recognize it as pain.

I discovered this when she came to me for some help with her riding. In answer to my questioning, she told me some of what had happened to her body. I kept asking her if anything hurt and she kept saying no, and I believed her. At the end of the lesson, however, it became clear that she was in extraordinary discomfort from the work at the walk and the *following seat* that we had been doing. It was then I realized that she hadn't recognized her pain, because she had simply shut it out.

In the next lesson, she had rested and the pain had eased so we experimented with finding a way in which she could ride without pain. It was evident to me that there was too much "hardware" in her sacrum and pelvis for her to ride in the conventional upright, deep seat. We explored the possibilities of the light seat. To remind you, in the light seat, the rider drops more weight down onto the thighs by gravity and takes the seat bones just slightly off the saddle. As a result, there is a minimal forward slant of the body. She tried this position and it worked well. Though she had previously not even recognized her pain, she was now definitely able to recognize its absence and was joyful at riding a whole hour without it. In the course of the next few days, she seemed to change her entire personality. She became much happier, cheery, and open. And the wonderful change occurred simply because we were able to give her a way she could ride without pain.

In another version of this tendency to shut down painful areas, a person sometimes discards a part of her body. A student came to me after recovering from a badly injured ankle. After the injury, her ankle had been put in a cast and she was told not to ride. She felt that the doctor didn't understand, so went ahead and rode before she was supposed to. The pain was intense. Her reaction was to ignore this part of her ankle and foot. She discarded it as if it were no longer a part of her body and paid no attention to it. It could hurt if it wanted to but she didn't care. The ankle got better and eventually the pain went away. However, when she came for a lesson this ankle was very stiff and when we started working with it she had no connection to it. It was as if it didn't belong to her. We had to reacquaint her with her foot and ankle. I first used very gentle manipulations asking her to recognize what I was doing with her mind and sensation. I then asked her to initiate some of the same motion herself—at first with some help from me, and eventually on her own. Little by little, she became reacquainted with that foot, and, recognizing it as a part of her body, she realized she could use it, and was not afraid to treat it as a normal appendage. Bringing a piece of your body back to be a part of the whole may take a little time, but it definitely can be done using your own awareness and intent, as well as help from someone else.

Some people continue to dwell on an injury even after the damage has been healed and the pain has gone. Though the disability no longer exists, they seem to want to use it as a crutch. For instance, their position or balance may need some correction but they prefer to continue as they are rather than make the correction. Perhaps it is reassuring to have an excuse. After using Centered Riding techniques, these people often discover that life can be more fun without using their crutch, and inadvertently wean themselves from it, because although Centered Riding is aimed toward body control, rather than mind control, the results often change mental attitudes and break up resistances.

Pain from Fatigue and Stress

Centered Riding can also help to alleviate a different kind of pain, the pain associated with prolonged fatigue and stress, sometimes associated with competition. In endurance rides, for instance, the demands on a rider's body can be overwhelming and frequently, on completion of these races, a rider has to be lifted off her horse. If a rider can stay in balance and help the horse to stay in balance throughout, some of this fatigue will be prevented.

Unfortunately, when we get tired, we tend to fall into bad habits. Probably the most important way to delay or alleviate pain from fatigue is to maintain your *centering* and *breathing.* The minute you start holding your breath the pain will increase. Keep your *soft eyes, building blocks,* and *grounding* as well, because losing any of your *Basics* will cause problems. It is essential for the rider consciously to use the *Four Basics* and *grounding* during times of fatigue.

World Champion endurance rider, Becky Hart, wrote in *Centered Riding News* of her ride in the World Championships endurance race in Stockholm in 1990 (fig. 18.2). She won this Championship in 1988 in Front Royal, Virginia, but shortly thereafter had been diagnosed with a degenerated disc. The doctor's orders were, "No riding." This wasn't Becky's plan at all. She had her heart set on riding in the World Championships a second time, and proceeded to do all kinds of therapy for her back, which included swimming and working with a sports therapist.

Finally, a new doctor gave her the OK to try riding, but not in competition. She got in touch with Mary Fenton who was teaching Centered Riding in Watsonville, California, and to quote Becky, "Through Mary's skill and wisdom my horse, Rio, and I began to work together more closely than ever as a team. Three months later, I rode in my first endurance ride in nine months and was amazed to find I wasn't sore the next morning, nor did Rio show signs of stiffness or soreness. With this much progress gained in three months, I knew that in a year I would be ready for Stockholm."

18.2 Becky Hart winning the Gold Medal for Endurance Riding at the 1990 World Equestrian Games held at The Hague in Holland.

cage to rotate, and breathe! Breathe! Breathe! Rio moved out very freely, doing some of the best trotting he has ever done. His canter was smooth and easy. For the most part, I let him choose his gait while I used my Centered Riding techniques to keep him nice and comfortable. Centered Riding has made a terrific difference to Rio and me. We are both more comfortable during a ride and not nearly as apt to stiffen up after. I feel that Rio's racing career will be prolonged due to Centered Riding. As long as he still wants to go, I'll be on him."

In a postcard to Mary immediately after the race, Becky wrote, "They are calling Rio a 'living legend' over here, partly because he looked so fresh at the finish. One of the big reasons he looked so good was the help you had given me. I have so many comments about how even and square his trot was. Thanks for getting my shoulders loose. That made a big difference especially on the pavement."

Two years later in Barcelona, she and Rio won the World Championships for a third consecutive time, breaking all records.

There are many times when Centered Riding techniques alone will alleviate a rider's pain. Sometimes, however, I suggest some additional avenues as well. The sports medicine specialists frequently recommend activities such as swimming as part of treatment. The Alexander Technique, which is so closely connected to Centered Riding, and the Feldenkrais Awareness Method are also beneficial. Rolfing and various types of massage, cranial osteopathy, and chiropractic treatment are additional methods to deal with pain. If you discover that your Centered Riding techniques are not enough to completely address your pain, you may want to add any of these several useful and related methods of treatment. ∼

That she was, and made history by winning the Championships for the second time. She had to carry 20 lbs of lead to make up the 165 lbs of weight required, so she needed to give Rio all the help she could. She goes onto say, "The day of the ride I used everything Mary had taught me. By this point many of the concepts were automatic while others required concentration. I ran a litany through my head—release your neck, allow the rib

19

What You Have Learned from Centered Riding 2

entered Riding 2: Further Exploration has turned out to be a much longer book than I meant it to be. I keep telling my instructors, "Keep it simple." That usually means short. The problem is that I want to communicate with a wide spectrum of people who are interested in one or more of the various riding disciplines, or in just riding with no other purpose but pleasure. The essentials of Centered Riding can help all of these people, but I needed to offer different approaches. In attempting to do this, the book grew larger. So, if parts of it have seemed to not apply to you, I hope you have said, "That's all right. I'll try another Centered Riding approach."

The book started with the uninhibited horse who moves freely until a human climbs on his back, and it started with the human who does well as a small child until the demands of society interferes with, and stultifies her movements. The book ends up with the horse and rider having learned to accommodate each other so they can perform in ease and harmony. The book's large middle part enlarges on what is needed to progress from the pure beginning through the often-not-even-realized obstacles to the time when you and your horse can dance together. The accompanying pictures in this chapter show the difference that a clinic of only two days in length can make for first-time Centered Riding riders (figs. 19. 1 A & B and 19.2 A & B).

In the process of moving through the Centered Riding work, you have become aware that it is all right to keep a *clear intent* of your *use of self* in all you do. It is not selfish to keep 75 percent of your awareness for yourself. It is more efficient. It builds harmony. It is the best way to take care of yourself, your horse, your students, your friends, and circumstances in your life.

These two sets of photos feature two riders at the very beginning—before any teaching—and at the end of a two-day clinic with me.

19.1 A & B

(A) *Before: this girl is self-consciously and desperately trying to catch up with her feet to find her balance. She has the right idea, but doesn't know how to achieve it.*

(B) *After: it's so easy when you learn how! See her relaxed expression and the greater freedom in her hip and knee joints, which would be even better if her foot was a little further through the stirrup. With more practice, she will become even more grounded, and her breathing will have more depth. Note the improved balance in the horse's way of going.*

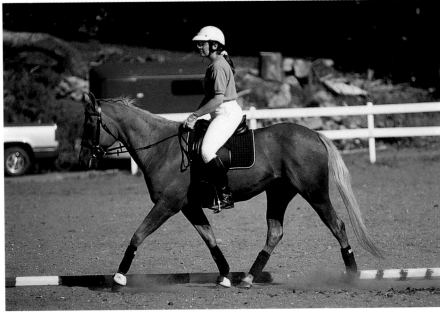

You have become aware that you do not need to be responsible for every detail. Nature is your best friend. Trust Nature to handle much of what you need to do better than you could yourself. But this is only possible if you will stay out of the way and let it happen. Your horse will love you for it.

You have learned a variety of exercises to develop improved musculature in your horse, and quiet strength and stability in your seat. You discovered the satisfying pleasure of the canter, the delicate but potent use of your hands from your center, and the joys of jumping.

19.2

(A) Before: this rider rides herself and her horse downhill. They are both looking down at the ground. The rider's shoulders are rounded with her heels jammed down, which are reflected in the heavy front end of the horse.

(B) After: here is a much improved attitude in both horse and rider. The rider has lifted and opened her shoulders and is showing improved balance and greater freedom of motion in her hips and legs.

Finally, and most important of all, I trust you have fully recognized the impact that the philosophy, and the use of Centered Riding techniques have on the rest of your life. Keep your balance, your *clear intent*, and of course, your *grounding* and your *Four Basics*. Allow changes. No forcing. Breathe and enjoy. ❧

Therapeutic Riding

It is widely recognized in Europe, and more recently in the United States, that physically and mentally disabled persons can be definitely helped by riding on a horse. In therapeutic riding, as it is called, the motion of the horse's body promotes motion and relaxation in the rider's body. The horse used needs to be very reliable, and all the work must be conducted so that the rider feels totally secure.

At first, there must be at least one person leading the horse, and two side walkers both holding a leg of the rider. Often, a skilled person, such as a physical therapist, will direct the operation. The rider, as she learns to follow the movement of the horse's body finds improved coordination and strength. Consider a person without use of her legs, for example. A horse that is walking will move the same muscles in the rider's torso that would be used if she was able to use her own legs to walk.

Centered Riding techniques apply to therapeutic riding in a natural and exciting way. When the rider has a distinct awareness of the area of the "center" in her body, the body will respond in remarkable ways even when the rider has no consciousness of the possibilities. As always in Centered Riding, the instructor's *use of self* is extremely important. When used in therapeutic riding, Centered Riding has given handicapped riders greater freedom of motion and, in some cases, greater comfort.

Virginia Martin, founder of Winslow Therapeutic Riding Unlimited, in Warwick, New York, explains how Centered Riding and therapeutic riding combine effectively. She says, "We need to promote relaxation. That is the main benefit of therapeutic riding, and absolutely the main reason why Centered Riding techniques are desirable, highly useable, and of great import to the disabled, in particular the physically disabled. Strengthening of muscles can only be done when there is relaxation."

For a number of years I have been conducting training sessions for instructors of the handicapped. Basically, I teach them as I teach any group of instructors. I do not teach them what to do in their therapeutic work. I let them feel the broad experience of the Centered Riding techniques and they can use whatever is appropriate in any portion of their work.

My first personal experience of the power of the tool of Centered Riding in therapeutic riding was at Winslow Therapeutic Riding working with Idrissa, a grown, very intelligent, well-educated man with cerebral palsy. He was not only spastic (hypertonic—with tight muscles primarily in the lower extremities), but also athetoid, which caused his hands and arms to make writhing motions and his face to twitch and grimace when he tried to speak.

With the horse standing still, I asked him to remember his Centered Riding instructions, especially the *Four Basics*. I put my hands on his lower body, encompassing his center. Keeping myself grounded, soft and centered, I talked about the quietness and power of his center. In a few moments the spasms in his lower body ceased. Hardly believing what I was feeling, I talked about the quietness in his rib cage and chest. Shortly, this area also became still. Since I could reach no higher with my hands, I stood by the horse's shoulder and talked about Idrissa's shoulders being open, wide, and floating on water. I talked about the stillness of the water–a total stillness. Gradually the jerking stopped. Then his arms and hands quieted as I kept talking about the stillness of the water and the quiet depth of his center. As I watched peace come into that spastic body, I had

a hard time choking back the tears. There were few dry eyes among the observers.

Next, I suggested that he walk off while still thinking about his center. He walked way around the ring before the twitching started again. He stopped, and I put my hands on his center again. The quietness returned and he walked off. The next time the twitching started, he stopped the horse and stilled the twitching without the help of my hands. Then he found he could stop the twitching while walking. After repeating this several times, he tried trotting. He had to stop a few times and reestablish his calm. The final triumph came when, at the trot, he quieted a bout of twitching without stopping. When he got off his horse, he walked out of the ring hardly wavering, very different from the wobbling, tight Idrissa who had come into the ring at the beginning of his lesson.

Later I worked at the Thorncroft Therapeutic Horseback Riding Center where owner, Saunders Dixon, and his instructors teach both able-bodied and handicapped students in mixed groups whenever possible. This system creates a positive experience for all concerned. The easy abilities of some do not look so unattainable to the handicapped riders, and the handicapped riders no longer seem odd to the able-bodied.

One woman in my class was Vivian, a very bright woman in her forties, also with cerebral palsy. Her condition pulled her legs up and tended to twist her body. Her hip joints were extremely tight, almost locked. With descriptions, demonstrations using Herman, my 18-inch plastic skeleton, illustrative drawings, and use of my hands, I showed her how the bones of the pelvic area and the upper body function, and how the joints articulate. Then, with Centered Riding techniques and my own careful *use of self*, I helped her find her center. By feeling my hands around her buttocks just above the saddle and then around her hip joints, she was able to imagine emptying these areas and release her legs downward. With work on her ankles and feet, she became much more grounded. She was able to balance her upper body, free and balance her neck and head, and find some rotation around her center. Finally, she was able to walk a figure-of-eight on her horse with some body rotation and level shoulders, which she had been unable to do before. It was a dramatic change.

When her instructor, Saundra Cabell, helped her dismount, she let Vivian stand beside her horse, holding onto the saddle to orient herself to being on the ground. Then we brought over her walker, a triangular lightweight one with a pair of close-together wheels in front and a pair on each side. The handlebars were like those on a bicycle and even had brakes. When I admired it, she said her arms got very tired when she used it. I could account for this because she placed her feet behind the handles so her body weight leaned on her hands. I held the walker steady and suggested she walk her feet up into it so they were under her hands. This position allowed her to stand upright. It was an exciting experience for her.

Someone said, "But how does she walk?" I asked her to center herself, put one knee forward from the hip and then the other, and allow herself to walk off. She did this with a grin from ear to ear while we all clapped. I saw her again that evening at the Devon Dressage Show, walking down the aisle still upright and still smiling.

Also at Thorncroft, Yoav, a talented instructor from Israel, presented Rena, a girl in her twenties with brain damage from an automobile accident. Her upper body kept tipping off to the right and Yoav could not get her to stay upright. I put my hands on the front and back of her center, one on top of the sacrum, the other just above the pubic arch. I suggested she become aware of that area, especially deep in toward the hand on her back. I, myself, stayed very *grounded*, *centered*, and *breathing*, with *soft eyes*, soft hips, knees, and ankles. Without my saying anything more, she grad-

ually began to straighten up until she was upright. She stayed there when I took my hands away, but when the handlers led her horse around, she tipped off to the right again. Yoav put his hands on her center, with careful *use of self*. I stood in front and watched Rena's body slowly become upright again. Yoav, being tall and strong, was able to keep his hands on Rena as her horse walked and she remained upright. It wasn't long before Rena could walk her horse and stay upright without the help of Yoav's hands. It is important to realize that when we use our hands in this way, we do not push, twist, or direct in any way except from within ourselves.

One more example of Centered therapeutic work was my experience with Nicky. Nicky at that time was a tiny 5 year old who was born with only 3% of his cerebellum. Nicky is bright and quick, he can understand what you tell him, but he cannot speak and his coordination is not good. He has a little walker, much like Vivian's, and he tootles around with it at amazing speeds. One of the coordination problems is that his head wobbles around as if it would break off. This happens when he walks on the ground, as well as when on the wonderful pony, "Frosty." Saunders, who is impressively talented in his *use of self*, is his instructor. When I asked Nicky if he could hold his head still when Frosty was led at a walk, he indicated an enthusiastic, "Yes," and when they walked off, he held his head steady with both hands. Though this was successful, it was not what I meant and somewhat impractical.

Once more, we worked on *centering*. Saunders put his hands on Nicky's lower body to let him become aware of that centered area and off they walked, big tall Saunders, tiny Nicky, and little Frosty. It was a wonderful sight, and all the more so because Nicky's head stabilized, no more flopping in all directions, as long as Saunders kept his hands on Nicky's center.

After a few repetitions, Saunders could take

his hands off and Nicky's head would stay stable for increasing lengths of time. A year later Saunders told me that the child who was supposed to never be able to walk, could now run without his walker, his head was almost always steady, and he had even said a few words.

In Nicky's case, we taught Centered Riding merely through touch and *use of self* by the instructor. It seems that if you can create for the body a sense of its center, with its quietness and security, it starts to produce a central control. Instead of the senses rushing to peripheral parts of the body in confused and unorganized ways, with the resulting conflicts and stiffening, we allow the senses to return to the center. From here, more normal directives can begin to emerge and allow the body more natural balance and movement. Once again, we see that without interference, the body will choose to work as efficiently as possible.

Some handicapped people seem angry. They push your hands away, they want to be left alone. They seem to say, "This is the way I am, so go away."

If, without antagonizing them, you can find a way to keep your hands around that center and stay with it, you will find that their bodies and faces relax, as they begin to find quietness and acceptance. They may even look at you with trust and gratitude. They are opening the door for further work. This reaction reminds me of the response I get from a horse when I am doing bodywork on his very tense and unbalanced rider. The horse will reach around and touch or rub me with his nose as if to thank me. In therapeutic riding, the bodies of these afflicted people are saying, "Thank you."

Though a physically challenged rider will need more repetitions of a movement or exercise than usual, he can learn and benefit from Centered Riding techniques much as an able-bodied rider. Students with brain damage depend on communication through the instructor's hands. If we repeat the exercises often enough with good *use of self*, we can help the bodies of these students gradually learn new patterns. Centered Riding techniques add a dimension to therapeutic riding and can help teachers as well as their students look with wonder at new possibilities. ⚜

PHOTO CREDITS

Courtesy of the AMERICAN PAINT HORSE ASSOCIATION
Page 170

Courtesy of SUSAN ASHLEY
Page 9

KAY BENNETT
Page 2

MICHAEL CAMBELL
Page 7

DARRELL DODDS
Pages 16, 34, 38, 41, 45, 47, 52, 55, 57, 59–61, 63, 70–76,
93, 94, 96, 97, 100, 108, 110–113, 115–117, 125, 127–130,
132, 136, 137, 139–142, 151, 152, 154–156, 165, 174, 248, 249

MARGARET HALPERT
Pages 37, 164, 193, 222, 223

Courtesy of BECKY HART
Page 246

CHARLIE HILTON
Page 8

Courtesy of JOSEY ENTERPRISES
Page 102

Courtesy of MARCIA KULAK
Page 5

BOB LANGRISH
Pages 33, 144, 178, 179, 182, 185, 192, 196, 198,
199, 212, 213, 216, 218, 219, 226, 227, 230, 231

MICHAEL MALONEY
Pages 148, 180, 181, 194, 197, 211, 228, 229, 236

TERRI MILLER
Page 3

ROBERT MISCHKA
Page 26

PHELPSPHOTOS.COM
Page 243

SPORT HORSE STUDIO.COM
Page 4

Courtesy of SALLY SWIFT
page ii, 25

INDEX